TWO BOLD SINGERMEN AND THE ENGLISH FOLK REVIVAL

Popular Music History
Series Editor: Alyn Shipton, Royal Academy of Music, London.

This series publishes books that challenge established orthodoxies in popular music studies, examine the formation and dissolution of canons, interrogate histories of genres, focus on previously neglected forms, or engage in archaeologies of popular music.

Published

An Unholy Row: Jazz in Britain and its Audience, 1945–1960
Dave Gelly

Being Prez: The Life and Music of Lester Young
Dave Gelly

Bill Russell and the New Orleans Jazz Revival
Ray Smith and Mike Pointon

Chasin' the Bird: The Life and Legacy of Charlie Parker
Brian Priestley

Handful of Keys: Conversations with Thirty Jazz Pianists
Alyn Shipton

Jazz Me Blues: The Autobiography of Chris Barber
Chris Barber with Alyn Shipton

Jazz Visions: Lennie Tristano and His Legacy
Peter Ind

Lee Morgan: His Life, Music and Culture
Tom Perchard

Lionel Richie: Hello
Sharon Davis

Mosaics: The Life and Works of Graham Collier
Duncan Heining

Mr P.C.: The Life and Music of Paul Chambers
Rob Palmer

Out of the Long Dark: The Life of Ian Carr
Alyn Shipton

Rufus Wainwright
Katherine Williams

Scouse Pop
Paul Skillen

Soul Unsung: Reflections on the Band in Black Popular Music
Kevin Le Gendre

The Godfather of British Jazz: The Life and Music of Stan Tracey
Clark Tracey

The History of European Jazz: The Music, Musicians and Audience in Context
Edited by Francesco Martinelli

The Last Miles: The Music of Miles Davis, 1980–1991
George Cole

The Long Shadow of the Little Giant (second edition): The Life, Work and Legacy of Tubby Hayes
Simon Spillett

The Ultimate Guide to Great Reggae: The Complete Story of Reggae Told through its Greatest Songs, Famous and Forgotten
Michael Garnice

This is Hip: The Life of Mark Murphy
Peter Jones

Trad Dads, Dirty Boppers and Free Fusioneers: A History of British Jazz, 1960–1975
Duncan Heining

Two Bold Singermen and the English Folk Revival

The Lives, Song Traditions and Legacies of Sam Larner and Harry Cox

Bruce Lindsay

eǝuinox

SHEFFIELD UK   BRISTOL CT

Published by Equinox Publishing Ltd

UK: Office 415, The Workstation, 15 Paternoster Row, Sheffield, South Yorkshire,
      S1 2BX
USA: ISD, 70 Enterprise Drive, Bristol, CT 06010

www.equinoxpub.com

First published 2020

British Library Cataloguing-in-Publication Data

A catalogue record for this book is available from the British Library.

ISBN-13 978 1 78179 917 8   (hardback)
         978 1 78179 918 5   (ePDF)

Library of Congress Cataloging-in-Publication Data

Names: Lindsay, Bruce (Music journalist) author.
Title: Two bold singermen and the English folk revival : the lives, song
   traditions and legacies of Sam Larner and Harry Cox / Bruce Lindsay.
Description: Bristol : Equinox Publishing Ltd, 2020. | Series: Popular
   music history | Includes bibliographical references and index. |
   Summary: "Two Bold Singermen and the English Folk Revival explores the
   lives and song traditions of two of the most influential English
   traditional singers: Sam Larner and Harry Cox"-- Provided by publisher.
Identifiers: LCCN 2020019604 (print) | LCCN 2020019605 (ebook) | ISBN
   9781781799178 (hardback) | ISBN 9781781799185 (ebook)
Subjects: LCSH: Larner, Sam, 1878-1965. | Cox, Harry, 1885-1971. | Folk
   singers--England--Biography. | Folk songs, English--England--History and
   criticism.
Classification: LCC ML400 .L718 2020 (print) | LCC ML400 (ebook) | DDC
   782.42162/200922 [B]--dc23
LC record available at https://lccn.loc.gov/2020019604
LC ebook record available at https://lccn.loc.gov/2020019605

Typeset by S.J.I. Services, New Delhi, India

Contents

Acknowledgements

I owe a major debt to the following, who were crucial in providing me with ideas, contacts, archive material and personal insights: Jenny Barker (Harry's granddaughter), Jim Carroll, Brian Gaudet, Chris Heppa, Chris Holderness, Jane Roberts (Sam's great-great-niece), and Steve Roud. Thanks also to Alyn Shipton and the team at Equinox.

Many people and organisations helped me with my research, providing valuable evidence or talking with me about local and family history. My thanks go to: Keith Bacon, Churchwarden at All Saints, Catfield; Alex Bartholomew at the East Anglian Traditional Music Trust; the British Library; Margaret Crowe; Cromer Museum; Megan Dennis at Gressenhall Farm and Workhouse; Rosemary Dixon, librarian at Archant (publishers of the *Eastern Daily Press* and other publications); Derek and Vivienne George; Mary Haslam, Churchwarden at St. Nicholas, Potter Heigham; Glen Johnson at Topic Records; Sandra Laws, Churchwarden at Holy Trinity and All Saints, Winterton; volunteer guides on the drifter *Lydia Eva*, at Yarmouth quay; Norfolk Heritage Centre and Norfolk Records Office; Janet Rowe (for her work on the Larner family tree and other Winterton research); Nathan Salsburg at the Alan Lomax Collection, American Folklife Center, Library of Congress; the Time and Tide Museum, Great Yarmouth; the Vaughan Williams Memorial Library at Cecil Sharp House.

The following people took part in interviews – either face-to-face, by phone, or by email – and gave me invaluable insights into many parts of this story: Christine Alden, Frankie Armstrong, Damien Barber, Mike Barber, Tony Baylis, Dave Burland, Martin Carthy, Peter Coleman, Shirley Collins, Andrew Fakes, Pauline Godbold, Reg Hall, John Harle, David Higgins, Katie Howson, Ken Hunt, Gemma Khawaja, Hugh Lupton, Sophie Miller, Sheila Park, Alex Patterson, Bob Pegg, Carole Pegg, Ken Saul, Joan Saul, Peggy Seeger, Georgia Shackleton, Sally Shreeve, Keith Skipper, Philip Underwood, and Martin Warren.

All extracts from Alan Lomax's interviews with Harry Cox are taken from the Alan Lomax Collection at the American Folklife Center, Library of Congress, and used by courtesy of the Association for Cultural Equity (culturalequity.org).

Lyrics from Stone Angel's "What Will Become of England" (words and music by Ken Saul) are reproduced by kind permission of Ken Saul, published in 2004 by Stone Angel.

Images from *The Bonny Labouring Boy* and *Now is the Time for Fishing* are reproduced by kind permission of Topic Records (topicrecords.co.uk).

As always, thanks to Julie, Sam and Alex for their love and support – even though I never could persuade them of Harry and Sam's talents.

Introduction

This is the story of Harry Cox and Sam Larner: working men from rural Norfolk who became two of the most important singers of traditional songs England has ever produced. They sang songs they liked; sometimes they were modern songs but usually they were old ones, songs that have come to be known as "folk songs" – not that they ever used the phrase. Other people call them "folk singers," "traditional singers," "field singers" or even "country singers" – but they never used those phrases either. Harry rarely left his home in the Broads, turning his hand to almost every trade that farming and rural life required. Sam was a fisherman, chasing the shoals of herring from Yarmouth to the Atlantic. Their homes were just a few miles apart, but they never met. They shared some songs, but differed widely in singing style. They both made it onto records, radio, and television, both telling stories and singing, portrayed by journalists and BBC presenters as rare examples of a soon-to-be extinct species – the English folk singer – and guardians of a repertoire that would die when they did. The songs didn't die – and we have singers like Harry and Sam to thank.

Harry and Sam grew up in Queen Victoria's England, fought in the Great War, worked through World War II and lived into old age and the Swinging Sixties. Within these long lives they developed vast repertoires of song and came to be crucial source singers for the English folk revival. They died over fifty years ago but the songs are still around, alongside many aspects of an English tradition that refuses to disappear. Morris sides still dance from pub to pub on warm summer evenings, bells jingling, sticks thwacking. Folk festivals attract thousands of fans each year. Youngsters still pick up fiddles, melodeons and concertinas and play old tunes together. Pub sessions take place every night of the week, even though hunting them down is not always an easy task. The folk world's leading lights draw large audiences to major concert halls. And, every few decades, the music comes to the surface yet again as the broadsheet newspapers enthuse about another "revival" of England's musical heritage; usually soon after they've enthused about another revival of the British jazz scene.

Even those of us who never set foot in a folk club or festival – who've never heard of Sam Larner or Harry Cox – recognise a few old songs ("The Wild Rover" and "The Black Velvet Band," for example) from Harry and Sam's repertoires. But most of these songs are obscure, remembered by the committed folk song fan or performer but far from the minds of the rest of us unless they pop up on TV, or soundtrack a film about love in the Edwardian countryside. Today it's easy to hear even the most obscure of them. Modern technology makes them accessible to us at any time of the day or night: shout "Hey, play Harry Cox" loudly at a small plastic box in the corner of your kitchen and it will immediately regale you with a selection of songs from Harry and his compatriots (assuming that you've shouted at the correct box). The technologies that make hard rock, metal, hip-hop, and EDM accessible also ensure that a few unaccompanied singers who were active over one hundred years ago can be heard whenever we wish.

When we *do* wish, what *do* we hear? Harry and Sam sang about events from everyday life and about events they could never have experienced. They sang the stories of adventurers, smugglers, pirates, poachers, maids, mothers, jolly ploughboys, and bold fishermen. Many of their songs were inventions, idealised romances or allegories; others were inspired by past happenings, but changed over the generations until their lyrics no longer made such events clear. They sang alone – except when listeners joined in on the chorus – and without musical accompaniment. Harry never played his fiddle or melodeon while he sang; Sam never learned to play an instrument. They were confident in their own talents, albeit in very different ways. To "sophisticated" modern listeners they can sound outdated, harsh, stark, or just plain odd. They sang about things that transcend time and musical fashion: of love, hate, bravery, trickery, loss, sex, poverty, wealth, cruelty, and happiness – things that we still understand and experience today. Their songs were stories, but never their own stories.

So this is the story of Harry and Sam.

1 Fields and Fishing

Pakefield for poverty, Lowestoft for poor,
Gorleston for pretty girls, Yarmouth for whores,
Caister for waterdogs, California for pluck,
Damn and beggar old Winterton,
How black she do look.[1]

Sam Larner was fond of rhymes, even if they did no favours for poor old
Winterton-on-Sea. Sam's home village doesn't look especially black these days:
it's a mix of old cottages, post-war bungalows, converted farm buildings and
recently updated detached houses, with a holiday park on its border. It's not
far from California, but Norfolk's California is a far cry from the west coast
state of redwoods, surfers, and Hollywood. The Church of All Saints dominates
the village, just as it has done for hundreds of years. Sam would recognise it at
once: after all, he lived within sight of it for most of his life.

Sam's cottage is still on Bulmer Lane, a modern extension adding space to
what visitors remembered as a tiny but cosy home. It's easy to spot, a blue
plaque in commemoration of Sam and his songs is firmly fixed to the front
wall. Sam's favourite pub, the Fishermans Return, is still in business and it's a
short walk from the village to the beach, but Winterton has lost one crucial
part of its life since the days of Sam's youth. The Yarmouth fishing fleet, an
industry that kept Sam and many of his friends in employment for decades,
is little more than a memory. As the industry was dying, J. Wentworth Day
nostalgically praised Winterton's fishermen as:

> a race of true North Sea sailors. Men of the herring drifters and
> the lifeboats, they have dwelt for uncounted generations in this
> little, lonely village, with its few sea-windy streets of flint-built cot-
> tages, crouching under the landward lee of the tawny sandhills,

sentinelled by the old lifeboat house and the squat tower of the lighthouse.[2]

Nineteenth-century Winterton relied on the fishing, but while Sam claimed that he and his siblings had one choice when they left school – "fishing or jail" for the boys, "service or jail" for the girls – the options weren't quite so limited.[3] Winterton's economy needed innkeepers, builders, shopkeepers, teachers, domestic servants, gardeners, and farmers but fishing was the biggest single employer of men and boys who, like Sam, would sign up for their first vessel at the age of twelve or thirteen.

Samuel James Larner was born in Winterton on 18 October 1878 and baptised on 31 January in the following year, the son of fisherman George Larner and his wife Jane. In the wider world of 1878, Wanderers beat the Royal Engineers 3-1 in the seventh FA Cup final, Frank Hadow won the second Wimbledon men's tennis tournament, anti-Russian demonstrations took place in Hyde Park, Thomas Edison patented the phonograph, Gilbert and Sullivan debuted their comic opera *HMS Pinafore*, and on the Thames the pleasure cruiser *Princess Alice* collided with a colliery vessel and sank with the loss of 650 passengers and crew. Norfolk life carried on much as it had done for decades. The railway network was not yet at its height, farmers still relied on horses to pull the ploughs and teams of men to work the land, and Yarmouth's fishing fleet was still under sail not steam. Despite its rural beauty and rich landscapes of rolling farmland, Norfolk's reputation was poor: "among the most ignorant, improvident, and criminal counties" in England.[4] Work was hard, wages were low, and its rural and coastal villages were a far cry from the sophisticated society of the county's nobility and rich landowners or the wealthy professionals of the city of Norwich. These small settlements did have one advantage, however: they were rich in song.

It's almost impossible to travel further east than Winterton on the British mainland. Ness Point in Lowestoft has the distinction of being the most easterly point in the country, but Winterton comes close. The foreland of Winterton Ness, two miles north of the village, was renowned for its dangers: Daniel Defoe knew of the area's reputation, writing in *A Tour Through the Whole Island of Great Britain* that this stretch of Norfolk coastline was "particularly famous for being one of the most dangerous and most fatal to the sailors in all England, I may say in all Britain."[5] In Sam's boyhood the dangers of Winterton Ness remained much as in Defoe's day, despite the local lifeboats, lighthouse and coastguard team. When he was six years old, out collecting birds' eggs with his friends, Sam caught sight of four sailors drowned and washed up on Winterton beach: "They were tooken up into the old church barn, they, and that was the mortuary then … We could see them laying up in the corner, you see. Four of 'em layin' there dead."[6] The village's lifeboat volunteers put their own lives in danger every time they launched to rescue fellow sailors. "The Wreck of the Lifeboat," one of Sam's songs, tells simply of the dangers from the point of view of the sweetheart whose lover is drowned within sight of land as he goes to help a vessel caught in a storm.

Despite the dangers, black old Winterton offered hospitality to the tourist. The *Yarmouth Independent* couldn't bring itself to wholeheartedly recommend a visit to the village at any time of year, but still felt that it had much in its favour as a "health-giving resort" and there are indications of a small-scale tourist industry. Albert Pratt rented out apartments as did James King, the shoemaker and landlord of the Three Mariners. King's apartments were close to the sea, offering spectacular views in wild weather, while his pub could cater for private parties for very reasonable rates. Some of these tourists formed Sam's first audiences.[7]

Sam was the second youngest of the Larner children, barely two years older than his sister Jane. He had nothing positive to say about his education at the village board school, but could still recall poems learnt in the classroom when he was eighty: "I can say all my poetries, what I learnt at school. I can recite all them now … *The Burial of Sir John Moore, The Soldier's Dream* and all that."[8]

Although Winterton relied on fishing, farming was the centre of the economy for the rest of the county. Norfolk farmers were some of the most technically innovative in Britain, at the forefront of the development of agriculture.[9] In contrast, the county's agricultural labourers had a long history of radicalism and were among the first to embrace unionisation in the late-nineteenth century; their relationships with their employers were often tense and occasionally violent. In the Broads, Harry Cox, his father and his brothers all worked on the land and experienced the poverty that was the regular lot of the agricultural labourer.

Harry Fred Cox was born at Barton Turf on 27 March 1885. His mother Sarah wanted to call him Henry or Harold, but when she was told that people would always call him Harry she decided to register him by that name.[10] Fifteen miles from Winterton, in the northwest corner of the Broads, Barton Turf lies mostly at the edge of Barton Broad. It stretches out westwards towards Pennygate, where Harry's family lived. Like Winterton, its parish church has been there for centuries; unlike Winterton, the church is not at the centre of the village but sits a mile to the southwest, on the top of a gentle incline. The Church of St. Michael and All Angels has been in place since the fourteenth century, an imposing structure, although invisible from Pennygate.

Barton Turf has rarely troubled historians or the news media. The church's medieval rood screen is significant and beautiful, the young Horatio Nelson is rumoured to have learnt to sail on Barton Broad, but that's it.[11] Barton Turf lacked a geographical feature of note, posed no threat to passing travellers and had little if anything to offer the Victorian tourist trade. The 1877 *Harrod's Directory* devoted barely a third of a page to this village of 408 people. Then, as now, there was no pub or inn in the village. But down at the staithe, on the edge of Barton Broad, James Yaxley sold beer to quench villagers' thirst.[12]

By the time Harry was ten years old the march of the railways meant that the village was just four miles away from a railway station at Wroxham, on the Great Eastern line, and five miles from Stalham station on the Midland and Great Northern. Barton's population had fallen to around 385 people and it was still without a pub, but James Yaxley carried on selling beer at the staithe, George Jones and Henry Watts kept shops, George Gales ran a market garden, and Henry Christmas Goulder managed to hold down four jobs: as assistant overseer, tax collector, farmer and miller. Four Coxes made it into the 1896 *Kelly's Directory*, at various levels of the local economy, though none of them were from Harry's family: Sarah, a farmer and coal dealer; Joseph the blacksmith; William the rat and mole catcher; and Jacob Salmon Cox, boat-builder and owner of apartments to let.[13]

In 1951 Wentworth Day, a writer and outdoorsman who was at his happiest when traversing the Broads in search of birds to shoot or fish to catch, declared that Barton Broad had not changed in over a century:

> [The Broad] has not been tamed ... Woods come down to meet the wild fens which surround it. There the bittern booms, coots clank, and the wild duck passes overhead on quick-cutting wings. Barton is the home of enormous pike, so large and so numerous that a twenty-pounder is regarded as very little out of the ordinary.

Beer was still on sale down at Barton Staithe. Wentworth Day sang the praises of "a little, old-fashioned off-licence which sells beer to the thirsty wayfarer through an open window. You have to drink it standing in the open."[14]

Harry's school was smaller than Sam's, but Harry shared his attitude to education. He started attending lessons at the age of six, but sending Harry and his siblings to school was financially difficult for his parents and his mother struggled to find the money: "You had to pay tuppence a week ... there were six went and she couldn't stand it, couldn't pay it. Shilling's a lot out of ten bob." As Harry remembered, the "ladies" of Barton Hall paid the money so that he and his siblings could get an education. It seems like the money was wasted, at least in Harry's opinion: "I never learnt nothing. You didn't try ... I learnt ten thousand times more since I left. I learnt myself."[15] Harry picked up one lifelong habit before attending school: when he was three years old his father gave him a clay pipe and tobacco and started his son on a lifetime of enjoyable pipe-smoking.[16]

Most Barton boys went to work on the land. The Broads offered work to others, in the boatyards or on the specialist Broads sailing boats known as wherries, and from time to time the adventure of the fisherman's life at sea proved attractive. But agriculture was an intensive user of labour and local farms and their supporting trades would always provide jobs to Barton boys like Harry. Agricultural labourers' wages were low and bringing up a family was a constant struggle, even with just one or two children. Winterton families also struggled along on low incomes and in both villages boys were expected to earn a living as soon as they could while their sisters went into service, earning a small wage but also easing the family's burden by leaving home to live with their new employer.

Harry and Sam came from large families: Harry grew up with eight siblings while Sam was the second youngest of seven children. They described the poverty of their early years in almost identical words. "Course, we were brought up the hard way we were, there's no mistake about it. We see more Sundays than we did Sunday dinners when I was a little boy," said Sam. Harry declared, "I'm like my uncle: 'Seen more dinner times than I've seen dinners'; that's what he used to tell us."[17] He added, "I have been hungry. We used to have it lotted out to us. My mother used to say: 'Eat that and your two elbows, there's no more.'" Sarah Cox would take on jobs whenever possible, especially if her husband Bob was away and not sending money home regularly. For trimming mangel (a root vegetable used as animal fodder) Sarah could earn ten pence a day, or five shillings for a six-day week. Harry was aware of how important this was: "She done a lot, else we shouldn't ha' been where we are now."[18]

Both agriculture and herring fishing were characterised by long hours. Life as a trawlerman involved weeks or months away from home, chasing herring from England's east coast across Scotland and down to Cornwall and southern Ireland before returning to Yarmouth. Sam learnt to keep an eye open for birds and sea creatures that would tell of the shoals: "The gulls and the blowfish used to tell us where the fish were ... the big blowfish, the big sparm [sic] whales that blow the smoke out ... they'll tell you where the herring are." When Sam was young, the herring were plentiful and so were the boats. Yarmouth was one of the most important fishing ports in Europe, with around four hundred trawlers registered in the 1870s and – according to Sam – almost a thousand by the early 1900s, when he would see Yarmouth harbour "chock-a-block with fishing boats, eight hundred or a thousand belonging to the home fleet. Then the Scotch boats as well and the Danes and the Icelanders and the Germans and Dutch ... fair solid it was."[19] Great Yarmouth was a town of two distinct sides. It was on its way to becoming a major tourist resort, drawing thousands of summer visitors – "jolly, unsophisticated, trippers, half from London and the great cities and the other half, ruddy-faced and broad-tongued, from the villages of East Anglia," according to Wentworth Day – but it relied heavily on its fishing vessels. This everyday, working side of the town was not for the faint-hearted, filled as it was with

> rough, dark places where dwelt rough men and slattern women. A place of midnight brawls which, when the Scots drifters were in port and the Scots fisher-lassies were ashore – girls as strong, uncouth and scaly-armed as their men – were places where no policeman dared walk alone.

Yarmouth Docks, c.1900: "chock-a-block" with fishing boats, just as Sam remembered it.

Instead, the policemen went about in threes, wielding truncheons in both hands when they burst into the throng to break up a midnight brawl.[20]

Winterton was peaceful and relaxed in comparison to the bright lights and dark places of Yarmouth. Inland, the villages and hamlets were even quieter. Farm workers might get back home each evening, but the working day could last from dawn until dusk, seven days a week – especially when livestock needed care. Harry enjoyed such work when he reached adulthood, but it was tough: "I took delight in feeding the cattle. I fed, oh, thirty years or more. Sometimes I done seven months at a stretch, Sundays and all, no rest, never had a holiday, nowhere to go." Free time at home or on shore was precious, the chance for relaxation and fun, even if Harry claimed that after work all there was to do was to "get round the old fire, get the music, [his term for any instrument] have a song ... Something to cheer yourself up, that was all the frolic we had."[21]

Both Sam and Harry were dismissive of their opportunities for entertainment. Harry blamed a lack of transport: "Where could you go, in them days, walking? Never got out the parish!" When he did get out of the parish, Harry enjoyed visits to the aquarium and the Hippodrome in Yarmouth.[22] Sam spoke of the village pubs as the main places for fun after a long voyage: "a drink, a song and a four-handed reel. Round we'd go and up we'd go and we used to have a rare old, good old time."[23] Singing and dancing were clearly vital sources of pleasure, but Sam and Harry are understating the range of entertainments on offer in turn-of-the-century Norfolk.

Church or chapel were important in village life, socially as well as spiritually. Young Sam may not have viewed the church as an entertaining place, but it did give him an early opportunity to sing in front of an audience and he was proud of his achievements as a choir member and as a soloist. He was a choir member for twenty years, by his own calculation, "and I was always picked out when we went festivals … my little tenor voice."[24] Harry was less involved, making use of the local church for baptism, marriage and burial but keeping away from the regular services, even though he enjoyed singing hymns at home on a Sunday.[25] There were plenty of other places to sing.

Ewan MacColl and Peggy Seeger claimed that East Anglia was the richest source of folk song and folk singers in England.[26] A decent voice and a repertoire of a few old songs could give a farm labourer a place in the affections of their fellow villagers and perhaps a free drink or two at the local pub. A degree of ability on a fiddle or a melodeon would be a useful addition to a person's talents, should a tune be called for; when Harry got his own melodeon it helped to liven up nights in the Cox family home and in local pubs.[27]

If a fiddler or melodeon player was present in the pub or at a frolic (the local term for a bit of a do, or a knees-up) but the confines of the room prevented a full-blown country dance, there was another solution: stepdancing. Both Harry and Sam would become known for their stepdancing, an energetic, on-the-spot form of dance for one or maybe two people with improvised steps, most frequently to a hornpipe tune. The noise of the dancer's feet plays an important role in its impact. It's freestyle, with an emphasis on rhythm and with a few basic steps from which an individual dancer can add their own stylistic touches.[28] Because the dancer can stay in one place, with their arms kept close to their sides, it's possible to stepdance in the smallest pub room. Most dancers wore their usual footwear, with leather or hobnailed soles capable of making a loud sound on a stone floor or sometimes on a board laid down expressly as a surface for dancing. When Harry's family was having a get-together, they would lay an old door down on the floor and dance on that – "the old-fashioned way," Harry called it.[29] In some pubs, tin trays were put down to make the sound even louder, while the more athletic and extrovert stepdancer might leap onto a table to perform. Sam was one such athlete, happy to jump up so he could be seen and heard by his audience and still willing to try when he was in his eighties. Harry, by contrast, was known to dance in rubber-soled footwear, making him one of the quietest stepdancers around.[30]

A third art combined dance, music and puppetry, needed very little space and could even be practiced without the use of an instrument or the ability to remember the words of a song: the art of the jig doll. Jig dolls (or dancing dolls) are carved wooden dolls around twenty-five centimetres in height, with jointed legs and arms. A stick protrudes from the doll's back, enabling its operator to hold the doll lightly over a length of flexible wooden plank. The operator sits astride the plank, most of which protrudes forward. Hitting the plank with a fist makes the plank bounce up and down, striking the doll's legs and making it appear to dance. In the absence of an instrumentalist the operator can vocalise a wordless tune – a process known as diddling – for the doll to dance to.

Jig dolls came in a variety of designs and were often made at home. Harry made his own, hand-carved with no attempt to give them any realistic facial features but with joints in the legs and hips which ensured that they were talented dancers in the hands of an expert. Evidence on film and from those who saw Harry operating his doll makes it clear that he was such an expert and it's also obvious that he enjoyed making his dolls dance.

No-one remembers how many jig dolls Harry made. His granddaughter Jenny Barker remembers one, now lost, which he painted green and which someone else later painted in regimental colours.[31] Sheila Park, a singer and a friend of Harry's in his last years, owns one which is unpainted and faceless but still in excellent working order. Carole Pegg, the singer and musician, owns a third: another plain doll, more crudely constructed than Sheila's but with rudimentary eyes, nose and mouth.[32] Harry's friends Cliff and Pauline Godbold passed a doll on to storyteller and author Hugh Lupton, who regards it as one of his treasured possessions: his doll is painted black, with no facial features.[33] The most unusual of Harry's surviving jig dolls is part of the Vaughan Williams Memorial Library collection. Harry gave this doll to Ewan MacColl – he may have made it specially for him – and it's notable for the presence of hair, made from a few short strands of ginger-yellow wool.[34]

Harry was still making dolls when he was in his early eighties. In 1968 his daughter Myrtle wrote to Lewis and Isobel Strickland, who owned at least two of the dolls: "How is the dancing man? My father has made several more since, they seem to be in demand." Myrtle took on the job of posting Harry's dolls to their lucky owners: when she forewarned the Stricklands of the imminent arrival of parts of a new doll she wrote, without making it clear that she was referring to a wooden doll: "I am sending the mans [*sic*] legs that my father promised you he says he hasn't smoothed them off very well you can smooth them off to your own liking."[35]

Harry enjoyed making jig dolls, but he enjoyed singing even more. At work, singing helped to while away the hours or to make easier work of the more strenuous and back-breaking tasks. Sam and Harry learnt songs from their fellow workers and used songs to pass the time when they were working alone. Such activities were not confined to Norfolk. In their home village of Rottingdean, in Sussex, the Copper family and their friends sang during haymaking or sheep shearing. One song, to accompany a game involving throwing your legs behind your head until your feet touched the ground, included the earthy but no doubt accurate lyric "O can you see my arse? O yes, quite plain enough." In her fictionalised account of growing up in the Cotswolds, Flora Thompson wrote of labourers and traders singing as they worked. The local professionals didn't sing, but "even the doctor and parson

on their rounds hummed a tune between their teeth." Such reticence probably stemmed from their wish to keep up appearances, but the village squire
showed no such concern when engaged in one of his own favourite pastimes,
playing the banjo and singing "negro songs."[36]

Informal songs and games could happen whenever the mood took you, but
across the year there were plenty of formal entertainments – even in villages
as small as Barton Turf or Harry's later home of Catfield. Weddings, baptisms,
Christmas, May Day and harvest were all celebrated with singing and dancing. Church services gave thanks for a successful harvest each year, and once
the crops were safely gathered in there would be a harvest frolic with singing,
dancing and plenty of drinking.[37]

Church bell-ringers were often skilled workers or artisans and their regular practice sessions were bookended by visits to the pub.[38] Handbell groups
offered another social activity based on music and brass bands were active
in villages across Norfolk including Castle Acre, which named its band the
Nelson Band in honour of the county's naval hero. The popularity of "blackface minstrels" meant that amateur groups of black-faced entertainers also
emerged. Flora Thompson's banjo-playing squire brought a few village youths
together in a "Negro Minstrel Troupe" to play at the annual concert. The
mid-Norfolk market town of Reepham was home to the Black Diamonds, an
ambitious minstrel troupe of around twenty-seven men and boys including
eight musicians, which boasted a musical director, a manager and a president,
with on-stage antics under the charge of the group's interlocutor, H. C. Peck.[39]
Sam enjoyed singing minstrel songs and gained his greatest early success with
his version of the minstrel favourite "Old Bob Ridley-O."

Norwich and Yarmouth could offer year-round professional entertainment
in their theatres, concert halls and – from the turn of the century – in cine-
mas but professional troupes would also travel to smaller settlements, especially during the summer months. When Kate Lee (one of the leading song
collectors of the first folk revival) went searching for songs in Wells-next-the-
Sea on the north Norfolk coast, the townsfolk advised her not to bother chasing after local amateurs, but to seek out one of the blackface groups: "There's
sure to be some minstrels coming to the town in a few weeks – they nearly
always do come in the summer time, and they sing some fine songs," one local
informed her.[40] It was a frustrating piece of advice for someone who was keen
to collect traditional songs, but it does suggest that some locals viewed pub
singing sessions as second best – something to make do during the winter
months, before the glamorous professional singers of modern songs returned
to the Norfolk seaside.

Italian organ players, brass bands, broadside sellers (who sang the songs
which featured on the broadsides as an advertising strategy) and German
bands (so-called because they included saxhorns and not because their members necessarily came from Germany) could be found in the cities, towns and
villages of the late nineteenth and early twentieth centuries.[41] They performed

for passers-by rather than for a ticket-buying public, playing for whatever people put in their hats or, as Flora Thompson remembered, for free drinks.[42] The members of the German bands were reputedly skilled in more than musical performance: Harry sang "The German Musicianer" about one such musician who pleases the singer's wife with his skill at "piano tuning" and the use of his "German sausage."

Holidays and celebrations brought fairs and circuses, for which locals expended time and energy in dressing up and decorating floats and village greens alike. Circuses might bring exotic animals: camels or elephants, as ragged and weary looking as the "dancing" bears that also appeared.[43] Fairs brought roundabouts, trials of strength and other exciting rides and activities, with varying degrees of success. Broadland native Jimmy Nicholson, born in 1910 and a friend of many of Harry Cox's neighbours and singing compatriots, remembered "Rhubarb" Underwood's amusements at the annual Sutton Fair, but the quality was disappointing. Mr. Dack's amusements, at the larger Ingham Fair just after Whitsun, were more successful.[44] In Sam's childhood Winterton could boast of one of the largest village events in the county, in the Winterton Marine Regatta. The regattas were held in August and in 1880 the first attracted several thousand people to watch the races between village vessels, join the yacht *Paragon* for a cruise and take part in the duck hunt.[45]

Rivalries between individuals or villages could be played out on the sports field. The north Norfolk quoits league brought village teams together, a Mr. Cox won a race between the men of Barton Turf and Neatishead in the late 1920s, and an all-male walking competition excited the people of Attleborough in the years before World War I. Cricket teams were popular – Catfield had one when Harry moved there in the early 1900s and Barton Turf's ground became the home of Norfolk's premier village side – and fetes might include informal athletics contests such as wheelbarrow races (with men in the wheelbarrows, giving an extra challenge to those doing the pushing). An intensive training regime was unnecessary – a Norfolk veterans' race in 1935 involved Harry and Sam's contemporaries running along a track while dressed in their best shoes, trousers, shirts, ties and waistcoats.[46]

Harry and Sam sang plenty of songs about the pleasures of country life. Harry sang of "Widdliecombe Fair" and the "jolly companions" who travelled there; other singers went to the same fair, but moved it to Barningham, Maligan, Donnybrook and a dozen other places around the British Isles. Sam's favourites usually involved romantic or sexual encounters in the fields or country lanes, such as "The Haymakers' Courtship" or "All Fours." In the folk revival of the 1960s a song about travelling to Scarborough Fair – possibly a reference to the resort's beauty rather than to a collection of amusements – would cross the Atlantic and become an international favourite thanks, in small part, to Sam Larner.

2 Two Norfolk Families

The Larners came late to Winterton – long after the Hayletts, Georges, Goffins, and Kings. Sam's great-great-grandfather was one of the first to arrive: Samuel Learner (spelled with the *e*) of Bradfield was in Winterton by 1816 and married Amy Warner from Yarmouth, who was five months pregnant with their daughter Amelia, on 29 October.[1] Samuel was a bricklayer, eventually becoming prominent enough to be listed in county directories and achieving the status of freeholder with the right to vote.[2] George Ezra Larner, Samuel and Amy's grandson, became a fisherman and married Jane Amelia Powles when they were both aged twenty.[3] Jane's grandfather was Robert Jones – Sam claimed Welsh ancestry through the Jones line:

> My great grandfather, now, his name was Jones and he came from Wales. He was supposed to be well off but he ran away to sea. He came and lived hereabouts as a coastguard – and that's where we reckon we get our Welsh voices from.[4]

It's hard to establish what Sam meant by the Larners' "Welsh voices." There's certainly no hint of a Welsh accent in Sam's singing: perhaps he's referring to the strength of his voice, or the passion he was capable of putting into his songs. Or perhaps he's just making up the story to add a bit of glamour to his family background.

Sam was Jane's seventh child. Sam's oldest brother George Ezra (named after his father) was already dead, buried at Winterton church on 27 December 1870 a month after his fourth birthday. Edward, Thirza, Alice, George, and Sarah Elizabeth (aged between seven and two when Sam was born) would grow up with Sam in the busy family home, as would his younger sister Jane Amelia. Sam's youngest brother Charles was born in March 1882, but died three months later. By the time Sam was three the Larners were living in Beach Road, near the Three Mariners. Sam's mother and older sisters were working as netmasters, mending nets to bring some extra cash into the home. Bread was a staple of the family diet and Jane baked eight or nine loaves every two or three days. She kept the house clean, scattering Winterton sand on the stone floor and changing it regularly to mop up spills and mess. The Larners loved to sing around the home: Sam's grandfather knew many songs and his father and mother sang songs such as "Barney and Kitty."[5]

Over in Barton Turf, the 1891 census recorded thirty-four Coxes in a village of 386 people. On Pennygate Lane, Harry was part of the largest Cox family of all, the seventh oldest of Bob and Sarah Cox's nine surviving children. Sophia was twenty, Robert was eighteen and working as an agricultural labourer like his father, while Eleanor was sixteen years old. Florence (aged twelve), Laura (aged ten) and Rosa (aged eight) were at school which left Harry, four-year-old Anna and two-year-old Fred at home with their mother and two older sisters during the day.

Naomi Whitaker from Smallburgh, just over a mile to Barton's northwest, gave birth to Sarah on 4 February 1850. Sarah's father's name was missing from the birth certificate, but less than three months later Naomi married James Nobbs, a kiddier or market trader from another Smallburgh family.[6] In 1868 Sarah married Robert Cox, then working as a fisherman, and the couple had thirteen children. When the American song collector Alan Lomax asked if Bob fathered any children with other women, Harry told him emphatically: "We're all in the flock, alright. No outsiders."[7] Four of the Cox children died young including Martin, buried at eleven days old in 1876. Such a loss was not unusual: the under-five mortality rate in Norfolk at the time was thirty-one percent.[8] At first, the couple made sure that their children were baptised, but after Laura's baptism in 1880 there is no record for Rosa, Harry, Anna or Fred, while Eleanor didn't receive her baptism until she was twenty years old.

In later life, Harry spoke of his childhood and adolescence as happy times, apart from his dislike of school and the family's often precarious finances. His parents treated their children well:"Never was hit. Never was knocked about," said Harry. His mother was a good cook and a good baker, an easy-going woman who was blessed with a good singing voice: despite a hard life, she lived to be ninety-four. He had a close relationship with his father – "I was his boy," recalled Harry – and Bob taught him farming skills as well as songs. Bob boasted of a large repertoire and claimed that when he was away at sea for the herring fishing season he could sing two different songs each night without repeating any.[9]

Bob may have taught his son how to work the land and sing songs, but Harry learnt other things on his own or with friends. Sex education was not on the primary school curriculum, so the Barton children learnt by watching the animals on the farm. Horses were popular sources of practical information, especially when stud horses were brought in: "If we got a chance to look we'd be there," as Harry remembered. The farm workers were less keen on assisting with Harry's education and, if they found any of the children peeking at the horses, "They'd come after us with a whip ... They wouldn't let you see anything. They let them see anything now!" The village girls were as interested as the boys and as a result, Harry recalled, "They knew just as much. They were rum times." When Lomax asked Harry if he had dreams as a child, Harry replied with a laugh: "I've had dreams – wet 'uns an' all."[10]

The pub offered Harry more opportunities to add to his education as he joined his father on trips to local hostelries, a small boy barely noticed by the men in the bar. He learned quickly. As a little boy he didn't understand childbirth – when his two youngest siblings were born, he "knew they come into the world, but how, I didn't know" – but careful listening soon clarified things. Down at the pub, "I learned some funny language ... I soon got to understand that." One drinker provided advice for men who wanted to conceive a boy rather than a girl: "Old bloke he say 'You wanna be like an old drake.' He say 'You wanna get a boy you've gotta come off other side.'" Harry burst into laughter at this point, rendering any further advice unintelligible. Lomax follows this story with one of his most personal questions: did Harry ever hear his mother "carryin' on and groanin' and moanin'?" It's not clear if Lomax is asking about Bob and Sarah having sex, or about Sarah giving birth. Harry ignores the first interpretation but treats the latter to a reply: "I never did hear a sound in that way, never. I didn't know there was anything. They all came into the world and I never did know there was any, any fuss whatsoever."[11]

Bob spent most of his working life on the land as an agricultural labourer, with spells of work on the sea or on wherries. According to Harry, his father first went to sea as a young man, working on the Yarmouth sailing ships: "My da, he didn't stick the land like I done, he went on the fishing."[12] Harry remembered his father as a tough, fearless, character:

> He was short, thick and strong, very tough sort of a kid he'd been, a sort of fighting man in his time. Been through several "batters," gunning, poacher, old hares and things ... wasn't afraid of anything night or day, he didn't care.[13]

The Broads are low-lying, sheltered waterways but they are not without their dangers. Wherries could weigh up to thirty-five tons when laden and needed careful handling – if the wind dropped, the wherry had to be propelled by means of a long pole and the wherryman could easily fall into the water and drown. In the early years of their marriage Sarah would sometimes travel on the wherry alongside Bob, bringing one or two of her young children with her, but the couple ended this way of life before Harry was born.[14]

Harry claimed that his father learnt most of his songs at sea. Sarah also knew many songs, which she often learned from broadsides she bought on trips to Norwich as a young woman.[15] Broadsides were cheap, poorly printed, sheets of paper containing the lyrics to one or more songs – though not usually the tunes – and decorated with simple prints. There are numerous broadsides from Norwich printers such as Robert Cullum, Davy & Berry, and Walkers of Church Street, the topics ranging from recent executions to tales of bravery in foreign wars or gossip about newsworthy celebrities: Walkers published the lengthy and dull "A New Song, Jenny Lind's Second Visit to Norwich," credited to S. Lane, in about 1850 to celebrate the famous Swedish Nightingale's concerts at St. Andrews Hall. Broadside sellers would hawk their wares on the streets, singing the songs they were hoping to sell in printed form. They even travelled to small villages: when Harry was a child a pair of sellers came to Barton Turf, carrying a sign on a pole and singing a song about a boxing contest between Jim Corbett and Charley Mitchell.[16]

Harry's grandfather, another Robert, was a singer and a dancer. He was born in 1806 – "in a cave," according to Harry – and worked as a farm labourer around Barton.[17] Harry recalled that Robert had attended dance school and that he sang many old songs, which he passed down through the family. He was still alive when Harry was a boy, in his seventies and "living on the parish" with his wife Eleanor, his widowed daughter Sophia Brackenbury and her three children.[18] With two song-loving parents in the house and a singing grandfather close by, it's hardly surprising that evenings were spent singing to each other – or that at least one of the Cox children would become a noted singer in turn. Harry's younger brother Fred was apparently another fine singer, but he was never recorded by collectors. This may be because he married and moved to the Yarmouth area, where he and his wife Esther were living in 1915. By the mid-1920s Fred and his family were back, living in High House in Catfield, and he was known to sing in the Crown at Catfield and the Catherine Wheel at Sutton. He was at High House in 1939, working as a horseman and living with Esther and their children, Laura and Frederick.[19]

Fred was not the only one of Harry or Sam's relatives to move away from home. Sam's brother Edward went to London, becoming a Church Army evangelist.[20] In the early 1870s Sam's grandparents George and Isabella were living at 51 Peel Street, Kensington, with two of their children, Samuel and Alice. Ties to family and to Norfolk were strong and many people returned to the county after trying their luck elsewhere. By 1891 George Larner, still a bricklayer at seventy-two years of age, was back in Winterton with Isabella, living a few doors away from Sam on King Street.[21]

Those who stayed closer to home often married into local families. Sam's sister Alice married Matthew Dyble, another Winterton fisherman. Sam's unmarried sister Thirza gave birth to George Edward in 1892 and married local fisherman Edward John Powles four years later. George Henry, Sam's older brother, married Louisa Daysh, an incomer who, like her father James and mother Louisa, was born in Portsmouth. When Louisa died in 1908 George married Florrie Popay, a Winterton native who was in service two houses away from George's.[22]

Around East Norfolk the tendency to name boys after their fathers, uncles and grandfathers led to a small number of dominant first names. Nicknames were invaluable in differentiating between the many Georges, Sams, Edwards and Williams. They could be distinctive and unusual and often remained with a man for life. This was fine if they were in any way complimentary; less so if they drew attention to an undesirable facial characteristic or personality trait. The tradition was widespread across England. In the Sussex village of Rottingdean, James Copper became known, rather predictably, as Brasser and as farm bailiff he oversaw labourers who rejoiced in the nicknames of Woblow, Dido and Shirty.[23]

In Winterton, Sam's uncle James Sutton was known as Old Larpin, a derivation of "loping lugs" in reference to his prominent ears. Sam's father was known as Bredler, for reasons now lost in the mists of time. He was a large and imposing figure, as Sam recalled, "a big man, about fifteen or sixteen stone ... and he could do the stepdance." The men of the George family were often nicknamed Starchy, supposedly after an ancestor who favoured starched shirt collars; Walter Rudd's nickname was Tuddy and Sam's fellow trawlerman Robert Hodds became known as Tuskin. Harry Cox's neighbours and fellow singers boasted similar nicknames. The shoemaker Walter Gales acquired the name Waxy because of the wax he used in his work, but the origins of John Salmons's nickname of Charger, Bob Parker's nickname of Sky or James and Tom Nickerson's acquisition of Slant and Crack are harder to decipher. As far as anyone can remember, Harry Cox never gained a nickname – perhaps his first name was rare enough for it to be unnecessary; perhaps attempts never caught on.[24]

Sam "Funky" Larner gained his distinctive nickname when he was still in his teens. In the post–James Brown era such a name might indicate a talent for dance, or a certain stylistic cool, but in Sam's case it was bestowed upon him as a result of his unpredictable moods which could result in him going into a "funk" – becoming bad-tempered, angry or aggressive. The nickname stuck with Sam throughout his life. Fifty years after his death, his great-great-niece still remembered the nickname being used and recalled his ability to be outspoken and "huffy puffy."[25]

Informal, rarely-if-ever written down and often misheard by visitors, these nicknames were open to being misunderstood and misspelt by the song collectors and researchers who took an interest in Norfolk's singers: Walter Rudd's nickname might be written as Tuddy or Toody, Tuskin could become Tuscan and Bredler might be misheard as Bradley. Christopher Heppa initially believed that Harry Cox's friend and fellow singer William Miller's nickname was Bullets, but later acknowledged that it was probably Bullards, after Miller's favourite beer.[26]

Winterton and Barton Turf had much in common in the late-nineteenth century: small, close-knit communities relatively isolated from major centres of population, with most of their inhabitants reliant on hard, physical work for their incomes after receiving a few years of basic education at best. The singing of familiar songs was another experience shared between the villages.

No-one called them "folk songs" or "traditional songs" or "vernacular songs"; they were simply songs that people enjoyed singing or hearing. Such a lack of discrimination could annoy those song collectors who were only interested in what they believed to be the "pure" musical tradition of the rural working class. During the 1960s TV show *The Singer and the Song*, Sam spoke of his love of a sentimental music hall ballad called "Mignonette," written in around 1901 by Harry Dacre. He sang a verse and told of its popularity until the interviewer broke in, sounding rather irritated: "These aren't really the old songs, are they Sam?" Sam agreed, then launched into a minstrel song that was unlikely to be more than a few decades old itself. He was not a man to care too much about a song's age.

Sam and Harry started to develop their repertoires at home and at school, well before they reached their teens, and carried on once they started work. Sam learnt "Butter and Cheese and All" from his father and remembered "Windy Old Weather" and "The Dogger Bank" being popular with Winterton boys.[27] Larpin Sutton taught him "The Dolphin," "Henry Martin" came from an old labourer on Yarmouth docks and he learnt others from crewmates on the fishing vessels: "Bold Princess Royal," for example, learned on a trip to Lerwick in 1906. As he told it, his method was simple:

> They'd be singing these old songs on the watch – the old skipper'd be at the tiller and she'd be sailing along to windward, and that's when you'd pick 'em up. That's how I picked *mine* up, got 'em off all the old men.[28]

The perils and the pleasures of the sea feature strongly in English folk song. It's unsurprising that a Winterton lad like Sam would grow up to sing of storms and shipwrecks ("The Skipper and his Boy"), of pirates ("The Golden Fenidier" or "The Dolphin"), of the life of a fisherman ("The Dockyard Gate" or "Coil Away the Trawl Warp") or of the joys of sex in words thinly disguised as the tale of a fast clipper ("Cruising Round Yarmouth").

Harry first heard "Betsy the Serving Maid" and "Bold Archer" from his paternal grandfather Robert who, Harry believed, knew hundreds of songs. "Where they came from, God above know where they came from. That's how that came into the family," Harry told Charles Parker. "Betsy the Serving Maid" was one of Harry's favourites: "Now that's what I call a song," he declared at the closure of one of his recordings.[29] He claimed that "Betsy" could be traced back for over two hundred years through the Cox line: it's possible, as the song was in print by 1800, but this claim contradicts his belief that it came into the family through his grandfather.[30]

When Harry was four years old he began joining his father at sessions in local pubs, often travelling to the White Horse in Neatishead where Bob played fiddle for a shilling or two and a couple of pints of beer: "I used to go along of him and sit on the window-board, back of him – 'a little old

James "Larpin" Sutton: Sam's uncle and one of the first Norfolk singers whose songs were collected by E. J. Moeran. (Courtesy of Chris Holderness, photographer unknown)

customer' I was."[31] After her marriage Harry's mother no longer travelled to Norwich, where she could buy songs on broadsides and penny songsheets, but she kept her collection. "I never see the sheets," said Harry, "my mother learnt them, and I learnt them off her. 'Down in the Lowlands Low', that's one she used to sing."[32] As a young man, Harry worked as a drover from time to time and would drive cattle to Norwich: it's possible that he bought a few broadsides on these trips to add to his mother's collection, but given his limited ability to read it seems unlikely.[33]

"Barton Broad Babbing Ditty" was one of Bob Cox's songs, the only song known to tell of adventures in Barton Turf. It's the story of a local landowner, Old Snuffers, who hires the broad for eel fishing (or babbing). The local poachers are soon stealing Snuffers's eels, despite his attempt to frighten the eels away from the poachers' boats by playing his "music," or melodeon. According to Harry, an unknown local wrote the song when Bob was a boy – no doubt to celebrate the victory of the working man over the wealthy landlord.[34]

Harry's family was an excellent source of songs for a young lad, but it wasn't the only one. He learnt "What Will Become of England" from a customer at one of the local pubs: "Well, a chap used to come into the pub, used to play a tin whistle, and that's a song he used to sing. And I learnt it. Course, I weren't very old then. I'd only just left school."[35]

A repertoire of songs was soon useful, for both Harry and Sam were performing in public before their teens. Harry's debut was a low-key affair:

> First pub I started to sing in was the Union Tavern at Smallburgh. I was 'bout eleven. I went along with my father, they kidded me up. Well, I made a gatherin', I sung two or three o' my pieces o' songs, I went round with a hat, I got a few pennies, got a copper or two. I didn't get a lot. I got some anyhow. Then I gradually worked into it when I got older.[36]

Sam started performing in public when he was nine years old and still at school, singing for pennies to groups of tourists as they passed through Winterton in horse-drawn coaches.[37] Once schooldays were over and working life beckoned, Harry and Sam would start building their repertoires in earnest.

3 First Work, First Songs

Sam and Harry left school without regret, eager to start work and, as Sam put it, feel like "a big man."[1] Both boys had another reason to start work: it meant more money for the family and relief from the financial strain of bringing up a large household on limited means. They were doing what all of their friends were doing: ending their formal education in order to learn a useful trade.

Sam claimed that when he was a lad around two hundred Winterton men and boys worked at sea, a number that increased to 320 by 1900 and included his father and brother George.[2] It's not surprising that Sam would want to follow in the footsteps of his friends, relatives and neighbours. What is surprising is how soon he started, going out on his first trawler for pleasure when he was six, on a vessel skippered by his uncle James "Larpin" Sutton and with his oldest brother Ted as a deckhand.[3]

Sam started his working life at thirteen, signing on to his first ship (the forty-ton sailing lugger *Young John*) as a cabin boy. Seventy years later, he remembered all of the luggers he served on: *Young John*, *John Frederick*, *Gemini*, *Thalia*, *Snowdrop*, the *Snowflake* and the *Breadwinner*.[4] The early voyages were an emotional struggle for Sam and his mother: as he left home on the 6:30 a.m. train to Yarmouth his mother cried, not knowing when or if they would see each other again. When Sam was on board, he would often cry from the exertion and pain of the hard, physical tasks, his hands blistered from hauling on ropes.[5] When Sam sings "Coil Away the Trawl Warp" with his usual enthusiasm and verve, it can be easy to dismiss its tale of hard toil as an over-dramatisation: hauling nets, gutting fish, storing them tightly in ice lockers to avoid damage which could reduce their market price. But Sam knew what he was singing about. The trawl warps are the ropes that attach the trawl net to the vessel: a single trawler might use well over a mile of trawl warp and the job of coiling it away for storage fell to the junior member of the crew.[6]

In the days of the sailing boats, Sam and his crewmates might be at sea for two weeks at a time, travelling between ports. Limited space for drinking water meant that there was no room for water to wash or cook with: salt water would be used for cooking and for basic hygiene, but the men never used it for washing their faces. Back on shore the locals steered clear of these filthy, wild-looking fishermen: "We used to come home, black as ace of spades. And people wouldn't travel or trade with us ... No, they wouldn't travel, not with those dirty fishermen," Sam recalled. He would be exhausted from a voyage, barely able to stay awake as he made his way back to the family home: "My poor old mother washed me; I didn't know she washed me, I was that dead tired. They worked us 'til we very nigh dropped."[7] Despite the exhausting work, Sam felt a strong affection for the sailing boats, claiming they had something human about them and would respond to being treated kindly.[8] He learned his seafaring skills on these boats: tying knots, splicing ropes, mending the nets, cooking, hauling the nets, and setting the rigging. On average, Sam spent no more than one season on each of the luggers. Once steam drifters replaced the old sailing vessels from 1899, Sam signed on board the *Lottie*. Life became easier and he had no desire to return to the sailing luggers: "As regards work, that was like heaven when we got into the drifters ... absolutely like heaven."[9]

In a life spent fishing in the North Sea, "Heaven" is a relative term. Work on the steam drifters was still hard and dangerous, even close to port in calm weather. When Sam was around the Shetlands in the summer of

The Lottie: Sam's first drifter. Sam is the man in the middle. (Courtesy of David Higgins, photographer unknown)

1908, the fishing fleet suffered a record number of accidents in a single week. The *Agnes* caught fire, rendering it unfit to put to sea, and there were eight separate collisions, most involving East Anglian vessels – the *Ant*, the *Coronation*, the *Twenty-Four* and the *Twenty-Six* from Yarmouth, and the *General Bruce Hamilton*, the *Boy Archie*, the *Commerce* and the *Morning Star* from Lowestoft. Lowestoft's *Morning Star* and Yarmouth's *Twenty-Four* collided with each other and the *Boy Archie* collided with the Banff-registered *Mignonette*, a vessel that shared its name with one of Sam's favourite songs.[10]

Unlike the trawlers, which pulled their nets along the sea bed in order to catch the fish that swam at low levels, drifters set their nets two to four metres below the surface of the sea and drifted. Herring rise to the surface of the sea at dusk to feed on plankton, so each drifter would lay out up to two miles of nets on the starboard side and allow them to drift for five or six hours, trapping mature fish by their gills. Hauling in the nets was a back-breaking manual task that demanded the coordination of the six crewmen whose job it was – the better the catch, the harder the work, the greater the potential reward. Catches were measured in cran, with one cran equating to about 1,320 herring and weighing around 180kg. Fifty cran was average and took the crew four hours to haul in, but a good catch could be two hundred cran – over thirty-six metric tonnes of fish that could take eighteen hours to get on board. By the 1930s such catches were the stuff of dreams, the Yarmouth drifter *Lydia Eva* returning from its final trip with just six cran.[11]

Sam and his crewmates followed the shoals of herring around the coast for weeks on end, eventually returning to the Norfolk coast for a period of "home fishing." At the fishing grounds they would lay their nets at dusk, drift, haul in the catch and head for the nearest fishing port the following morning. A crewman would take a sample of the catch to the market to find a buyer, then the entire catch would be offloaded. A few hours later the drifter set out again, six days a week for weeks on end. By tradition English crews took Saturdays off; Scottish crews rested on Sundays. At the end of the season the profits were divided between the vessel's owner and the individual crew members, with the owner taking around fifty-seven percent and junior crew getting two or three percent each.[12]

Sam's early voyages were "poor doin's" and for a twenty-week voyage in the North Sea he earned five pounds. Even with a job on the drifters and a share of profits, money was tight and the Larners were often "poor as church mice."[13] High-earning years did occur from time to time. Sam recalled one lucrative season when the herring were plentiful, when he claimed he earned a hundred pounds – excellent wages at a time when farm labourers were making twenty-five pounds a year. "I came home with it … cor, my poor old mother burst out crying, never seen so much … All sovereigns." Sam claimed that he always looked after his mother: "She never went short with me, my boy … After I was married she didn't. No, no, she never went short as long as I lived."[14]

Good wages or bad, there were always herring. Once landed ashore, the herring would be sold on the quayside – Sam recalled "Russian Jews" buying up vast quantities of the fish at Yarmouth – and Sam and his fellow fishermen would go to the nearby pubs where they would eat plates of pickled herring. One of the few perks of the fisherman's job was the right to take home a supply of the fish, which could be smoked and stored for eating over winter. Sam never lost his taste for the "silver darlings":

> What! I love 'em! We were brought up on 'em and I still love 'em. When I was a boy you could come to Winterton about half past five on a winter night and the herring were cookin' all over – a lovely smell, would make your mouth water.[15]

Working in wet, windy conditions for much of the time, a fisherman's clothes were crucial to his comfort. Sam and his crewmates wore long leather boots beneath oilskin coats, trousers and sou'wester hats to keep out the worst of the weather, replacing the heavy waterproof jackets with a cotton twill smock in warmer and calmer times. Under these layers was a gansey: a woollen jumper with a tight weave that offers a high level of warmth and water resistance, decorated with distinctive patterns on the top half of the body and sleeves, representing items such as herringbones, ropes or chains – patterns that might be peculiar to a village, or even to a family.[16]

Some fishermen were skilled knitters, capable of making their own ganseys, but most were knitted by the women of the coastal towns and villages. Gansey-knitting offered the chance of paid employment and a few Winterton women worked at this skilled trade: census enumerators were unfamiliar with ganseys, recording these women variously as jersey knitters, guernsey knitters and fancy knitters.[17] The women knitted for husbands or sons and earned money as home workers for outfitters such as Yarmouth Stores.[18] The fishermen bought ganseys and other clothes from commercial outfitters in the ports, wherever and whenever the need arose. If possible, however, clothes would be darned, patched or mended – each item was expected to last for years.[19]

Although Sam remembered his early voyages as poor doin's, they gave him plenty of opportunity to sing and to learn new songs and rhymes. Most songs were sung for pleasure, or to help stave off boredom when things went quiet. "Green Broom" is one – a story of a lazy young man who, forced by his father to get to work cutting broom and selling it door to door, finds himself marrying a "maiden in bloom" – but it was also used as a work song. Sam remembered singing it when the catch was light and hauling it in was relatively easy: "We used to start singing, and I used to sing it right through ... Then they'd start, 'maiden in bloom.' They'd all go like that, man, it used to sound lovely, going hauling the nets." Sam recorded this song on more than one occasion, enjoying the "nice swing" of its rhythm. His stressing of the first and third beats makes it easy to imagine his crewmates hauling the nets on each of those beats.[20]

Young seamen were supposed to learn their trade on the job and rhymes and songs helped them to do so. Sam recorded some of these educational rhymes in later life: rhymes which taught about navigation, the points of the compass, coastal landmarks, and some of the characteristics of local ports and the people within them. There were no classroom sessions or theory exams, he remembered: "Ours was all practical know, no book learning … Experience teach knowledge, that's how we done." They were generally short rhymes, encompassing important information in a four- or five-line verse such as this:

> When in danger or in doubt,
> Always keep a sharp lookout;
> If you haven't got room to turn,
> Ease her, stop her, or go astern.[21]

Fishing was tough, dangerous, work for every man, but as a junior member of the crew Sam also had to be wary of his fellow fishermen. The romance of a life at sea soon faded once the older men administered a few beatings, or threw buckets of cold water on you if you fell asleep. When Sam spoke of these men in later life there was admiration for their toughness, but also bitterness about the treatment they sometimes gave him:

> A rare old bulldog breed they were, they didn't care for nothing, neither God nor man they didn't … they were wicked old men. Now and again you'd find a kind old man but some of 'em, oh, they were cruel. You wasn't allowed to speak … put the rope onto your backside if you give 'em any trouble.[22]

Even when a crew included a family member there was no guarantee that treatment would be more favourable. Sam remembered that his uncle Larpin Sutton, who sailed with Sam on the *Breadwinner* and taught him many songs, used to flog him and then cry afterwards.[23]

Kitty George, landlady of the Fishermans Return in the 1920s and 1930s, shared Sam's disdain for many of the retired fishermen who frequented her pub, describing them as "selfish, cruel old men who were only interested in drinking, fighting and fornicating."[24] Sam's own generation may not have been as cruel as their forebears, but they were not all the jolly fellows of nostalgia. One of Sam's relatives, a child in the late 1950s and early 1960s, remembered them without fondness:

> They were rough types. Goodness me. The old fishermen used to go and sit outside their huts on the beach and if any children went

anywhere near, whoa! They frightened us. The same at the top of the lane, they'd sit there and they'd say: "You come anywhere near me and I'll give you a good faggin', you little varmin." Yes, children were quite rightly scared of them.[25]

Sam showed no inclination for fighting, but he was fond of beer and of sex, as his singing of "The Reckless Young Fellow" suggests:

> I once was a reckless young fellow,
> I never took care of my life,
> I sailed the salt seas all over,
> And every port a fresh wife.
>
> I wish the wars were all over,
> And I safe ashore on the main,
> God bless me forever and ever,
> If I ever go whoring again.[26]

As he finishes the song Sam laughs and declares: "I been a naughty boy in my time ... little bit naughty. But no harm, no harm." It's as if he's the subject of the song, not merely the singer.

Harry may have been reticent to speak about his sex life, but Sam had no such concerns. He spoke proudly about his exploits to MacColl and Seeger, but was aware that such days were long gone:

> "I been a wicked man in my time," he said, with obvious relish. "Ain't that right, Dorcas?" (This to his wife, who was sitting by the fire, opposite him.)
>
> "You have, Sam, you have," agrees Dorcas philosophically.
>
> "Yes," says Sam, his one good eye alight with concupiscent memories, "I done some wicked things."
>
> "You been a wicked bugger, Sam," comments Dorcas again, and Sam shakes and wheezes with delight.
>
> "See? She knows what I mean. Don't you, my old dear?" Then, with passionate intensity, he says, "And I loved it. Yes, I loved it! And now that I'm too old for it I don't care whether I live nor die. No, I don't, truly I don't!"[27]

During the same recordings Sam sang "Blow Away the Morning Dew," a song about a "pretty fair maid" who foils a man's attempt to seduce her. This song brought back more memories of sexual adventures: "I always loved a young woman, always. And I could always get one ... had one in every port ... Course, I been a lustful old boy in my time, you know, I loved 'em." He loved the Irish girls he met in port at Fenit, in County Kerry, when he was fishing for mackerel off the Irish coast. He learnt local songs while he was there too, perhaps finding them useful in forming relationships with these young women.[28]

"The Dogger Bank" epitomises the toughness and glamour of the fisherman's life and Sam sang it with relish. Sailing from the Dogger Bank to "Great Grims-bee" is hard work, but there's pride to be had in sailing the ship successfully and a joy to be had when the wind's blowing freely in the right direction and there's a chance to "Give her sheet, let her rip." The crew are dubious characters – the captain's a "shangaroosh," the mate's a "roadstone inspector" who's been inside many a gaol, the third hand's a "bush ranger" from the "African Isles" and the cook is "hoppity wild." But they can do the job and once on shore they're ready to get drunk, roll around on the pub floor and create something of a "jubilee."[29]

According to one Norfolk historian there were two types of herring fisherman. One, epitomised by "Wilks" Larner or William "Wee" Green, saved his money and invested wisely, eventually owning his own vessels. The other went to sea to earn a "latch-lifter" – enough money to be able to lift the latch of the pub door, go in and spend it all.[30] The crew in "The Dogger Bank" were eager to spend their latch-lifters, Sam would have felt comfortable in their company.

The life of a single man away from home for large parts of the year obviously appealed to Sam, at least for the first few years, but after a decade at sea he returned to Winterton and married Dorcas Eastick on 29 December 1903.[31] Winter weddings were common in the area, perhaps because fishermen were more likely to be at home during that time. Even Christmas Day and New Year's Day weddings were routine, as these were two of the rare holidays granted to working people – Harry's sister Sophia married on Christmas Day 1895.[32]

When Mr. Wrenford, the curate of Great Cressingham parish church, baptised Dorcas on 14 July 1878 he recorded her name as Ellen Dorcas Eastwick, with a superfluous *w*, but she was always known as Dorcas (named after a woman who St. Peter raised from the dead) and her name was recorded as Dorcas Ellen in later documents. Dorcas's father Arthur was a village postmaster and baker when he married Anna on Christmas Day 1877, less than seven months before Dorcas was born.[33] By 1901 he was the landlord of the Bell Inn at Anna's home village of Saham Toney; Dorcas was in Winterton, working at Hill House for eighty-one-year-old widow Mrs. Eliza Hurne, and her two nieces. Mrs. Hurne employed three servants: a lady's maid, a cook, and Dorcas – at the bottom of the domestic pecking order as house parlour maid. Hill House was on King Street, as was the Larner family home, so it's not difficult to imagine Sam and Dorcas meeting up on their way around the village. Details of their courtship are long-forgotten, although one story has Sam travelling to London to court Dorcas, possibly when Mrs. Hurne spent time in the capital.[34]

By the time of Dorcas and Sam's wedding, Arthur was running the Green Man in Watton – the wedding register lists both Arthur and Dorcas as licensed victuallers.[35] Sam recalled singing to Dorcas when they were courting and singing in the pub on their wedding day.[36] The celebrations were tinged with sadness, however: earlier that week, Sam's niece Marjorie died at the age of three.[37]

Was it a happy marriage? It was certainly a long one, lasting for sixty years. Peggy Seeger, who interviewed Sam in his final years, remembered Dorcas being present at the interviews from time to time, seemingly content but saying little – usually nothing more than short responses to Sam's comments or questions. Seeger also thought that she had sight problems. Dorcas is pictured in a couple of photographs – a grey-haired, elderly, woman wearing a floral housecoat, with a slightly bemused smile on her face. In recordings Sam refers to her as "Mother," despite the fact that the couple was childless, and when he struggles to remember facts or gets dates wrong he often turns to Dorcas for help.

Family members remember Dorcas as "absolutely lovely" but question her relationship with Sam, who was variously described as "an old sod," "a dirty old bugger" and a womaniser who did not treat his wife well. Sam seems savvy enough to know who he was talking to, the showman persona revealed to interviewers and audiences contrasting with the tougher, funkier personality reported by relatives and others. There is a belief in the family that Sam contracted syphilis and passed it on to Dorcas. There's no clear evidence for this, but it may be an explanation for their lack of children and for Dorcas's eye problems: the fact that the story is accepted by family members says something about their perspective on Sam's personality and behaviour. If it's true, Sam would not have been unusual. Research into syphilis among men in their mid-thirties in the decade before the Great War suggests that the prevalence was between three and eleven percent, with an average prevalence of around seven percent.[38]

Sam sang plenty of songs about the joy of the single life, or about the heady days of courtship and the early promise of a wedding, but songs about married life are far less frequent. In "When I was Single" he moans, "when I was single I had a black shawl, now that I'm married I get bugger all" – but he immediately adds, "Still I love her." "Before the Daylight in the Morning" is another "bad marriage" song. It opens with the singer wishing he'd been "killed on the banks of the Nile" – making it clear that this tale of married life will not be a happy one – before going on to describe a beard on his wife's lip "like a wandering Jew" and the beatings he'd receive if he failed to carry out his domestic duties. Sam found the line about the beard to be especially funny, laughing as he repeats it to Ewan MacColl while trying to remember the next verse.[39]

After marriage Sam carried on with the fisherman's life, spending long periods away from Dorcas as he continued to journey around the coasts of

Britain and Ireland. The work was still hard even on the steam drifters, but it was easy to come by and the fishing was good, ensuring that Sam and Dorcas had enough money to live comfortably. Dorcas wasn't happy about Sam's life at sea, telling him that it made her feel miserable. She knew she was marrying a fisherman, Sam reminded MacColl, but he was sympathetic towards the fishermen's wives at home, "the wind a-roarin' down the chinley, ah, they lay awake and thinkin' about on you at sea." He was also a realist, aware that jobs on land could be hard to find and paid little, and the drifters were less dangerous than the old sailing vessels.[40]

A steam drifter saved Sam's life when he experienced a severe storm off the Norfolk coast on 1 October 1911, a storm that might have proved too much for a sailing lugger. Sam was serving as mate alongside the skipper, his brother-in-law and fellow singer Bob Green. Sam remembered the storm as occurring in "the year after King Teddy died": the sea was "like smoke" and the ship was lucky to reach safety at Cromer. The Hull-registered drifter *Montrose* was less fortunate – the vessel sank in the storm with the loss of four crew. This may have been the most extreme weather that Sam faced, but it was not the only time he escaped tragedy: "Me, I'm one of them people who seem to bear a charmed life. I've been overboard four or five times, and I'm not dead yet."[41]

Sam joined the Royal Naval Reserve Force a month after his wedding, serving for five years before being discharged with the rating of trained man, seaman class.[42] The RNRF was a volunteer group of merchant sailors and fishermen prepared for call-up in the event of war to supplement the Royal Navy's full-time force. Sam was like many of his fellow fishermen in joining up, although doing so just a few weeks after getting married is unusual.[43] Shortly before Sam completed his service Louisa, the wife of his brother George, died two weeks after giving birth. Louisa's death put pressure on George and support from the couple's extended family was vital: Sam and Dorcas took baby William (or Willy) into their home and cared for him as one of their own.[44]

As the drifters sailed north on their summer voyages, stopovers in the Shetlands offered the chance of organised entertainment for the crews courtesy of the Church Army, St. Margaret's Mission and various willing local supporters and volunteers, who organised "smoking concerts" for the fishermen. Full houses were the norm in Lerwick's Rechabite Hall, providing a talented young singer like Sam with a large and boisterous audience. After a long and difficult voyage any entertainment would have been popular, but the extent and variety of the Rechabite Hall's evenings made them doubly welcome. Sam was a popular and well-known performer – despite later writers' insistence that he was "discovered" in the 1950s. Sam was fond of telling the story of his success in a Lerwick singing competition, where a rousing rendition of his song and stepdance number "Old Bob Ridley-O" brought him first prize:

The Lerwick ladies, they had to judge and the gentlemen, to judge the singin'. And I got the most encore of the lot for that song. They won't let me sit down, I had to sing 'em another song. That was in 1907. These people all know it about here, I aren't telling stories. And I got the first prize.[45]

Sam did win first prize, but contemporary accounts in the *Shetland Times* tell a slightly different tale. The concerts began in 1907, taking place each Saturday night during the fishing season and often featuring singing competitions, where a panel of judges awarded prizes. At each concert tobacco and cigarettes were provided free of charge to all the attending fishermen thanks to the generosity of local donors. The Church Army's Captain W. J. Ford, a Lowestoft man, organised the events and was also a popular performer, noted for his singing of music-hall favourites such as "Boom with a Ra Ta Ta." The wide range of performances at a typical concert, from piano soloists to comics and singers of maudlin ballads, suggests that the fishermen had broad tastes – or were prepared to put up with the duller aspects of the programme in order to get their free tobacco and cigarettes. The *Shetland Times* reported that the concerts were so popular that hundreds of eager fishermen were unable to gain admission. Eventually, they were moved to the larger Town Hall.[46]

There's no record of Sam appearing in the 1907 season, but his reputation preceded him in 1908 – the *Shetland Times* eagerly announced the 25 July concert with the news that "Sam Larner, the well-known comedian and dancer, has promised to appear." Faced with a large audience, mostly consisting of his fellow fishermen, Sam shone. He won an encore when he sang the humorous "Butter and Cheese," despite facing stiff competition from Joe Great, with "The Wonderful Musician" and "Timothy Toodles"; Mr. A. Leeder, a singer, pianist and impersonator who imitated the cornet and the banjo at the same time; and Miss Robertson, whose singing of "A Pattern to the World" gained her an encore. Mr. W. Hall was less of a competitor for Sam, merely singing "Sentenced to Death ... well." If this is the turgid, melodramatic song by W. C. Robey and W. H. Fox that tells of the execution of a young Irish soldier, Mr. Hall is to be congratulated for singing it at all. It hardly seems like the sort of musical number that herring fishermen on a night off would be demanding to hear.[47]

The following Saturday evening Sam was back at the Rechabite Hall for another "right-down good evening's enjoyment," in the words of the *Shetland Times*. Joe Great was there again as were Miss Robertson, the singer, and Mr. Leeder, the impressionist. Royal Navy torpedo boats were in port and one of the crew, Mr. Richards, proved popular when he sang "How'd You Like to Spoon with Me?" Sam, the "well-known and popular Winterton comedian," sang two comic songs, recited *Christmas Day in the Workhouse* and was one of nine performers to win prizes.[48]

Sam's biggest success that season came a couple of weeks later. Warrant Officer Snelling of the torpedo boat *HMS Spanker* took on the role of judge for the singing competition and awarded a total of sixteen prizes. Joe Great took second prize, having created "much amusement among his fellow-fishermen from the south." Best of all, Sam took first prize for a performance of "Old Bob Ridley-O" (reported as "Bob Bridley-O" by the newspaper) that "fairly brought down the house with laughter and applause."[49] "Old Bob Ridley-O" is a song and dance number from the American minstrel tradition, the lyrics making it clear that the singer is a black worker from the plantations of the south recalling, surprisingly cheerfully, his tough life in the cotton fields. Sam's recording of the song, made in the 1950s, is bright and cheerful enough, although he always sings of young Bob rather than old Bob. It's easy to imagine the much younger Sam singing and dancing his way to victory in front of the Shetland crowd.

Sam's friend Tuskin Hodds informed Winterton of Sam's success in the Lerwick competitions and concerts by letter. Tongue firmly planted in cheek, Tuskin told his friends and neighbours of Sam's fame with admirable hyperbole, speaking of a level of success that "has been absolutely astonishing in the history of the Shetlands" and claiming that Sam's popularity now exceeded Harry Lauder's. He also claimed that adoring fans had showered Sam with enough bunches of carrots to provide the horses of the London Fire Brigade with fodder for the entire winter – a ludicrous if amusing claim that would be picked up by the Norfolk newspapers in Sam's old age.[50]

There were contests around the Broads villages, too, but Harry took a more jaundiced view of such things and refused to enter them. He was sure that such competitions were fixed in favour of a local singer, no matter how good other entrants might have been:

> They went for a show of hands ... if I'd had a go, I shouldn't have got nothing, 'cos that was set. They'd set for any other body they think ought to have it, you see. If one wasn't half so good at singing they'd show hands to him ... They wanted him to have it.[51]

Young Harry had little time to enter competitions, even if he wanted to. He started his working life at about the same age as Sam, leaving school when he was twelve-and-a-half: "I've been knockin' about on the land ever since I've been able to do anything," he claimed.[52] As a boy his wages were small, just two shillings and sixpence a week, making Sam's first wages seem generous. By seventeen his earnings had risen to nine and sixpence a week but seven shillings went to his mother to pay for room and board, leaving little to spare for clothes or entertainment. When his wages rose to thirteen shillings for a sixty-hour week he took his spare six shillings and spent it at the pub: "I never did trouble about the money, I used to spend it as I got it, make myself happy," said Harry, who would take a different approach to finances as he grew older.[53]

Shetland Herring Fishing

*(Reproduced by kind permission of Mr. H. C. DYBLE
January, 1964)*

My dear Friends of the North Shed,—

No doubt you and other Winterton friends have heard with pleasure the success of the Winterton Comedian—Mr. Funky Larner. His success has been absolutely astonishing in the history of the Shetlands.

His popularity here is now even more than Harry Lauder's. You remember when the famous Scotch (not Winterton) Comedian set sail for America on the Lusitania, the thousands that saw the popular Harry off to earn £500 a week, will be a mere flea-bite when the good ship Thirty-Two leaves here. Unfortunately the ship cannot carry the prizes and presents that have been won and given him since he arrived in the most Northern Burgh in the British Isles.

For instance, he won a Tan Copper on Saturday, also a Box of Cutch the previous week. That will take up a lot of room. The bouquets of White Heather, Bunches of Carrots, etc., that have been hurled at him are sufficient to provide the

"LONDON FIRE BRIGADE HORSES"

with fodder for the winter. Popular Sam Larner is not like the "Village Blacksmith," who on Sundays went to church. Something above that, he goes with, not his daughter who sings in the village choir, but with his brother Bradley to the "Rechabite Hall." There these two brave Lifeboatmen lead the choir. Poor Sammy's pathetic speech relating to the death of poor little "Nelly" brought tears to the eyes of everyone. For in "Uncle Tom's Cabin" the death of poor little "Eva," everyone knew was a child. Sam with his London and Bressay experience of telling a yarn, forgot to tell the audience that poor Nelly was a dear little "Dorg."

Please arrange to see that popular Sammy has a fitting reception at the North Shed on his arrival from here.—

Yours faithfully,

TUSKIN HODDS

The Shetland Letter: Sam's first taste of fame, as reported by his friend and fellow fisherman, "Tuskin" Hodds. (Courtesy of Chris Holderness)

Agricultural work was poorly paid and tightly controlled, but union activity in the 1870s and 1880s had won concessions from farmers and the government so Harry was employed under slightly more liberal conditions than those of the previous generation. His father Bob started farm work before the union's success and would struggle to earn ten shillings a week as a married man – much less than was needed to support a large family. When Harry speaks about his father's working life it's easy to hear the anger and bitterness in his voice, especially when he talks of a farmer called Mac who reduced his father's wages to nine shillings at one point, with Bob threatening to drown him as a result.[54]

Harry left Barton Turf before he started full-time work. He'd lived in the village "all my young life, my word, crawlin' bout round there … we moved away there, in the finish … we went away Thurgarton way, when I was about ten." Harry met his first sweetheart Maud Hewitt in Barton. The daughter of a marshman, Alice Maud Hewitt was a few months younger than Harry, a fellow pupil at Barton school and a close neighbour in Pennygate. When he left the village he left Maud behind and never saw her again. It would be some time before he embarked on another romantic relationship: "I didn't trouble 'em a lot, I never did go after 'em much," he said. He was taking his father Bob's advice: although Bob regretted not having more relationships before he married, his advice to his son about women was "don't have nothing to do with 'em." Eventually, Harry restarted the activity: "I wish I'd kept away from 'em then," he reflected in later life.[55]

Thurgarton – about fifteen miles northwest of Barton Turf and closer to the North Sea at Cromer than it is to the Broads – is even smaller than Barton, but luckily for Harry there was plenty of singing in the area: "I used to go to the pub over there and hear a lot of good old singing and it was my delight to sing."[56] Perhaps Bob Cox's night-time activities around Barton Turf brought him to the attention of the local gamekeepers, necessitating a move away. As Harry tells it, his father was a skilled and canny poacher:

> Old hares and things, he'd been through all that. He'd do anything, he weren't afraid o' anything. He used to go out after old hares at night in Barton. Porch, church porch, that's when he got two or three old hares and he was goin' far away he'd go an' lay 'em in there … 'til he came back. He used to say they'd never touch them in there, they're frightened by the churchyard. He shot many a hare in there, Barton churchyard, at night.[57]

Bob was not the only Barton local to creep out at night with a gun or a net. As Harry explained, a poacher could take a night's catch home to feed his family or could sell it on for much-needed cash: "There was plenty like him, then. That was a right do. A good old hare was worth half a crown."[58] Landowners and gamekeepers were keen to catch poachers, but working families understood the need to go out poaching game and Harry was on their side: "pheasants and things, they're as good for you as anybody else. Then they made the law up so you mustn't touch 'em. That's what caused people to poach." Harry called it the eleventh commandment – "steal, rather than starve."[59]

There's one tantalising hint that Harry may have followed in Bob's foot-steps, although both Harry and his granddaughter Jenny deny that he did.[60] When Michael Grosvenor Myer and Bob Thomson visited Harry they asked if he remembered a specialised item of poacher's clothing: "Have you ever seen one of those old coats they [poachers] used, with big—" asked Myers. Before he could finish the sentence Harry responded with, "Mine's hanging up over there."[61] Harry's ownership of such a coat is, of course, far from defin-itive evidence of illegal activity – after all, Yarmouth Stores openly made and sold hard-wearing, waterproof coats with internal "hare pockets" stitched in place.[62]

The Cox family soon moved from Thurgarton. Harry remembers that he first sang in public at the Union Tavern in Smallburgh, around sixteen miles from Thurgarton, when he was about eleven years old.[63] It's a long way to travel just to sing in a pub when your only means of transport is your feet and when pubs nearer to home were good for singing, which suggests that the Cox family was already back in the Broads by then. Harry's oldest sister Sophia married at Potter Heigham in 1895, which also suggests that the fam-ily was living in the area. In 1901 Bob, Robert, and Harry were working as agricultural labourers and living with Sarah, Rosa, Anna, and Fred in Decoy Road at Potter Heigham. Florence had married earlier in the year, Laura was in service with the Jarvis family in Cromer, while Eleanor was probably in service elsewhere.[64]

The family soon moved again, this time taking a house in nearby Catfield – a village that lies equidistant between Hickling and Barton Broads. The village was small, around six hundred inhabitants, but well-served by tradespeople. The Crown and the White Horse were the village pubs and the Rational Sick and Burial Society kept an office in the village. There were numerous farms and the main crops would have been familiar to Bob and Harry – wheat, oats, barley and turnips.[65] Cox was a rare surname in Catfield: of around eight hundred burials recorded in the parish between 1881 and 1983 only three had that surname. One of them was James Cox, who drowned in Yarmouth harbour on 18 December 1908. His body eventually washed up on the beach three weeks later and it was a further month before he was buried in his home village.[66] Harry described him as "a little bit of a relation," and remembered how "Jimmy got drowned in Yarmouth harbour, off a wherry. He could swim, but he couldn't get hold of nothing. They say he just held his hands up and went down."[67]

The 1911 census recorded six members of the family. Laura was absent from the census again and Rosa too was not at home. Eleanor had married in March of 1902, with Rosa as witness.[68] The household had gained an extra wage as Fred now joined Bob, Robert, and Harry in farm work while sister Anna was helping her mother on "house duties." The 1911 census differed from previous ones, requiring the head of the household to complete a return instead of relying on an official enumerator. Bob undertook the role diligently, filling out the form in legible though rather ragged handwriting and recording Anna as Annie. He recorded six rooms – "Count the kitchen as a room but do not count scullery, landing, lobby, closet, bathroom: nor warehouse, office, shop," the instruction read – and gave the address as "Nr. Heath, Catfield." Fred was now twenty-one, Harry was twenty-six. With four out of six members bringing wages home, the family may well have been more comfortable financially than it had ever been.

Farm work changed with the seasons and varied from district to district. Around Stalham and Martham soft fruits such as blackcurrants and raspberries were important summer crops, grown for Yarmouth. In 1911 a sugar beet factory opened in Cantley, ensuring that beet production would become a major part of Norfolk agriculture.[69] In the same year, the first bitterns to breed in England for fifty years did so on Hickling Broad: perhaps the male's distinctive "boom" kept Harry company at dawn and dusk in the fields and reed beds.[70] These local differences and longer-term changes gave variety to the long days of labour on the land. Harry found enjoyment – in one of Harry's favourite phrases, he "took delight" – in most of the tasks. If the work involved a group of labourers this was an opportunity to "get into a gang, have a club, jug or two of beer, happy as the birds in the wood." His favourite activities involved hooking, cutting or chopping wood or rushes, or scything crops.[71] Harry often worked alone and took the chance to sing to himself as he went about his tasks: "You got a nice job, you could sing all day long, 'muse yourself."[72] Harry loved living and working in the country: "I think that is the best … all the lovely sunshine … You can lay down and have a nap, nobody to come by you." In his opinion, the high buildings of a city like London hid the sunshine and there were too many people around to disturb his rest.[73]

Harry enjoyed his own company, fond of taking time for himself, at work or at leisure. Singer and vocal coach Frankie Armstrong connects Harry's love of being alone with the style and tone of his voice:

> That sense of Harry's heavy, plodding, voice. That's not a criticism.
> It's a very particular kind of voice. It's not a "giving out to the world"
> voice, it's a voice to occupy your time in isolation, therefore you're
> feeding it back to yourself. It's a voice that circles out of you then
> feeds back to you. I don't know if that makes any sense, except as
> a kind of metaphorical image … He's telling stories to himself. …
> Harry's singing doesn't have that physicalising thing of people using
> their bodies and hands and eyes as part of their expression.[74]

Harry developed talents in many different aspects of farm work. He was skilled with a scythe, good at wood cutting, able to look after livestock or operate a horse and plough. He could take on work outside the fields as well, as a thatcher or a reed cutter: "I done any old farm work, anything put before me, any kind of work you like. … I didn't care what I done, I done anything in the agricultural way."[75] He took particular delight in tying sheaves of corn, a job at which he was especially skilled: "I was never afraid of nobody on that job … I could do that as quick as you like, I done acres and acres."[76]

According to Fred Cox's grandson Reg Reeve, Fred could turn his hand to as many jobs as his big brother. Like Harry he made frail baskets from rushes, was skilled at tying and stacking corn and had a talent for making things: "He could build anything, he could make anything out of wood; he was brilliant … He was a brilliant gardener … he could thatch like second to none!"[77] Fred found work on a local farm but Harry started working on a self-employed basis, hiring himself out to farms across the area. Billy Durrants, a younger farm worker who knew Harry, explained the older man's strategy:

> He was all piece work, Harry, he wasn't a regular farm worker. He used to go and work for himself where he could earn more money. Harry was more of a businessman than the rest … He'd do thatching, beet hoeing, anything.[78]

Work as a self-employed agricultural labourer was precarious. Harry had to be more widely skilled than the average worker, reliable, honest, trustworthy, and physically fit. He would need to be a determined and dogged negotiator as well, to ensure that he earned the maximum possible income. It seems that Harry was all of those things, as well as being blessed with good health for most of his life: "Never knew what it was to have any sort of illness, that sort of thing, I been a-goin' all the time."[79]

As a single man living at home, Harry spent a great deal of time with his father and could spend time (and money) with friends in the pubs around Catfield, singing his favourite songs and learning new ones. This lifestyle may have been crucial in his development of an extensive song and tune repertoire: living a bachelor life and regularly visiting local pubs filled with friends and fellow singers meant that he was more likely to hear new songs. However, Harry worked long hours as a single man and didn't change his working habits after marrying so it's unlikely that marriage played a great part in reducing his pub-going activities.

Alan Lomax, who interviewed Harry extensively in the early 1950s, was keen to know what Harry's relationships with women were like and unafraid to question him in very personal terms. Harry was initially reluctant to reveal too much – after all, in an earlier conversation he'd stressed his lack of interest in women – but Lomax persisted. "In all these here songs it looks like all the girls laid down pretty willing," Lomax suggested in one interview, drawing out Harry's opinion that "it looked like how you hear. But I think that funny doin's is about now."[80] Lomax didn't pursue the concept of funny doin's, but he returned to the theme of sex in other discussions. "When you were a young man, could you fool around with the girls in the countryside or did you have to go to town to get a whore?" Harry replied, "Ooh … these here that led that life, that's where you'd find them, they're not so much in the country."[81]

Harry was careful to avoid giving away any personal details, keeping his responses general so it's seldom clear if he's speaking from experience. When Lomax asked if he could get a country girl "to give you a piece," Harry told him, "Yes. There was them about. Yes, that was going on … Course, town's the main part … they do it for a living in these towns." Lomax enquired after the health of the town girls: "Did they mostly have diseases?" Harry replied, "In country places you were alright. In towns, I wouldn't trust 'em."[82] Harry is always polite during these interviews, but on more than one occasion he does sound surprised at Lomax's persistent questions about his sex life. In a later interview he spoke with distinct disapproval about Lomax's desire to record one bawdy song:

> That old fellow who come from America, I told you, he wanted "The Long Peggin' Awl." I sang that, he took it on his recorder. I didn't like dirty things like that. I mean, I used to be ashamed to sing it. But I ain't ashamed of nothing now.[83]

Harry's reference to Lomax as "That old fellow" is amusing and perhaps a deliberate slight: Lomax was around forty when he undertook his recordings of Harry, while Harry was about sixty-eight. "The Long Peggin' Awl" is one of the ruder songs in Harry's repertoire – he remembered his father would never sing it at home, only in pubs "when he got among the rough crowd."[84] The title gives a strong hint about the song's content and its use of phallic symbolism; anyone seeking subtlety and nuance should listen elsewhere.

After his marriage, Sam "Funky" Larner carried on with his fisherman's life: visiting ports around the coasts of Britain and Ireland, singing on board and entertaining on shore and coming back to Dorcas when the fishing was over for another year – whether or not he carried on pursuing a girl in every port. A few miles north Harry took delight in work, song and the single life. Things might have stayed that way for many more years, but the Great War was looming.

4 The First Folk Revival

At the end of the nineteenth century folk song was dying, the last generation of singers soon to disappear, leaving no-one to remember their songs. These tales of pirates, murders, shipwrecks, lost lovers, battles, cuckolds, and seduction – already limited to the farming communities of the rural counties – would disappear from England's culture. The illiterate, ill-educated and poverty-stricken singers and their friends would leave no record for others to follow. Who could save these invaluable treasures of English life? Enter the folk song collectors: enthusiasts from the Victorian and Edwardian middle classes who were ready to work tirelessly across the country to secure these songs for future generations.

That's one version of the story. The debate about what is generally known as the first folk revival (at least in England) continues to this day with varying degrees of discussion, argument and (occasionally) anger and rancour – even without considering the thorny issues of what English folk song actually is and whether it was ever dying in the first place. Singer and musician Martin Carthy makes the important point that it's wrong to think of English folk song as stylistically constant, from Newcastle to Newquay, from Lowestoft to Liverpool:

> The mistake some people make is to talk about an English style. There is no such thing. What you get is a whole panoply of noises coming out of those singers all across the country. That whole patchwork is an English style. Each square on the eiderdown is wildly different from the one next to it.[1]

It takes only a few minutes of listening to Harry and Sam to feel like Carthy's point is incontrovertible. Born within six years of each other, living only a few miles apart and sharing some of the same songs, the two men are as stylistically different as Janis Joplin and Maria Callas or Martin Carthy and Captain Beefheart.

It's been said that a "folk revival" has never been clearly defined, so what can safely be said about the first folk revival in England?[2] It took place around 1895–1920, predominantly in farming counties such as Lincolnshire, Sussex, Dorset, Norfolk and Suffolk. There, middle-class men and women sought out "traditional" singers (almost all men), asking them to sing a few songs and noting down the tunes (and less frequently, the words). The Folk-Song Society was established in 1898, the English Folk Dance Society followed in 1911 and the English Folk Dance and Song Society (EFDSS) was formed when the FSS and EFDS amalgamated in 1932. The revival's impact on the country as a whole was minimal, compared to the many popular songs emanating from the music halls and theatres, but it did lay down a body of songs and tunes that would be eagerly taken up by later enthusiasts. Whatever the motives and biases of the first revival's collectors, they created an invaluable archive for later generations. Without them, many songs and tunes could have been lost: good things happened thanks to the first folk revival.

Magazines and journals – notably the *Journal of the Folk-Song Society* – published some of these songs and tunes, often arranged for voice and piano so that respectable ladies and gentlemen could sing and play them in musical *soirées*. Folklorists and musicologists engaged in lively debate about whether a singer favoured major scales or modal approaches, but they largely ignored the singers once they had performed for the collector – Jim and Tom Copper from Rottingdean were unusual source singers, as they became members of the Society after singing for Kate Lee.[3] Most collectors would not record songs that they viewed as too modern, or as coming from popular sources such as music hall. Lyrics that were too earthy would be censored or altered by the collector or even by the singer, anxious not to assail the collectors' delicate ears with rudeness. There were plenty of those bawdy songs, with words too shocking for the sensitivities of a well-mannered, middle-class audience: as one writer put it, "the rude rustics were rude indeed, and liked their dirty songs."[4] Harry might have taken issue with this characterisation, although he knew many such songs: "His repertoire of sexualia is extraordinary," as one source put it.[5] Sam would likely have agreed wholeheartedly about the popularity of a *risqué* tale.

There was something of a social disconnection between the collectors and the singers. Cecil Sharp and Ernest Moeran both attended Uppingham School.[6] Kate Lee was a professional musician who trained at both the Royal Academy and Royal College of Music. Ralph Vaughan Williams, Percy Grainger and George Butterworth were talented composers.[7] Lucy Broadwood, who started song collecting in the 1880s, was the niece of the piano-maker John Broadwood and the cousin of music critic J. S. Fuller Maitland.[8] Peter Kennedy, a leading figure in the 1950s "second revival," was the son of Douglas and Helen Kennedy – respectively the director and first

Honorary Secretary of the English Folk Dance Society and the nephew of song collector Maud Karpeles: the Honorary Secretary of the English Folk Dance and Song Society (EFDSS). Peter Kennedy joined the EFDSS as an employee after World War II.[9]

Kate Lee's early experiences of folk song came during Christmas visits to wealthy friends. On one such visit Lee decided to note down songs from a group of locals, but her host told her not to "because he said 'it would spoil the men very much if they thought they sang anything worth writing down.'"[10] In 1907 Cecil Sharp felt able to claim that

> twenty years ago … it was only by a very few people that folk-songs were known to exist in this country … At that time, and for several years afterwards, it was generally assumed that we had no folk-songs of our own, and that the English peasant was the only one of his class in all Europe who was unable to express himself in dance and song.[11]

Sharp's definition of "people" appears to exclude the thousands of men, women and children who were regularly singing these songs, listening to them and dancing to them in pubs, houses and meeting places across England. Sharp set out his ideas in *English Folk Song: Some Conclusions*. He was adamant that no singer under sixty years of age was worth hearing, because their songs would nearly all be modern.[12] When he wrote these words the thirty-year-old Sam Larner was winning song contests in Shetland, Harry was making a few bob and free beers in Broadland pubs while still in his early twenties, and the younger members of the Copper family were developing their extensive repertoires in Rottingdean – all singing songs from decades and even centuries past.

The revival didn't enforce strict rules about collecting. Some collectors concentrated on tunes, caring little for the words being sung. Some collected in a single county, or a small area within a county. Some would do their best to note down tunes and words as the singer performed; others would ask the singer to repeat a song over and over until they had as accurate a record as possible. (Sharp was such an in-depth collector, visiting some singers at least twenty times.)[13] Most collectors gathered songs in public spaces such as pubs – which may explain in part why the great majority of the collected singers were male – but on occasions they would collect in the singer's home or perhaps in their own home, although this was a strategy to be used cautiously. Kate Lee invited an elderly female singer to her home, where she sang many songs, but at first Mrs. Lee was nervous: "I had qualms when she first threatened to come and sing to me; I thought she might be a burglar in disguise, so when she first arrived I took down songs with one eye on the umbrellas and the other on the paper."[14] Lee's writings suggest that she had a sly sense of humour, so the qualms may be as much for comic effect as real, unless her umbrella collection was particularly valuable (or useful as a source of weapons). In the north of Ireland, Sam Henry started collecting songs in 1908 when he took on the job of assessing people for their old-age pensions. He travelled with his fiddle as a way of forming a friendly relationship with the people he visited and often found himself accompanying a song or two. Over a thirty-year career he collected around 850 songs.[15]

By the early 1900s a new technology was beginning to ease the task of noting down tunes and lyrics: the phonograph. The machine and its wax cylinders were readily available, transportable with care, and increasingly affordable for the middle classes. Although many collectors preferred to retain the notebook and pencil approach to recording, others were enthusiastic about the phonograph: Sharp, Vaughan Williams and Lucy Broadwood all made use of phonographs with varying degrees of success.[16] Percy Grainger became its most fervent advocate, dismissive of the complaint that the machine's presence would negatively affect a singer's performance even if, as the Lincolnshire singer Joseph Taylor quipped, it was like "singin' with a muzzle on."[17] Unfortunately, none of the collectors who descended on Norfolk at this time brought a phonograph with them. Unfamiliar dialects led to lyrics being misheard or misunderstood – by singers when they learnt the songs, as well as by collectors trying to write them down. One man sang "Dimmy Darey ran through the wood" to Kate Lee, then informed her that a Dimmy Darey was a dromedary. When she discovered a written source for the lyrics, she found that a "little timid hare" was doing the running.[18] The possibilities for bias or error were endless; even the use of audio recording devices didn't always ensure clarity.

The collectors who arrived in Norfolk, notebooks and pencils in hand, visited much of the county and heard a variety of singers – although neither Harry or Sam were among their number. In Wells-next-the-Sea Kate Lee met a singer she identified only as Tom C. He proved to be a disappointment musically, as he was so nervous "that not a note could he utter, and he gave way to groans, interspersed with whistling when he got anywhere near the air." Even worse, the one song Lee did manage to note down from Tom's singing turned out not to be traditional. Tom redeemed himself by introducing Lee to an old gardener, whose name she noted as Mr. Edge. He was a veteran of the Chinese War and told Lee that "he had been 'a great singer in his day.'" Edge sang a song called "Llandaff" which he first heard during his army service in Wales.[19] Lee included "Llandaff" in her 1899 *Journal of the Folk-Song Society* article, along with songs collected from the Copper family.

Ralph Vaughan Williams visited Norfolk on at least five occasions between 1905 and 1911, collecting over 170 songs.[20] In Hickling Peter Knight sang him "Turkish Lady," "'Twas Early One Morning," and "Spurn Point"; at Ranworth he collected songs from Sally Brown, Walter "Skipper" Debbage, and Mr. Saunders; at the Bridge Inn in Acle, Christopher Jay sang a handful of songs including "The Foggy Dew" and "The Bonnie Bunch of Roses."[21] George Butterworth collected songs across Norfolk in the years immediately before

William "Shinny" Crowe: another singer from Larpin's generation. Shinny was, like Harry, an agricultural worker. He sang for George Butterworth. (Courtesy of Margaret Crowe, photographer unknown)

World War I. In California John Woodhouse sang him "O Father Dear Father"; in Filby, five or six miles south of Winterton, Butterworth met "Shinny" Crowe who sang him at least eight songs including "Saucy Ward," "On the First of November," and "Scarboro' Town." In March 1913 he collected the tune of "Spanish Ladies" in Winterton from a source noted simply as "a young sailor."[22] It's tempting to think that this was Sam, but he was almost thirty-five – no longer a young man – and the sailor remains unknown.

This fervent collecting activity helped to save many songs from oblivion, but it failed to enthuse the great mass of the English public. Ronald Pearsall, writing in the middle of the 1970s, argued that the "general public" (in particular, the urban working class) "was suspicious of folk song, of its being foisted on it for its own good." As for folk dance, this "was eternally risible, and still is."[23] Pearsall, an ex-professional musician, carried out his entire discussion with regular references to individual collectors and composers, but without mentioning a single source singer by name.

Even if the first revival failed to enthuse the mass of the great British public, Norfolk proved to be a rich source of songs that appealed to the Folk-Song Society's members. As the Great War approached, a young and enthusiastic music student with no connection to the society became attracted to the county's folk songs. He would become the most important early collector of songs from Harry and Sam's singing communities.

5 A World Turned Upside Down

Ernest John Moeran, a student at the Royal College of Music, failed to get a ticket for a Bach concert and went to a concert at Queen's Hall instead. He was prepared to be "bored stiff," but found himself moved by the music and filled with enthusiasm to hear more. One of the pieces was a rhapsody by Vaughan Williams, based on songs from Norfolk. Moeran decided to explore the source music and "to lose no time in rescuing from oblivion any further folk-songs that remained undiscovered." This sounds romantic and perhaps a little excessive, but the singers he met in the months and years that followed assured Moeran that these old songs were dying out.[1] Helpfully, his father was the vicar of Bacton, on the east Norfolk coast, so the newly converted lover of English song could begin his quest in his own back yard.[2]

After one church service Moeran approached William Mayes, the senior church chorister and head team man at Abbey Farm. Mayes mentioned that he knew "The Dark-Eyed Sailor," but refused to sing it on a Sunday. He did sing it (along with other unnamed songs) the following day, but the immediate area around Bacton proved to be devoid of an active singing community.[3] Other places in east Norfolk would be more fruitful sources of songs and tunes, but before Moeran could begin to explore their possibilities Britain went to war.

World War I impacted on every corner of the British Isles and on every aspect of life, including social life and the arts. Unknown numbers of men and women who enjoyed singing in choirs, at parties or in pub sessions died with their songs unrecorded, their singing voices lost forever. George Butterworth was killed in action at the Somme, aged thirty-one. Moeran was seriously injured during service in France.[4] The Norfolk Regiment took heavy losses and the county itself came under German attack. Harry and Sam joined up.

Britain declared war on 4 August 1914 and Norfolk soon felt the direct impact of hostilities. On 22 September a German submarine destroyed three Royal Navy cruisers with the loss of almost fifteen hundred sailors, many of them reservists from East Anglia. On 18 November the Yarmouth drifter *Seymolicus* hit a mine and sank, nine of its crew dying. The Government requisitioned more than five hundred drifters from Yarmouth and Lowestoft – fifty-four of them were lost in action. Yarmouth became a submarine base and an air station, while Lowestoft served as a base for minelayers. On 3 November a group of eight German vessels bombarded the Yarmouth coastline: there were no casualties, but the attack showed Norfolk's vulnerability. Then on 19 January 1915 Yarmouth gained the unwanted distinction of being the first British town to suffer fatalities from a German air raid, when a bomb landed on St. Peter's Plain killing fifty-three-year-old cobbler Samuel Smith and seventy-two-year-old Martha Taylor.[5] By the end of the war, twenty-five men from Catfield had lost their lives in the fighting (twice the national average) and eighteen Winterton men had been killed. They included seventeen-year-old James Sutton of the Royal Naval Reserve, the son of Sam's uncle Larpin.[6]

The Battle of the Somme, which began on 1 July 1916, devastated the Norfolk Regiment. The regiment's so-called Kitchener Battalions – the Seventh, Eighth and Ninth, all popular with the county's farm workers – suffered seventeen hundred deaths and injuries during the battle's first week. Bill Curtis, from Salhouse in the south of the Broads, managed to survive but his friends did not:

> We went in a full battalion, we come out twenty-four of us … When we couldn't get through we got in a shell hole. There was five people all from Salhouse in that shell hole. I was the only one that got back.[7]

Moeran, aged nineteen and a keen motorcyclist, volunteered for army service when war was declared and became a despatch rider in the Norfolk Regiment. In mid-1915 he gained a commission and spent some time on leave at Bacton before going to France.[8] He travelled to Winterton, where he heard the singing of Larpin Sutton and noted down five of his songs – "The Bold Richard," "The Captain's Apprentice," "The Royal Charter," "The Pressgang," and "The Farmer's Son" – but didn't meet Sam, who may well have been at sea. Moeran didn't make it to Catfield during his leave and he was soon back on the front line, but he eventually discovered Harry and his friends thanks to a serendipitous meeting with an old road-mender.

Sam and Harry volunteered for active service. For Sam, an experienced seaman and an ex-Royal Naval Reserve Force member, the navy was an obvious choice. The army may seem the likeliest destination for landlubber Harry, but he decided to join the Royal Naval Reserve. His father's experience of life at sea and his own knowledge of the Broads waterways may have played a part in his decision, or he may simply have decided to follow his friends and neighbours: of the thirty-six Potter Heigham villagers who served in the armed forces, sixteen of them joined the Royal Naval Reserve.[9]

Naval records offer some insight into Harry and Sam as young men, although the records are not as reliable as they should be as the urgency of wartime recruitment led to incomplete and sometimes conflicting information. Sam's service records give one or two clues to his appearance: a fresh complexion, blue eyes and scars on both wrists. There was space to record his height and chest measurements but no-one did so. Harry's basic training log records him as being five foot eight inches tall, with brown hair, hazel eyes and a fresh complexion but no distinguishing scars or marks. One record gives his chest as a scrawny twenty-eight inches, but another shows it as thirty-eight inches, which seems more likely for an active labourer.[10]

Many years later, some of the people who met Harry and Sam gave their own descriptions of the singers. Ewan MacColl described Sam as "short, compact, grizzled, wall-eyed, and slightly deaf but still full of the wonder of life"; words that sit neatly alongside Peggy Seeger's description of "a little pudding of a man, square face, very stolid."[11] Sam's great-great-niece Jane Roberts remembers him as five foot eight or nine at most. Photographs of Sam in old age support these descriptions: one picture of Sam and Dorcas standing at their cottage door suggests that Sam was just a couple of inches taller than Dorcas. Harry, the younger by seven years, wore his age more easily than did Sam. In 1942 Francis Collinson estimated Harry's age as early to mid-forties and was astounded to find that he was in his late fifties.[12] When Bob Pegg and Leslie Shepard saw him more than twenty years later, both men thought Harry still looked younger than his years.[13] However, while Collinson remembered Harry as tall and lithe, and Shepard described him as tall and wiry, Pegg thought he was far smaller than he had expected from photographs. Jenny Barker, Harry's granddaughter, questioned the Royal Navy's record of Harry as five foot eight; her father, Lenny Helsdon, was five foot ten and Jenny remembers her grandfather as being taller than her dad.[14] An early-1960s photograph of Harry, Myrtle, and Jenny (all seated) suggests that Harry was no taller than his daughter – just to add to the confusion. Alan Lomax was impressed with Harry's hands and felt moved to tell him: "You've got strong hands. Big, powerful, hands."[15]

Sam enrolled as a Royal Naval Reserve deckhand on 12 December 1914, although it would be another two years until he saw active service. Sam and Dorcas lived at seven Miriam Terrace in Winterton when he enrolled but at the time of his transfer to Ramsgate his records listed his address as "Nr. Railway Gates, Ormesby, Great Yarmouth." Sam gained promotion to the rating of second hand on 16 February 1917 and went to serve on armed drifters, which were fishing vessels commandeered for military service and fitted with light guns. Dorcas moved to the south coast, joining Sam at 52 Hertford Street in Ramsgate where they lodged with a Mrs. East.[16] One stormy night, Sam's vessel ran aground near Ramsgate. One of his crewmates was scalded by a kettle of boiling water as the ship was driven towards the rocks at a place Sam called the North Break and the vessel sent out a distress call, so loud that Dorcas heard it onshore. Sam, clad only in shirt and trousers, helped to rescue the scalded crewmate and the lifeboat took all of the men off safely.[17]

Sam joined the *Dewey*, a Lowestoft-registered drifter commandeered as a patrol boat and armed with a single six-pounder gun. He was unhappy and nervous from the start of his brief time on board: "I said to Dorcas … 'I'd like to get out of that ship. … There's something about her ain't right.'" Sam's fears were compounded when he saw some of his fellow crewmen sleeping on their stomachs – he took this as a sign that he was being "forewarned" – and he was relieved when he was transferred. On the night of 12 August 1917 the eighty-three-ton *Dewey* was on patrol in the English Channel when it collided with the SS *Gleniffer*, a comparative giant of a ship at 9,428 tons. The *Dewey* sank off Beachy Head and eleven of the twelve crew were lost.[18]

Sam's closest brush with the enemy took place in the Downs, a sheltered area of sea between Deal and the Goodwin Sands, when he was on board a patrol vessel. Once again Sam was "forewarned," this time by the sight of one of his crewmates blowing up an inflatable lifebelt, but this time the warning came just hours before the event. A group of German destroyers evaded detection, entered the Downs and opened fire. Sam was in his bunk but unable to sleep and at the sound of the first explosion he leapt up: "I was out there and into the wheelhouse before some of them were out their bunk. I was like lightning." The German destroyers soon fled, their attack a failure, but Sam was in no doubt about his escape: "If they'd hit us we wouldn't have known a thing about it."[19]

Sam was demobbed in March 1919 at *HMS Vivid*, a Royal Navy shore base in Devonport, and went home to Norfolk. He may have been injured or taken ill towards the end of the war, as he received five shillings and sixpence a week disablement pension from his discharge until the end of September 1919, with an additional one shilling and fourpence a week from early April "in respect of child," his "adopted" son Willy.[20]

Harry volunteered for service in the Royal Naval Reserve on 1 January 1917, for "hostilities only" as his war record phrased it. He served as an ordinary seaman until his discharge on 12 April 1919, getting his basic training at *HMS Pembroke*, a shore station at Chatham.[21] Harry stayed there for six weeks and then, as Ordinary Seaman Cox, he began a two-year posting to his first and only active ship, the *Blanche*, one of seven *Boadicea* class scout cruisers named after the famed warrior queen of Norfolk. In that role it was part of the British Grand Fleet at the Battle of Jutland, but on the day Harry joined the ship it was re-commissioned as a minelayer and spent the next few weeks being refitted for this new role. A few months after Harry completed his training a group of German Gotha bombers attacked Chatham and hit the drill hall at *HMS Pembroke* killing 131 men, mostly young ratings undertaking the same training programme as Harry had done. It was the war's largest loss of life from a single air raid.[22]

HMS Blanche undertook sixteen mine-laying missions during the last eighteen months of the war.[23] For most of that time the *Blanche* was under

Harry Fred Cox, RNR: c.1917. (Courtesy of Steve Roud, photographer unknown)

the command of Captain (later Admiral) Reginald Aylmer Ranfurly Plunkett-Ernle-Erle-Drax. Plain old Harry Fred Cox, as far down the chain of command as it was possible to get, arrived on board with his ditty box – a wooden box about the size of a large shoe box, in which sailors kept their most valued personal possessions. This was filled with two or three homemade wooden puzzles, a tin whistle and – kept in a small Ship brand matchbox – a tiny model of a black cat, which Harry hoped would bring him luck. As the *Blanche* was based in Scotland, Harry travelled to and from the ship by train via London, his first trips to the capital.[24]

The *Blanche* was attached to the Fifth Battle Squadron of the British Grand Fleet when the German fleet surrendered and Harry was on board to witness the event.[25] His granddaughter Jenny remembers him telling stories of how scared he felt when twenty-foot waves reared up alongside the ship, but his only published story of action comes from an interview a few months before his death. Looking through Harry's photographs, Bob Thomson found a picture of two sailors. Harry told him: "That's me with one of my pals. During the war I was a sailor three years. Mine laying most of the time. Light cruiser. One night, there was one bugger got fouled. That blew up." According to his son-in-law Lenny, Harry thought "that was the finish o' us."[26]

Bob Thomson believed that Harry had "a touch of guilt" about surviving the war.[27] It was a common reaction in the men and women who came home, especially if friends and neighbours didn't return: historian Simon Schama described it starkly as "guilt, for missing the slaughter."[28] There was no justification for such guilt on Harry or Sam's part: they volunteered and they did their bit.

Harry and Sam continued their Royal Navy service for a few months after the armistice, returned to their home villages in mid-1919 and, at least at first, to their old working practices and social circles. Harry's name was added to the Potter Heigham Roll of Honour, still displayed in the Church of St. Nicholas. Songs of war, soldiering, and combat on land and sea would feature strongly in their repertoires for the rest of their lives, but none of these songs emerged from World War I. The revivalists would sing many songs about the conflict but Harry and Sam, like many who had direct experience of the war, preferred not to remember it in song.

E. J. Moeran recovered from his head wound, went back to England and returned to his musical career, teaching music at Uppingham then studying once again at the Royal College of Music.[29] At first he made no attempt to collect songs:

> As most of what I heard had been sung to me by elderly men, who assured me old songs were fast dying out, by the time the war was over I assumed there was no more to be had, and did not immediately make any serious efforts at collecting folk-songs.[30]

Moeran soon found that his assumption was wrong, but Harry also felt that the singing tradition of his youth was on the way out. "Most of that died away after the first war. Ah, that did," he told Charles Parker in 1963, "That went then. That might go a year or two after. Then there wasn't much more singing after that."[31] A visit to east Norfolk in the autumn of 1921 rekindled Moeran's enthusiasm for collecting, thanks to "an S.O.S. for me to come at once to Stalham." The emergency call came from Arthur Batchelor, a friend and fellow enthusiast who overheard an old road mender singing softly to himself as he worked.[32] Robert "Jolt" Miller was the singing road mender and he would prove crucial to Moeran's next phase of song collection.

Jolt was modest about his talent, but he sang in pub sessions and invited Moeran to spend an evening with him at one of the regular sessions around the Broads villages. Moeran thought Jolt was "a bachelor of absolute integrity," even though his repertoire included several "scandalous ditties" which Moeran politely refused to name. Jolt's respected place in the Broads singing community enabled Moeran to become accepted in the pub sessions. As he heard more and more old singers, Moeran began to form opinions about their styles and their knowledge of song:

> There seems little doubt that the traditional singers unconsciously adapt their tunes to their own personal fancy and singing idiom. Jolt was one who liked a tune with a wide tessitura. Also, he was fond of the drop of a major sixth … I heard many songs that were not traditional … The people who sang had little idea of what was the nature of a folk-song.[33]

Whether Jolt was aware of his love of a wide tessitura is debateable. The singers' love of non-traditional songs was common across England and could be a source of concern to some collectors, who worried that the popularity of these new compositions would sully the purity of the rural singer's repertoire. Other aspects of the singers' personalities and perspectives seemingly passed Moeran by. He told a story of one singer as a means of explaining their lack of understanding of folk song:

> Perhaps the most surprising appearance of an old song that was not a folk-song was when a greybeard, wearing ear-rings … suddenly announced … a song. "That's a rare old-un," he said turning to me, "I'll lay you hain't heard it afore." I was somewhat startled when the song turned out to be "Rule Britannia," and still more so when the whole gathering not only sat it through, but solemnly joined in the chorus.[34]

The possibility that the assembly was having a joke at his expense doesn't seem to have occurred to him.

At one pub session Jolt introduced another singer, hitherto unknown to Moeran. "Here's Harry," Jolt announced, "he've come over from Hickling purpose to sing to you tonight."[35]

6 Mr. Moeran Comes Collecting

Harry Cox impressed Moeran with his repertoire, his talent for memorising a new song after hearing it only three or four times and his ability as a singer. Moeran hailed Harry as "probably unique in England to-day as a genuine traditional singer combining comparative youth with a style of artistry which has almost disappeared."[1] Over the next twenty years, he revisited Harry to collect more songs. The experience affected Harry greatly: even in the late 1960s, said his friend and fellow Norfolk singer Peter Coleman, he would talk of his meetings with Moeran "as if he'd just come last week."[2]

Harry saw Moeran as more than a collector. He liked Moeran's ability to note down tunes and was pleased that the younger man published his songs in the *Journal of the Folk-Song Society*:

> He used to come to Sutton. Come that way I first met him. He put me in those books. They never were all in there though. He did well, he did a lot of writing. You used to sing for him, he used to get the music – take the tune down you see, a little in this line, a little in that ... He was a good chap.[3]

Harry told Bob Thomson that Moeran "was going to do a book of all my songs … we was gonna share profits … we never did finish that."[4]

The 1921 pub sessions brought together many of the Broads singers who would be part of Harry's social circle for decades. As well as Jolt Miller, Moeran met and collected songs from Jolt's nephew William (Bullards), Walter Gales, Ted Goffin, Shepherd Taylor, Charlie Chettleburgh (Moeran called him "Mr. Clittleborough" when he published his version of "The Groggy Old Tailor") and Elijah Bell.[5] He also met Harry's father Bob, but could not persuade him to sing. Bob was in his mid-eighties and aware of his declining vocal ability so it's not surprising that he refused Moeran's offer, leaving the family's reputation as talented singers to his son and ensuring that his own reputation remained intact.[6]

Harry was a single man for most of the 1920s, a drinker of mild rather than bitter, and a regular customer in the pubs of at least four Broads towns and villages.[7] Moeran collected songs from Harry at an unnamed venue in Potter Heigham, probably the Falgate or the Railway Tavern – or possibly Harry's home, where he could take note of a complicated song without having to deal with the noise of a busy bar. Harry's participation in some pub frolics went well beyond the singing of a dour ballad or bawdy song. Billy Durrants recalled Saturday nights at the Falgate, when Bullards would dance while drinking a pint and Harry would dance while playing his melodeon above his head, years before T-Bone Walker and Jimi Hendrix started doing the same with electric guitars. Durrants's memories conjure up a very different Harry Cox from the one familiar to those who only knew him in his later years.[8]

The *Journal of the Folk-Song Society* published three selections of songs from Moeran's Broadland collecting trips. The 1922 selection was prosaically titled *Songs Collected in Norfolk* and included Larpin Sutton's songs from 1915. The second and third collections (published together in 1931) were titled *Love Songs and Ballads* and – enticingly – *Humorous and Disreputable Songs, and Ballads of Adventure*. Of the thirty or so songs spread across these three selections Harry was the source for nine of them, including "The Bold Fisherman" and "The Pretty Ploughboy." It's possible that Harry contributed more than this, as Moeran listed some songs simply by the place where he heard them being sung without naming the singer – for example: "As I Was A-Walking One Morning in Spring" at the Pleasure Boat in Hickling, "The Girl of Lowestoft" (a.k.a. "The Hole in The Wall") at the Star Inn in Martham, and "The Publican" at the White Horse in Neatishead.[9]

The *Journal* published most of the songs in full, lyrics and tune, but some were incomplete and the footnotes added by Moeran's co-authors show that there was dispute about the "authenticity," origins or quality of others. "The Captain's Apprentice" appears twice in *Songs Collected in Norfolk*: one complete version from Larpin Sutton and one, the tune only, collected from Harry at Potter Heigham in 1921. It's something of a morality tale although the message hardly needs telling: don't beat, torture and murder a young orphan cabin boy even if you are the ship's captain, for if you do you will be hanged. Frank Kidson gave Harry's version of "The Bold Fisherman" short shrift, describing it as "very imperfect" compared to the version published on a broadside by Such.[10]

"The Fowler" (a.k.a. "The Shooting of his Dear") attracted most discussion. Harry recorded the song in 1959 for Mervyn Plunkett but the version Moeran used in *Songs Collected in Norfolk* came from Harry's friend Waxy Gales. A young man goes out bird shooting (probably poaching, as he's happy to blast away at a swan), unaware that his lover (Polly in Waxy and Harry's versions, Molly in others) has also gone out, foolishly wearing a white apron. The young man mistakes his white-clad lover for a swan and shoots her dead: he confesses to his uncle and goes to trial, but his lover's ghost appears and begs that he be freed. The theme appears in songs from America, Ireland, Germany, Scandinavia, and France. Sometimes the lover is seen as a fawn and not a swan, so "Dear" should be "Deer." In a footnote, A. G. Gilchrist claimed that "there seems little doubt that this ballad is a degraded relic of something very old, and that fair (lit. *white*) Molly can trace her descent from either swan-maiden or enchanted white doe." Waxy and Harry sing of how Polly was shot "in the room of a swan." Perhaps she was shot in the room of The Swan. How and when did "form" become "room," if that's what happened? Shirley Collins's version is clearer, with Johnny shooting Polly "in the place of a swan." The Shackleton Trio's recording (as "Molly Vaughan") is even clearer, Georgia Shackleton singing that young Jimmy shot Molly when "he mistook her for a swan." One of the earliest collected versions also makes his error plain. Sharp collected "The Shooting of his Dear" from Mrs. Louie Hooper and Mrs. Lucy White in Hambridge, Somerset, in 1903: the women sang of the young man setting out to shoot a swan, but shooting Polly by mistake when he "took her to be a swan."[11] (Folk songs – such simple things.)

The Shackleton Trio (l-r: Aaren Bennett, Georgia Shackleton, Nic Zuppardi): a twenty-first century band that takes inspiration from Harry and Sam. (Courtesy of the trio, photograph by Sam J. Cook)

Humorous or disreputable songs were acceptable, as long as they didn't go too far. This third collection opens with a verse of Harry's "The Soldier and Sailor," which is neither disreputable nor humorous (nor adventurous). Harry's "London Town" tells of a visitor to London who is seduced by a woman who plans to rob him after sex. He manages to sneak out of bed as she sleeps and turns the tables on his would-be robber, stealing her gold, silver, and "five hundred pound." "The Groggy Old Tailor", a tale of marital infidelity with victory going to the cuckolded husband, also appeared in full. Harry called his version "The Bold Drover," after the heroic husband, but it's otherwise almost identical to Charlie Chettleburgh's version which Moeran chose to include here. The mildly amusing lyrics attracted no comment but some debate arose regarding the tune, with Gilchrist asserting that it resembled "Kate Kearney" while A. Martin Freeman doubted its authenticity: "Is this a folk tune? Bars five to eight especially are suspicious."[12]

"The Girl of Lowestoft" fared less well than most of the songs: just one line of the chorus was given, with Moeran's footnote stating that "The words are indecent and not of interest or value, so they have not been noted." They are indeed indecent, if not obscene, but it's an act of censorship that runs counter to Moeran's later criticism of the Bowdlerisation of English song lyrics and his wish for a collection of English song "in which nothing worthwhile is glossed over or left out for reasons of squeamishness or timidity."[13]

Moeran arranged six songs from his collection for voice and piano, publishing them as *Six Folk Songs from Norfolk*.[14] They included Harry's version of "Down by the Riverside," from 1922. Harry's version of the song is seven verses long and tells the tale as if the woman and the supposed fisherman have never previously met. So, when he "gently lays her down" and she notices his gold chains, she's shocked to discover that he's no mere fisherman (bold or otherwise) but a rich young lord. Moeran edits the song, eliminating any suggestion of improper behaviour on the part of the woman or the fisherman: the resulting romanticised mush is a mere three verses long and tells a different story. In Moeran's brief and bucolic tale the fisherman rows up to his lady (clearly, they are already well acquainted), ties up his boat, takes her hand, and proposes that they go at once to his father's hall so that they can be married. There are no gold chains, no hint of sex on the riverbank, and no suggestion of the fisherman's noble birth – it's all rather dull.

Moeran was the first person to bring Harry's singing to the attention of the members of the Folk-Song Society. Harry also has Moeran to thank for giving him his most *outré* fans, a group of folk song lovers from England's artistic and cultural *avant-garde* who provide the first evidence of one of Harry's songs being performed in Winterton and offer the tantalising prospect of his work being admired by fans of "the wickedest man in the world" – the occultist Aleister Crowley. Moeran's friend and fellow composer Philip Heseltine was the link between Harry's world and a free-living, bohemian group of artists, writers, musicians and composers that included Augustus John, D. H. Lawrence, John Goss and Jacob Epstein. Heseltine was born in the Savoy hotel, went to Eton (and, for a year, Oxford University) and became a music critic and composer. Along the way he developed a love of the music of Frederick Delius, became close friends with the older man, enjoyed high-speed motorbike-riding while naked, began to call himself Peter Warlock, met Moeran, and became interested in English folk song and the mysteries of the occult – including the "magick" of the "wicked" Crowley.[15]

Heseltine and Moeran were friends by the autumn of 1923, when they spent time travelling around East Anglia with a phonograph on what Heseltine called a "folk-song hunt." Sadly there's no evidence of any surviving recordings from this road trip, but Moeran's artist friends joined him on further trips to the Broads, keen to hear the area's singers. A couple of years after their folk song hunt Heseltine and Moeran shared a cottage in Eynsford, a small village in Kent, where they gained a reputation for heavy drinking and wild weekend parties filled (it was rumoured) with nefarious and morally suspect activi-ties.[16] They still found time to visit the Broadland singers.

Augustus John was an enthusiast, calling Harry Cox "a first-rate singer with a large repertoire of traditional songs." John, the singer John Goss, Heseltine and his then-partner Barbara Peache travelled from Eynsford to the Windmill Inn at Sutton expressly to hear the singers at one of their regular pub sessions. The singers and their fans seemed to get on well: in a photograph taken on a wintry day in the mid-1920s, Moeran and the Eynsford quartet stand with six unidentified local singers outside the Windmill Inn.[17] The group are relaxed, singers and artists mixed together: Goss with a pint in his hand, John with a cigar and walking cane, everyone wearing hats and overcoats. One of the singers bears a resemblance to Fred Brown of Catfield while another could be Bullards Miller, but Harry seems to be absent.[18]

John tells the tale of a performance of Harry's "Down by the Riverside" in Winterton one dark and spooky evening. John, Goss, Heseltine and Peache visited the village's Church of All Saints and Heseltine regaled his friends with a rendition of the "beautiful but profane song" on the organ – presumably Heseltine sang as well as played. Things started to go awry, John wrote:

> Moved by a perverse whim, I proposed to revive the rites of a more ancient cult by there and then offering up Miss [Peache] upon the altar. My ill-timed pleasantry had hardly been uttered when, with a deafening crash, a thunderbolt struck the building, instantly filling the interior of the church with smoke and dust.[19]

Lightning dislodged a pinnacle, but luckily there were no casualties.[20] It seems churlish and inaccurate to blame Harry's "profane" song for such a disaster: John's attempt at ancient sacrificial rites seems far more likely to be the cause of the thunderbolt. Heseltine was familiar enough with Harry's song to be able to spontaneously perform it for his friends: that John sees no need to further explain Harry to his readers offers further evidence that Heseltine's friends knew him and his songs. The incident occurred on 26 April 1926, so such familiarity is not too surprising as Moeran had published *Six Folk Songs from Norfolk* only two years before.[21]

Heseltine respected Moeran as a song collector, writing that his friend's collection of over a hundred songs was one of the finest in Britain, gathered together "from no antiquarian, historical, or psychological reasons, but because he loves them and the people who sing them." He was in favour of Moeran's approach to collection – informal, friendly, remembering that "old throats grow dry after an hour's singing" – and wrote that the finest tribute to his friend's popularity among the singers of the Broads "was the remark of an old man at Sutton after a sing-song to which Moeran had brought a visitor from London: 'We were a bit nervous of him; with you it's different, of course – you're one of us.'"[22]

Visions of night-time frolics in Broads public houses filled with singers, attentive audiences, and colourful groups of visiting bohemians conjure up an impression of idyllic rural life where everyone is content and comfortable. It's an impression that speaks to our contemporary sense of nostalgia, but it's not one that would be recognised by many of the customers in those village inns. When Harry was a young man, agricultural workers' wages were still poor and unrest was close to the surface. Despite some improvement in wage levels, in 1923 this unrest peaked and farm labourers came out on strike, demanding a minimum wage of thirty shillings a week (up from the previous national minimum of twenty-five shillings) and reduced working hours. For six weeks from mid-March, the strike crippled Norfolk's farming industry. The dispute was often rancorous and violent and the Farmers' Federation brought in blackleg labour to break the strike.[23] The union responded to this move by forming bands of flying pickets: groups of strikers on bicycles, which could reach farms quickly to act against strike-breakers.[24] If persuasion failed, direct violence could be employed – including attacks on magistrates, who pickets pelted with eggs, rotten vegetables and stones.[25]

Groups of men whose task it was to intimidate non-strikers and scab labour became known as "wild gangs." One wild gang member, Ernie Cornwall, remembered that some police were willing to support their violent actions:

> Well there was one place where our policeman he come past us wheeling his bike and they (the strikers) see these here (the blacklegs) and he say to the men he say, "Stop somewhere out of the way then you can go after them."[26]

Strikers' spirits were high, a mood helped by George Hewitt's sighting of a white blackbird – a local sign of good luck.[27] However, after two or three weeks without progress the authorities toughened up their responses to the strike and the union's costs mounted. It was agreed that the twenty-five-shilling wage would remain as the standard minimum and the strike ended. Its aftermath impacted negatively on the county's rural communities. Mechanisation, already underway, led increasingly to a loss of farm jobs. Around a thousand Norfolk strikers were not re-employed after the dispute was settled.[28] Friends and neighbours were divided, as strikers and non-strikers lived and worked side by side.

Harry refused to strike: he was concerned for the animals under his care, cattle or horses that would not be properly fed or looked after if the normal routine of farm work was interrupted. His self-employed status may also have influenced his decision: he could easily have found himself *persona non grata* among his potential employers. He was not the only Norfolk farm worker to cite animal welfare as a reason for staying at work and initially the union was happy to ensure that animals were looked after in certain circumstances.[29] But as the strike hardened, strikers resented such activities and Bill Curtis, survivor of the shell hole at the Somme and member of the Salhouse wild gang, spoke of this with contempt:

> There was three blokes on the farm where we were on, they wouldn't strike. They was "Oh my master can't let me go. Whose gonna look after the horses?" "Bugger the old horses" I said "We don't want to worry about them. They can feed, turn 'em out to grass."[30]

Harry ended up in confrontations with the strikers: being "set upon" on the road, experiencing difficulties getting fodder delivered, and having fodder bins tipped over. However, when Moeran and others visited the Broads in September 1923 and April 1924 they found Harry singing in pub sessions, which suggests that he was still welcome in his singing community and his local hostelries.[31]

Harry's life as a single man came to an end in 1927 when he married Elsie Mary Amis, a dressmaker. He was forty-one. Alan Lomax tried to establish a few facts about Harry's relationships with women in the years between Maud Hewitt and his wife-to-be by suggesting that he would have been a handsome man in his younger days, but this approach got him nowhere. Harry replied: "I don't know how I looked. I weren't ugly. When I had my teeth, my proper teeth, in. I was different to how I am now. I was round, you know, more."[32] Harry and Elsie married on New Year's Day at Potter Heigham's St. Nicholas Church, with Fred Cox as a witness.[33] Elsie was born in Potter Heigham to Robert, a farm labourer, and Anna Amis (or Amiss) and she was baptised into the Primitive Methodists on 7 August 1892. Anna died a year later and Robert remarried in December 1895. His new bride was Sophia Cox, who was just nine years older than Robert's son Edward. She was also Harry's older sister and so, when Harry and Elsie married, Sophia became Harry's step-mother-in-law.[34]

With close family ties in a small and relatively isolated community, it's not surprising that Harry and Elsie met. It's more surprising that neither of them married until the advanced ages (for the time) of forty-one and thirty-four. Harry told Alan Lomax that he met Elsie when she was picking fruit, after which they courted for more than a year. When Lomax asked Harry if she was good-looking he said simply, "Weren't too bad." When he asked him about Elsie's eyes Harry replied "I don't know what colour her eyes were. I don't take much 'count of eyes." In response to Lomax's enquiry about whether he and Elsie had sex before they married, Harry was matter-of-fact: "Oh, yes. That's what you gotta do. Gotta try 'em first." He was chattier when asked about Elsie's domestic abilities:

> She was a good cook. A dressmaker, too. She could make anything. I had all my things made at home. She made everything I had: trousers, stockings, shirts, jackets and all. I never had to go and buy anything when she was alive.[35]

Elsie's dressmaking skills and the influence of his time in the Royal Navy gave Harry a distinctive style of dress that hardly changed from season to season, as he was convinced that what kept you warm in winter would keep you cool in summer. He wore a flat cap, a long-tailed collarless shirt, a gansey, and a canvas smock – also known as a slop. He favoured long woollen socks for his feet with short rubber boots – slip-on for work, lace-up for leisure time. His trousers were particularly distinctive. They were tweed with a flap front, closed with buttons rather than the usual fly, and with braces rather than a belt to hold them up. To ensure the braces did their job and didn't fall off his shoulders, Harry tied a piece of string across them at chest height. Outdoors in colder weather, a tweed overcoat completed his ensemble. After Elsie's death Harry took his business to Sparlings of North Walsham, which made his clothes to measure and sent them to Catfield by post.[36]

Harry told Alan Lomax that he thought Elsie was in love with him from the beginning of their relationship, though a surviving photograph from the day does nothing to support the claim. It shows bride and groom staring hard at the camera.[37] Harry looks uncomfortable in a suit, tie and oversize flat cap. Elsie wears a dark skirt with a light-coloured, smock-style top and a cloche hat that falls too far over her forehead. Harry has a neutral expression, maybe a slight hint of a smile at the right corner of his mouth. Elsie's mouth is down-turned, not even the pretence of a smile. They stand side by side but without touching. It's as if neither of them wanted to be there.

Ten weeks after the wedding, on 19 March, Elsie gave birth to the couple's first child, a daughter named Ethel. The little girl was born with what Dr. Evelyn Kempson Brown diagnosed as "misformation of the spine," and her brief life ended just three hours after her birth.[38] Later on Elsie gave birth to a boy, but his life is a mystery. Harry spoke about him to Alan Lomax but he didn't name him and there is no reference to him in official records of births, baptisms or deaths: he was possibly stillborn, unregistered and buried in a quiet corner of the churchyard. Harry told Lomax that one child was buried in Potter Heigham churchyard and one in Catfield, but he didn't name either of them. He was most affected by the death of his son: "The boy died; that's the one I wanted to live. I should ha' taught him everything I knew. I'd a given him all my knowledge, so he could have kept everything, and gone on." A boy was vital to the survival if the family name, something that was of great importance to Harry: "The old race has been goin' on several year, our class of Coxes. They're gradually dying out." As far as maintaining the family line was concerned, to Harry daughters "don't count. They change their names … so you're gone then."[39]

At first Harry and Elsie lived in a Decoy Road cottage owned by farmer Billy Balls, who Harry had worked for over the years. Myrtle's description of the situation suggests that Elsie was Balls's housekeeper and they may have been living in his home, but this arrangement didn't last long. A week after the wedding Harry bought a dog licence, which was a legal requirement for anyone owning a dog older than six months – perhaps Balls didn't like the animal.[40] Harry bought a terrace of three old cottages on the border between Catfield and Potter Heigham parishes for a hundred pounds and turned them into a family home, knocking two cottages into one and retaining the third as a workshop-cum-shed-cum-lounge. He called the new home Sunnyside and he and Elsie were living there by August. Both the living accommodation and the shed, which Harry called "yon ind [that end, or the far end]," were two-storey areas. In the living area, staircases that were little more than ladders ran through hatches to the bedrooms. Yon ind boasted a fireplace and a comfortable armchair, which enabled Harry to use the space year-round for storage, working, or quiet contemplation. The lavatory – as with most rural properties – was at the far end of the garden, unconnected to mains water and unlit.[41]

Harry made good use of yon ind. He stored fruit and vegetables in the upper level, but downstairs was the space for a host of different activities. In this small room Harry cured and stored his home-grown tobacco, made handles for scythes and reap hooks, sawed firewood, and maintained or mended his collection of American wall clocks. In the evenings he would braid rushes, attaching bunches of rushes to the door latch to maintain tension before braiding them together to make mats or frail baskets which local farm workers used to carry their food and drink.[42]

Whatever the impact of the 1923 strike may have been on Harry's social or financial situations, by the time they were married Harry and Elsie were financially comfortable compared to most of his workmates. Soon after they moved into Sunnyside they bought a range of new furniture from Brett's of Yarmouth, spending £29 15s. 1d. at a time when a farm labourer's wage was just over sixty pounds a year. A leather suite (costing £8 8s.), a leather armchair (possibly for yon ind), mattresses, tables, chairs and other furnishings duly arrived at the cottage.[43] As Harry and Elsie settled into Sunnyside, Bob Cox's health deteriorated and he died in 1929, aged ninety-two. On 12 April 1931 Elsie gave birth to Myrtle – baptised Myrtle Freda Mary at Potter Heigham on 5 May – and the family settled into life in Catfield.[44]

On the east coast, Sam and Dorcas Larner spent the 1920s untroubled by agricultural unrest or by the attentions of folk song collectors. After the war they returned to Ormesby, before moving in 1926 to the Bulmer Lane cottage where they would spend the rest of their lives.[45] Their adopted son Willy followed in Sam's footsteps and in 1928 he joined Sam on board the *WPG*, a Yarmouth-registered drifter owned by William "Wee" Green and named after his parents William and Phyllis.[46] With Sam as mate and young Willy as a deckhand, the vessel headed north.

When the *WPG* was off the Shetlands Willy's arm became infected, swelling so much that Sam had to cut Willy's shirtsleeve in order to take the shirt off. A Lerwick doctor put the arm in a sling, told Willy to rest and the drifter sailed off towards Wick, on the northeast tip of Scotland. The doctor's conservative approach proved to be inadequate. Willy's condition worsened and by the time the *WPG* reached Wick his arm had turned purple. Sam insisted that his son went to hospital and this time he was admitted and operated on – "Oh father, they cut my arm," said Willy when Sam visited him. It was to no avail. Septicaemia set in and Willy died on 29 August, just twenty years old. An uncharacteristically quiet and melancholy Sam told the story thirty years later. "We put him in [to the hospital] the Saturday, he was dead by Wednesday ... We brought him home in the boat and he's buried in this churchyard." The people of Wick paid their respects as Willy's body was taken to the *WPG*: "Salesmen, shopkeepers, they all followed him down," Sam remembered.

As Sam and his crewmates prepared for the journey back to Yarmouth, the weather turned and a storm loomed. Sam was not a religious man, but he prayed: "'Oh, God', I says, 'please send a calm.'" His prayer was answered, the storm failed to materialise, and it "came as flat as that table." The *WPG* made the voyage back to Yarmouth swiftly and without incident and Willy was laid to rest.[47]

Sam's sorrow at the loss of his adopted son was still obvious in the late 1950s, when he spoke of "poor Willy."[48] Although Willy died in an urban hospital, he is commemorated in the Fishermen's Corner in Winterton church as one of the nine village men who were lost at sea between World Wars I and II – the first name on the memorial is that of Sam's friend Tuskin Hodds. Sam continued working on the drifters after Willy's death, but life at sea was beginning to take its toll.

7 Harry Finds Fame

Sam's first fifteen minutes of fame were over by the start of the 1930s, his days of success in the Lerwick singing contests long past and no new opportunities taking their place. Harry had attracted attention in the 1920s but his admirers, though they included famous (or infamous) members of the artistic community, were few and his fifteen minutes were yet to begin. Thanks to E. J. Moeran's enthusiasm for his singing, however, he made his first entry into the "music business" by the middle of the decade. It would prove to be a tentative beginning – a wise move, considering what happened twenty-five years earlier when Britain's biggest record company tried to bring English folk song to a wider world.

Percy Grainger met septuagenarian estate steward and singer Joseph Taylor during song-collecting trips to Lincolnshire and recorded him on phonograph cylinders. Taylor enjoyed competition, gaining a degree of local fame by winning prizes at the 1905 and 1906 North Lincolnshire Music Festivals.[1] In 1908 he went to London to record some of his repertoire of English songs for the Gramophone Company: a selection including "Creeping Jane," "Worcester City," "Lord Bateman," and "Brigg Fair" which HMV released with special labels declaring them to be part of *Percy Grainger's Collection of English Folk Songs by actual peasant singers*.[2] It was the start of a catalogue of recordings by "genuine folk singers," hoped Grainger, who declared himself delighted with the company's decision.[3]

Grainger acquired copies of all of Taylor's Gramophone Company discs but few record buyers followed suit.[4] The Gramophone Company gave Taylor a gramophone and a set of his records but he never returned to the studio.[5] Grainger was going to be disappointed, the commercial failure of these records drawing to a premature end the flood of singers that he hoped to see trooping into London's recording studios. Record buyers were seeking exciting, aspirational and glamorous music from the world of the theatre or music hall – not the songs of the rural working class. It would be more than twenty-five years before another English traditional singer released a record.

By the mid-1930s, entertainment technology had changed out of all recognition from the acoustic system which the Gramophone Company used to record Joseph Taylor. Electrical recording systems arrived in the mid-1920s and were able to produce recordings of previously unimagined quality. A singer could give a far more nuanced and subtle performance, as electrical microphones could record soft whispers as well as powerful roars. Harry's style was well-suited to the new technology. Success awaited – except for the small matter of the competition. Hollywood was producing talking pictures, making a trip to the cinema in Yarmouth or Norwich even more exciting. Staying at home, or nipping down to the pub, could be rewarded with entertainment from an international range of artistes now that gramophones were cheap enough to be within reach of the skilled worker, or the enterprising pub landlord or landlady. The British Broadcasting Corporation's radio broadcasts were available nationwide with their Reithian commitment to educate, inform, and entertain. And if a radio was still too costly to buy, many a home hobbyist with a talent for wiring a few valves, power cables, and speakers together could build a serviceable wireless set. Faced with such an array of competitors, it's not surprising that Harry's first foray into a recording studio produced a limited output for a limited market. Moeran persuaded the London-based Decca Record Company to record Harry singing two songs – "Down by the Riverside" and "The Pretty Ploughboy" – for limited release by the EFDSS. Writing in 2000, Peter Kennedy claimed that Moeran and Peter's father Douglas accompanied Harry to the studio – it's unclear, but thirteen-year-old Peter may have met Harry during this visit. The resulting 78 rpm record went on sale for three shillings at Cecil Sharp House, the headquarters of the EFDSS, or by mail order for an extra ninepence. Norwich's Willmott's Music Shop was the sole Norfolk stockist of the disc, possibly the sole commercial stockist in the UK.[6]

Mr. Harry Cox, as he was credited on the label, was forty-eight when he made these recordings but sounds much older. The recordings have a commendably crisp and clear sound to them and Harry's diction is excellent: his accent might sound alien to the Society's more refined, urban members, but there's no mistaking the stories he's telling. These are not Harry's finest performances, though. His vocal on "The Pretty Ploughboy" is strong but he forces the tempo, as if he can't wait to get to the end, and he seems somewhat distracted during "Down by the Riverside." The recording studio is far removed from the warm and comforting atmosphere of a pub full of friends and sympathisers and this was Harry's first studio session, so it wouldn't be surprising if he was somewhat overawed by his experience.

"Whiffler," a columnist for Norwich's *Eastern Evening News*, wrote an extensive and favourable story about Harry's record on its release in February

1934, devoting most of that week's *Over the Tea Table* column to enlightening readers about the disc and the singer.[7] Whiffler was favourable, but combined enthusiasm with a patronising attitude and a reinforcement of the rustic stereotype, quoting Moeran's description of Harry as "a typical Norfolk son of the soil," and his singing as "utterly unsophisticated." The newspaper added to this stereotype by printing a picture of Harry in a field, staring unsmiling at the camera and holding a scythe ready for action. Still, at least Harry was getting some publicity: the story is the first reference to Harry to be found in the popular media, rather than a specialist, low-circulation journal.

Whiffler was unaware of Joseph Taylor's brief foray into the record business, telling readers that Harry's disc was the first commercial release "to reproduce folk song singing in its absolutely ungarnished form." Harry isn't named until half way through the article and it's clear that the writer doesn't expect the readers to have heard of him. It's clear too that Whiffler knows nothing of Harry's singing friends and feels able to boldly state that surviving traditional singers are all "old and decrepit." Jig dolls were also an alien concept to the columnist, who repeated E. J. Moeran's information that Harry had recently "constructed a figure of a dancing man which, when he beats his fingers, dances on a board."

Despite Whiffler's favourable review, Harry made no further visits to Decca. A modern perspective on Harry's disc is provided by record collector and YouTuber "EMG Colonel." He's less impressed than Whiffler, comparing Harry unfavourably with Kenneth Williams's comic folkie from BBC radio's 1960s series *Round the Horne*: "Yes, it is Rambling Syd Rumpo, but without a sense of humour," he declares before playing "Down by the Riverside" – although at the end of the disc he's softened his criticism, reflecting that "it's not a bad song, really." The Colonel believes "The Pretty Ploughboy" sounds "like something out of Tolkien." Maybe there is something of The Shire about the Norfolk countryside.[8]

Moeran was the first collector to pay Harry for a song: "He got '[The Pretty] Ploughboy.' I don't know what happened to that – he sold that or something or other. He got ten pound for that. We went halves."[9] As Harry tells it, the arrangement was an informal one and it's not known what Moeran eventually did with his new-found song that made it worth paying Harry a fiver. Harry did record "The Pretty Ploughboy" at his 1934 Decca session, but his comment that he didn't know what happened to it suggests that Moeran had another use for the song. Moeran's payment represents two to three weeks' wages at the time. Harry's later arrangements were formally agreed, but not necessarily as lucrative.

Harry may not impress EMG Colonel, but according to Moeran his performance at the Decca studios did impress a famous (but anonymous) baritone singer who overheard Harry during recording. The singer arranged an audition with the BBC and Harry was invited to broadcast a recital of Norfolk songs.[10] Harry wasn't the first traditional performer to appear on radio, but the

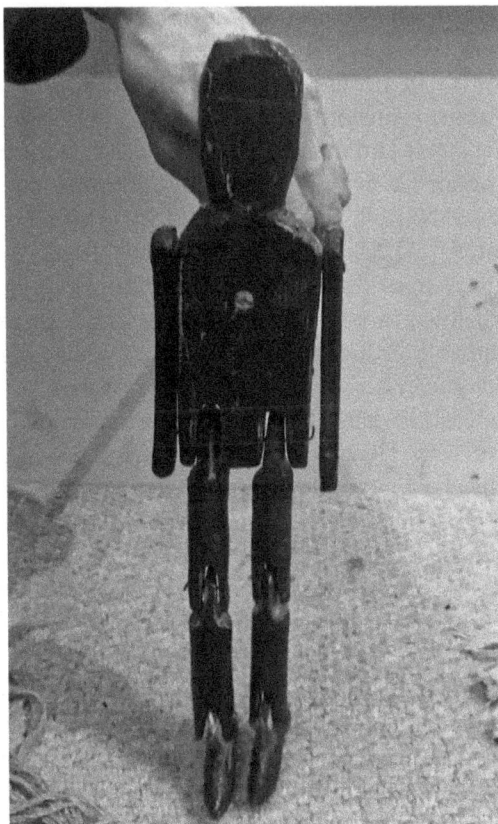

A jig doll. Made by Harry, probably in the late 1960s, it was given to the Godbolds and is now owned by storyteller and writer Hugh Lupton.

engagement was a departure for the BBC, which had broadcast "folk songs" from its early days but usually placed them in the hands (and vocal cords) of classically trained performers like the Wireless Singers or the English Singers, with pianoforte accompaniment. The *Radio Times* gave notice of one such broadcast by the baritone John Thorne with a cautionary note:

> It has always been a temptation to composers to make new settings for traditional folk songs. It is a risky adventure; even when a folk song is not of itself a really good tune, it very often has so firm a hold on the popular affections that it is not easy to displace it. Indeed, sad to relate, it is often the worst tunes which are the best loved.[11]

Harry made his first appearance on the wireless at 7:05 p.m. on Monday 5 November 1934, on the BBC National Programme's *From Plainsong to Purcell:*

The Foundations of English Music, under the direction of Sir Richard Runciman Terry. The series of twenty-minute programmes did what its title suggests, taking listeners on a trip through English music from medieval plainsong to Henry Purcell's late-seventeenth-century sonatas, performed almost exclusively by classical singers and musicians. Harry was an anomaly, a traditional singer with a programme of traditional songs and the sole artist in a programme devoted to "Norfolk Folk Songs sung by Harry Cox." He sang "The Captain's Apprentice," "The Shooting of His Dear," "The Transports," "Young Edmund," and "Just as the Tide was Flowing."[12] The positioning of this episode at almost exactly halfway through the series suggests that someone at the BBC – perhaps the estimable Sir Richard – thought these songs were being sung in the reign of Good Queen Bess.

After his broadcasting debut Harry returned to Norfolk, his agricultural work, and his gardening. His garden was large and filled with fruit and vegetables – though he was fond of flowers, they would not feed a family and so the only flowers to be found were in a narrow border next to the front path. He grew broad beans, peas, cabbages, potatoes, and other vegetables, carefully choosing a selection to provide food across the year. Harry ensured that fruit was also plentiful, growing a selection that included raspberries, apples, plums, and strawberries.[13]

Harry entertained himself with a few songs as he worked and sang, played and danced for fun – alone or with family at home, or with friends in the pubs. At some point he acquired a portable wind-up gramophone and began taking it to his favourite pubs, strapped to the back of his bike. As Myrtle remembered, other drinkers would add to the selection of discs Harry owned: "He was taking it to all the pubs and they were going absolutely mad to hear these records ... And no doubt some of them, if he hadn't got a certain record, they'd probably take theirs."[14] Maybe we should add disc jockey to Harry's list of talents.

Harry's brush with fame gave him a little local celebrity which he put to good use after a major Broadland disaster. On the night of Saturday 12 February 1938 a combination of a high tide and a severe gale burst the sea defences at Horsey, near Winterton, opening up a gap three miles wide and rushing five miles inland. Horsey was evacuated and up to twenty square miles of Broads land was covered by salt water: at one point, Winterton officials feared that the floods would reach as far as Norwich, along an old stream bed that had been dry for two hundred years. A relief fund was established to help Broads residents and Harry performed in Ludham village hall in aid of the fund.[15]

Harry's appearance in *From Plainsong to Purcell* was a one-off, but another BBC radio show brought traditional song to the airwaves on a more regular basis. *Country Magazine* started broadcasting on Sunday 3 May 1942 and continued until September 1954. For most of that time Francis Collinson was its musical director and arranger. Although Collinson collected traditional songs from singers across Britain, professional musicians and singers such as the Wynford Reynolds Sextet, tenor Robert Irwin, soprano Joan Stirrup, and the Dunelm Singers performed the songs. In mid-1952 Collinson presented and arranged the music for *The Postman Brings Me Songs*, a weekly Light Programme show of "songs from the countryside sent in by listeners."[16] As with *Country Magazine*, he arranged the songs for classically trained singers. Collinson first collected songs from Harry in the spring of 1942 when he noted down a dozen songs including "Bonny Labouring Boy," "The Bold Fisherman," and "Newlyn Town." Over the years he collected around sixty songs from Harry: he noted down the tunes, Myrtle wrote down the lyrics and sent them to him. When he struggled to capture the rhythm of "Bonny Bunch of Roses" he persuaded a BBC producer, Edward Livesey, to take the corporation's recording van to Norfolk to record Harry.[17]

On two occasions the BBC broadcast a special television edition of *Country Magazine*. On 5 October 1946 the TV show featured Harry Cox. However, the songs were credited to Robert Irwin and this Harry Cox was not the Norfolk singer but the naturalist and broadcaster of the same name, who was a regular contributor to BBC radio. Folk singer Harry Cox appeared on the BBC Midland service again in 1945 on *The Microphone at Large*, which the *Radio Times* billed as a series "in which the microphone visits cities, towns and villages."[18] This episode came from Norwich. Harry's role in the programme is unclear, his contract merely states "Contribution to *The Microphone At Large*."[19] However, he took part in a rehearsal arranged by Edward Livesey and was paid five guineas – a substantial fee compared to those he and Sam would receive for some of their 1960s broadcasts.

Harry's singing friends didn't follow him onto the airwaves, but they were well-established entertainers in the pubs of Catfield, Potter Heigham, Ludham, and Sutton. They were all men but otherwise they were a mixed bunch, mostly older than Harry and from a variety of working backgrounds. Walter "Waxy" Gales, the Sutton shoemaker born in 1863, was the oldest member of the group. Charlie Chettleburgh and Bullards Miller were farm workers, like Harry. Bullards was a team man, in charge of horses (Fred Cox did the same job at one time) and Charlie was a general labourer. Elijah Bell also worked on the land but, having made some money in the United States, he was able to buy his own smallholding at Pond Farm in Sutton. This gave him a higher social status than his singing friends while his Methodist religion and repertoire of religious songs, often performed in a duo with a Miss Hamblin, gave him added respectability.[20]

Jack Riseborough, a steam engine driver from Catfield who often worked in a threshing gang with Chettleburgh, was another regular group member. Jack, Charlie and other members of the group were noted drinkers – Harry enjoyed a pint of mild, but he wasn't in their league. Despite heavy drinking and long years of hard manual labour, Harry and his close friends lived to old age: only Jack Riseborough failed to reach his allotted three score years and ten, dying of stomach cancer in 1948. Riseborough was a tough man who could turn violent at times, but his singing and song repertoire show a more sensitive and romantic side. He was fond of a mixture of traditional songs, music hall numbers, Victorian parlour ballads, and sentimental songs. He owned a gramophone and was particularly fond of records by the Irish musical star Josef Locke, although his favourite song was reputedly "The Black Velvet Band." His repertoire included "When You Were Sweet Sixteen," "The Rose of Tralee," "Far Away in Australia," and "The Pretty Ploughboy," which he learnt from Harry's 1934 record.[21]

Harry was one of the youngest of this group, but by the beginning of the 1930s they were occasionally joined by the much younger Sam Howard, born in 1909. Waxy's grandson Brian "Pinky" Gales started to learn his grandad's repertoire in his early twenties and would sometimes join in with the group's sessions alongside Waxy. John "Charger" Salmons joined the group in 1942, the last addition to Harry's community of singers. A retired wherryman, he was living in Yarmouth at the outbreak of World War II but moved to Stalham Green to live with relatives and escape the German bombing raids.[22]

As with the Great War, Norfolk felt the impact of hostilities from their beginning. Fuel rationing started across the country in September 1939 and bus and train services were soon cut back. On 9 July 1940 Norwich was bombed for the first time, with twenty-seven fatalities. Yarmouth was bombed repeatedly: by the end of 1942 the Luftwaffe had attacked the town twenty-six times and one raid on Yarmouth and Gorleston caused the heaviest damage of any raid on East Anglia. Even little Winterton wasn't immune: it was bombed on 6 May 1943, killing Katy Brown and Edna Hodds.[23] Despite these losses some commentators though that the war was little more than a minor inconvenience for the people of Norfolk, claiming that

> workers in the rural parts of Norfolk had never had it so good
> – their pay was fine, there was no shortage of food and, unless a
> bomb dropped or an aeroplane crashed, there was no need to think
> of the war at all.[24]

Even if the Germans didn't bomb your village or your house, the war's impact on Norfolk's landscape and its farming community was inescapable. The RAF and the United States Army Air Force moved into Norfolk *en masse* and established bases across the county, including a radar station at RAF Neatishead and one of the country's most easterly air bases at RAF Ludham. When Francis Collinson first visited Harry in the spring of 1942 he found Catfield and Potter Heigham in the centre of the RAF's bomber airfields. The villages, he wrote, were

> hedged round by the strictest of security precautions. I had first,
> therefore, to persuade the local police, Home Guard, and not the

least the vigilantly patriotic *habitués* of the bar parlour of the inn at Catfield that I was not an enemy agent before I was allowed to walk the mile or so ... to Harry Cox's pleasing little flower-surrounded house of "Sunnyside."[25]

Harry and his singing friends were too old for active service, helping the war effort through their jobs on the land instead and carrying on with their sessions in their favourite pubs in the evenings. Moeran knew the group from their sessions in the 1920s, but by 1945 he assumed that most of them were dead and that "the spontaneous singing of old songs when men foregather on Saturday nights has now died out." He was pleasantly surprised when he returned to the Broads after the war to find the sessions in full swing: "to my delight and surprise, I found that not only were many of my old friends still living, hale and hearty, but that they were still having sing-songs."[26]

Moeran's belief that the sessions had ended is surprising – he made the same assumption at the end of World War I and was proven wrong. Fellow song collector Francis Collinson spent the war years unearthing songs in Norfolk and elsewhere, confidently describing Harry Cox as "too well known as a singer of folk-songs to require any comment from me."[27] The BBC even devoted an entire programme to a group of East Anglian singers, only six weeks before the outbreak of World War II, of which Moeran was apparently unaware.

Much to Norfolk's chagrin, Suffolk played host to this programme. On the afternoon of Saturday 29 July 1939 the BBC broadcast selections from the Eel's Foot in Eastbridge; *Saturday Night at the Eel's Foot* became the first national radio show to feature traditional singers and their songs in a genuine pub session, albeit a recorded one.[28] A. L. "Bert" Lloyd, a key figure in the post-war folk revival, visited the Eel's Foot in early 1939 at the invitation of his friend Leslie Morton, decided that he had experienced a vital part of English culture (he was another believer that folk singing had died out) and persuaded the BBC to record one of the regular Saturday night sessions.[29] The presence of Lloyd, producer Maurice Brown, and their recording equipment may have tempered the exuberance of the evening's activities but the recording captured much of the vibrance and humour of a pub singalong.

The BBC decided that the programme was important enough to merit an article in that week's *Radio Times*. It's another romanticised take on the lives of the rural working class, as Brown writes of the session as "a dramatic rite" in which everyone present knows all the songs and "labourer and roadman, tradesman and gamekeeper, young and old, women and men, they all sing." A musician was on hand to play a few dance tunes – curiously, Brown describes him as "a 'fiddler' with his concertina" – but most performers were singers, such as father and son William "Velvet" and William "Jumbo" Brightwell. Philip Lumpkin took charge as "chairman," calling the crowd to order by bashing a cribbage board onto a bar table. As for the songs, the earring-wearing

Velvet sang "Pleasant and Delightful," Mr. Cook sang "The Blackbird," Jumbo sang "McCassery," and the evening closed with a rousing ensemble chorus of "Auld Lang Syne."[30]

Harry's singing companions came to the BBC's attention almost a decade later, when the BBC commissioned Moeran to produce a radio programme devoted to East Anglian singers. In October 1947, he recorded at the Eel's Foot and at the Windmill in Sutton. The BBC's Third Programme broadcast the fifty-minute show *East Anglia Sings* at quarter past seven on the evening of 19 November, advertising the programme as: "An October journey made by E. J. Moeran and producer Maurice Brown in search of folk songs. Recorded by traditional singers in the countryside and inns of Suffolk and Norfolk."[31] Moeran – continually convinced of the imminent deaths of East Anglia's singers – was glad to see that they "were not all coughing and wheezing octogenarians." The engineers set up microphones so that the men could sing in their usual way, with the exception of one session where technological problems meant that five performers took it in turns to sing directly into a microphone. They "took delight" in the technology, in Moeran's words, treating it as if it were a new toy.[32]

At the Eel's Foot, Jumbo Brightwell was joined by three more singers and a stepdancer known only as "Mrs. Harding." The singers at the Windmill were all Harry's friends: Salmons, Chettleburgh, Bell, Miller, and Gales sang one song apiece, but Harry took the lion's share of the programme with "Barton Broad Ditty," "The Bonny Bunch of Roses," "The Barley Straw," and "The Fowler."[33] The recording provides a unique opportunity to compare Harry and his fellow singers: Salmons has a light voice, a little tight-throated but clear; Chettleburgh hesitates over one or two of the words but is otherwise confident, with a gentle swing in his rhythm; Gales sings slowly, his voice is weaker than the others' but he sounds more involved in the song than Charger does. Bullards Miller sings strongly and confidently, getting the crowd involved in the chorus of "Happy and Delightful." Elijah Bell is more tight-throated than Charger, sounding at times – without wishing to be unkind – like a folk-singing character from *The Goon Show*. In such competition, Harry is a revelation: a strong voice, clear projection and unhesitating delivery combine to put him well ahead of the rest, at least on that occasion.

One regular member of Harry's group was missing from the Windmill recording, despite being present on the night. Sam Howard reckoned Jack Riseborough to be "a very useful singer" and Jack did take part in the session that evening, but when his family gathered round a neighbour's radio to hear him sing they were disappointed – they tuned in again the following week, just in case there was a second part of the Windmill programme, but to no avail.[34] Christopher Heppa described Jack's non-appearance as "a mystery" and continued:

His family thought he hadn't gone [to the Windmill], or changed his mind, but he would never talk about it … He told one of his sons that he only sang one song, which they all did except Harry. I've seen the BBC's recording notes and he's not listed. I think he got drunk. He was a noted drinker and the recording crew supplied free food and drink.[35]

The programme may have helped to spread the word about English folk song, but it was not the most opportune week for it to appear. It was the week in which the BBC celebrated the twenty-fifth anniversary of British broadcasting with a series of special programmes and, on the day after *East Anglia Sings* was broadcast, Princess Elizabeth married Philip Mountbatten – an event that the BBC covered for many hours on radio and television. Despite these nationally newsworthy events, *Radio Times* managed to find space for a short story about the show under a title that set out to counter the widespread belief that no-one sang folk songs anymore: *Folk Songs are not Dead*. On the contrary, wrote Maurice Brown,

they are a part of the everyday life of ordinary men and women … They are sung because people enjoy singing them. We visited one little pub [the Eel's Foot] and found thirty-five villagers in the bar singing "The Dark-Eyed Sailor" at the top of their voices.[36]

Brown didn't consider whether the singers would usually attract thirty-five locals without the excitement of a BBC recording team.

Radio programmes such as *Saturday Night at the Eel's Foot* and *East Anglia Sings* brought Harry, Velvet, Jumbo, Bullards, and their friends to the attention of a national audience, but this attention soon wandered. Charabancs filled with talent scouts from the major record labels did not roar up the A11 to the Broads. BBC television did not wave contracts in Harry's direction. Sam and his friends in the Fishermans Return carried on singing as the rest of the world passed Winterton by.

Sam's singing community was markedly different from Harry's. For forty years Sam spent months at a time on small vessels whose crews might change from voyage to voyage, putting into ports around the British Isles and meeting fellow fishermen and singers at pubs and singing nights before returning to Winterton for a few weeks on shore. Such a lifestyle gave Sam the chance to sing with many different individuals but made the formation of a strong, consistent group of singing companions much harder to achieve. Only when he left the fishing fleet could Sam sing regularly throughout the year in Winterton's pubs. However, he rarely mentioned fellow singers by name during interviews with radio presenters or newspaper journalists.

When Sam does mention fellow singers they're usually members of the extended Larner family, notably his father, his uncle Larpin Sutton, or his brother-in-law Bob Green. (Bob was the skipper and Sam was mate when they experienced one of the most frightening storms in Sam's entire life at sea.[37]) Sam credited another uncle, Billy "Wilks" Larner, as the source of the "bad marriage" song "Before the Daylight in the Morning" and "Now is the Time for Fishing," which Sam described as "a little ditty I used to sing in the wheelhouse."[38]

Other Winterton fishermen, from Sam's generation or younger, were also singers – whether or not they were regularly part of Sam's social set. Sam's nephews Bob and Dick Green (the sons of Bob Green), Jack "Starchy" George, Walter "Tuddy" Rudd, and Johnny Goffin all sang.[39] Suffolk collector Neil Lanham recorded a few songs from Bob, Tuddy, and Johnny in the village in December 1966. Bob and Johnny sing clearly, but while Johnny manages to bring a degree of drama to "The Bold Princess Royal," Bob's singing of "The Maid of Australia" and "Cruising Round Yarmouth" is rather staid and detached – until Bob starts giggling at some of the ruder lines of "Cruising." Tuddy's performances of "The Dolphin" and "Blow Away the Morning Dew" are more entertaining and engaging but, as with Harry and his fellows on *East Anglia Sings*, none of these recordings suggest that Sam's position as the king of Winterton singers was ever under threat.[40]

The comforts of modern life gradually made their way to east Norfolk during the 1930s. Winterton benefitted from mains electricity in 1930, a public telephone arrived in 1934, and mains water was connected in the same year.[41] Sam ended his time as a fisherman in 1933, in the midst of this modernisation, worn out by forty years at sea. At the Norfolk and Norwich Hospital he saw a specialist, whose name Dorcas remembered as Barfield. Sam summarised the consultation for the benefit of Charles Parker: "He said, 'What have you been?' I said, 'Well, I been a fisherman all my life, sir.' He said, 'Do you do [a lot of] pulling, then?'" Sam told him it was a large part of a fisherman's job. "'Well,' he said, 'Don't go no more.'"[42] Sam took the doctor's advice and left the sea, but he was too young to collect his pension and too poor for a life of leisure. So he spent the next few years working odd jobs around Winterton, gaining the money he needed to support Dorcas and himself by breaking stones for road mending, planting trees for the Forestry Commission, and spending periods on the dole.[43] The 1939 National Register – prepared at the outbreak of war – recorded him as a general labourer, with Dorcas engaged in "unpaid domestic duties."

Hard, repetitive labouring work on shore was not what Sam wanted, but it failed to diminish his extrovert personality. Funky Larner was still in evidence around Winterton, a man who could be "wild and argumentative – not the avuncular image of the revival."[44] According to one story, Sam fell out with a fellow drinker at the Fishermans Return; seeing the man walk past the pub Sam jumped in front of the pub window, dropped his trousers and bared his backside towards his foe. Pranks like this gave him a reputation around Winterton as a bit of a "wildman."[45] Perhaps they also helped Sam to come to terms with the end of his life at sea. Despite its dangers, Sam loved being a fisherman and the years spent working on the land were no substitute for it: "I liked the sea, it's in our blood. Our forefathers were all fishermen. It's in our blood."[46]

8 Building the Repertoire

Sam and Harry's reputations owe much to their extensive repertoires of songs; repertoires, as Karl Dallas put it, that were "later to be ransacked by the younger traditionalists of the revival who felt, rightly, that they could not imbibe the true spirit of the tradition from the printed page."[1] But how extensive were these repertoires, where did the songs come from, how did the two singers decide which songs they would sing of the countless number they heard, and to what extent did they alter words and tunes – deliberately or accidentally?

Sam's known repertoire totals around sixty-five different songs. Harry's is substantially larger – at least 112, possibly over two hundred.[2] Recordings of songs in slightly different versions, toasts and spoken rhymes and fragments of songs no longer fully remembered can be added to the lists. Some recordings may still be hidden from view, lost and forgotten in attics and garages the length of the country: an unknown archive of song. Recordings of Harry and Sam were made for the most part by men and women with an interest in "folk songs" and a tendency to ignore popular, modern songs – however much Harry or Sam enjoyed singing them – so they don't represent the entirety of their repertoires. For Harry, exercise books and sheets of paper show songs that don't appear on any of his recordings. Friends and relatives remember other songs for which no written or audio evidence exists, perhaps sung privately and kept out of pub sessions. Adding all of these to the mix results in potentially larger and more diverse repertoires for both singers.

What is a "folk song"? In 1954 the International Folk Music Council defined folk music as "music that has been submitted to the process of oral transmission. It is the product of evolution and is dependent on the circumstances of continuity, variation and selection."[3] Steve Roud, creator of the Roud Folk Song Index, describes folk songs as being

> learnt and performed by non-professionals in informal, non-commercial settings. They are "traditional" in that they are passed

on from person to person, and down the generations, in face-to-face performance. It is not the origin of a song that makes it a "folk song", but the process by which ordinary people learn it, perform it and pass it on.[4]

By these definitions, any song can become a folk song. But no song starts its life as a folk song and, no matter how old it is, it can't be a folk song unless it's transmitted orally across generations. It seems simple, but is it? If Sam went to the theatre and added a song from the show to his repertoire then that song is not immediately a folk song. But if a younger singer learns it by listening to Sam in the Fishermans Return and mucks about with it so it becomes theirs, then maybe it starts to become a folk song. Fred Woods raised a similar issue regarding the difference between "traditional" singers and "revivalist" singers:

> Is a revivalist singer who learns his songs from the records of a traditional singer actually a traditional singer and not a revivalist? … is the child of a revivalist singer, who has learned the songs through hearing his or her parents sing them, a traditionalist or a revivalist?[5]

Christy Moore's description of how he found and crafted his version of "Little Musgrave" should perhaps have been the last word on the matter: "I collected it in a book which had no music but I was lucky to collect a tune from a Nic Jones album discovered on a field trip through Liam O'Flynn's flat." A statement made in jest, perhaps, but it serves to illustrate the complexity of song transmission and "traditional or revivalist" arguments. Was the book a primary source published many decades ago, or a secondary source reproducing an older book's contents? In either case it's a book, so Moore didn't learn the words in the accepted traditional fashion. As for the tune, Moore may have learnt it by ear but it comes from a recording by a leading revivalist – not from a face-to-face encounter with an ageing source musician. The revivalist Nic Jones listened to Sam's recordings with fellow performer Dave Burland, deriving great enjoyment from Sam's singing. With a bit of imagination, Sam's tune for "Blow Away the Morning Dew" bears a passing resemblance to Moore's tune for "Little Musgrave." So Sam, via Nic Jones, might just have influenced Christy Moore. But did he do so in the approved "folk song" style?[6]

The BBC defined a folk song as one "which has passed by oral tradition at least two or three generations, the original version usually being unknown or perhaps obscured by variants which have subsequently appeared."[7] Maud Karpeles – a first revival collector and compatriot of Cecil Sharp – held a simple, time-limited definition, telling Peggy Seeger that no song could be considered a traditional song unless it was at least three hundred years old.[8] This rigid definition immediately rules out any song about Napoleon or Nelson, most of the Industrial Revolution, Bonnie Prince Charlie's Jacobite rebellion

– the list is endless and includes the bulk of Harry and Sam's repertoires. Sharp himself defined a folk song as "the song created by the common people." As for the common people, they are

> those whose mental development has been due not to any formal system of training or education, but solely to environment, communal association, and direct contact with the ups and downs of life … who have never been brought into close enough contact with educated persons to be influenced by them.[9]

There's a romantic (if patronising) quality to Sharp's definition, a vision of uneducated rustics crafting songs as they tend their sheep or cornfields, unencumbered by the influence of educated persons or literacy. Sam and Harry never troubled themselves with defining what they sang: from the early days of their childhoods they heard a variety of songs and they sang the songs they liked. For Harry they were mostly, but not always, the "old 'uns" – or at least those that sounded old. For Sam, age was unimportant: tune, story, and rhythm were the elements that attracted him to a song.

Sam enjoyed songs of the sea: of pirates, bold seamen, jolly sailors, shipwrecks, and fishing. He was also fond of a bawdy song. These "rude 'uns," as he called them, usually went no further than being mildly *risqué*: "Clear Away the Morning Dew" or "Butter and Cheese and All" (the tale of a "jolly old cook" who supplies the singer's wants in terms of butter, cheese and more). In "Butter and Cheese," the cook's husband returns unexpectedly and the singer is forced to hide up a chimney, which is as Freudian as folk song gets – a similar tale can be found in Boccaccio's fourteenth-century collection of stories, *The Decameron*.[10] "She Said She Was a Virgin" is a combined bawdy/nonsense song about a nineteen-year-old girl who takes her lover to bed then surprises him by unscrewing her wooden leg. When Sam tried to sing it for Ewan MacColl he managed one verse before collapsing with laughter.[11]

Other songs were subtler: a fine example is "The Game of All Fours," which is ostensibly about a card game (all fours was a genuine card game, with a usefully ambivalent name) but manages to tell of a sexual encounter without recourse to obviously sexual language or (much) innuendo. "Cruising Round Yarmouth" uses seafaring terminology to thinly disguise the tale of another sexual encounter, in which a Dutch woman seduces the singer by lowering her "tops'l" and then empties his shot bag – a popular song with the women in his audiences, Sam claimed.[12] Still others were more explicit, without making the subject blatantly obvious to those of an innocent mind, like Sam's much-loved "Maids When You're Young, Never Wed an Old Man." He claimed that he knew "The Jolly Young Coachman" when he first went to sea: it's one of his ruder songs, telling of a young lady demanding to see the coachman's whip before she gives him permission to enter her coach box and drive her.[13]

Sam may have revelled in these bawdy songs, but even he could be sheepish about singing them in certain company. Singing "Cruising Round Yarmouth" for Ewan MacColl, he mumbled one or two of the more explicit phrases despite MacColl's assertion that "we're all grownups." Dorcas was in the room and, though she made no protests, Sam seems a little embarrassed: "Poor old Mother, sat down listening to all that," he says over MacColl's increasingly irritated pleas to carry on.[14]

Sea songs such as "Now is the Time for Fishing" or "Coil Away the Trawl Warp" tell of the life Sam experienced first-hand: when Ewan MacColl recorded "Coil Away" during preparation for the Radio Ballad *Singing the Fishing*, he told Sam that the song was "very useful for this programme."[15] Other sea songs tell of adventures from the past – real or imagined – like "Will Watch" (the tale of a smuggler) or "The Bold Princess Royal," with its story of a ship's escape from murderous pirates. "The Ghost Ship" is one of the darkest of these songs. A young man murders his wife-to-be and her unborn baby with a "long-daggered knife" – presumably because he has no desire to become a husband or a father – hides her body and escapes to sea. The ghost of the woman appears on board the ship and takes her revenge by ripping, stripping and tearing the murderer in three. Just the sort of thing for a jolly pub singalong.

Sam kept a few romantic songs in his repertoire. "The Haymakers' Courtship" and "The Green Broom" are two examples in which no-one is killed or forced to flee to the colonies. In songs such as "The Outlandish Knight," things begin with the hope of romance but end in death and despair. Some of his songs feature Irish events or protagonists: "Over There in Ireland," which he learnt in County Kerry, is the most saccharine of this group while "Donnelly and Cooper" tells the story of a bare-knuckle boxing match between Donnelly the Irishman and Cooper from England, with Donnelly emerging victorious.[16]

Sam's favourite song was "Henry Martin," which he usually called "The Lofty Tall Ship." It's one of his sea songs, in which the pirate Henry Martin attacks and sinks a vessel filled with valuable cargo. Sam told Ewan MacColl and Peggy Seeger that he learnt the song from an old labourer on Yarmouth docks in around 1894–95. It's a song that just fits into Maud Karpeles's strict definition of folk song, having first appeared in the early years of the seventeenth century.[17] Sam was aware of its age, telling Charles Parker: "The best one as I always did like was 'Henry Martin.' That's one of the oldest folk songs there is. In history, that one is. 'Henry Martin.' That come right down from Scandinavia."[18] Ewan MacColl was a fan of Sam's rendition of the song, telling him that it had "impressed me, I think, more than any song I've heard in a long, long time."[19]

Harry's recorded repertoire is, like Sam's, a varied collection: songs about farming, adultery, cuckolded husbands, sailors, fishermen, poachers, transportation, murder, marriage, domestic violence, romance, sex, pregnancy, sexually transmitted infection, and occasionally most of the above. It includes a couple of "bad marriage" songs, bemoaning the lot of the poor man (always the man) whose idea of a romantic and love-filled relationship soon turns sour. "There's Bound to be a Row" is sung by a husband who complains that whatever he does for his wife an argument will ensue. When Harry sung this for Charles Parker and Ewan MacColl, he found it impossible to avoid laughing at numerous points – a contrast to his usual calm and straight-faced style, even when singing humorous ditties. "A Week's Matrimony" begins with courtship and tells a similar tale of marital disharmony, adultery, physical violence – both parties "muddling" each other – and drunkenness, adding the wife's suicide to the mix and closing with the singer boasting that the night after the funeral he "made love to another." The mysterious "I Will Level with Her" (it has no Roud number) describes a particularly dysfunctional relationship in which the "tartar" of a wife reduces her husband to skin and bone through a catalogue of abuses, including giving birth to the lodger's child. His solution is simple: he'll cut her throat.

By contrast, Harry sang plenty of songs in which the promise of a long and happy relationship is fulfilled. "The Watercress Girl" is brief but romantic. A young man spies a damsel as she collects watercress, they court, marry, and live happily ever after. Harry's pronunciation of watercress as "wartycress" adds to the song's naive charm. "The Cabin with the Roses Round the Door" – written by Harry Hunter and John Guest in about 1900 and which Harry acknowledges "ain't an old folk song" – is a reflection on a long and happy marriage. There are humorous and nonsense songs as well. "I Had an Old Hoss" tells of the results of putting a plaster on the arse of a horse, a cat, and a wife. "The Bumblebee Song" is brief and mildly *risqué*. Oddest of all is "Mr. Morrison's Pills," which sings the praises of James Morison's Vegetable Pills – first produced in the 1820s and still on sale a century later, they were so efficacious that the singer could "cure all that come to me with a box of Morrison's pills."

Harry enjoyed a bawdy song. "The Knife in the Window" is one such, the story of a young couple whose night of sex is thwarted by Johnny's tight-fitting breeches until Nancy lends him a knife. It's a fine example of a seemingly nonsense phrase being used repeatedly to (barely) mask a spot of sexual imagery: in this case, Johnny's "long fol da riddle di doh" which hangs down to his knee. "Firelock Stile" also fits neatly into this category. In it, a young woman deliberately or accidentally draws the attention of a young rake by catching her clothes on a nail and revealing her quim – a sight that "dazzles his eye." He agrees to pay her twenty guineas and they head for the woods to have sex; six weeks later, he's contracted a sexually transmitted infection. Harry's slang term for the female genitalia is a rarity in folk song, even though the term was widely used in the nineteenth century. Harry enjoyed singing this song to the collectors, recording it for Kennedy, Lomax, and MacColl. It was one of the songs Collinson noted down from him in 1942.

Harry claimed to have "made up" two or three songs, but only one, "Threshing Time," still exists. Peter Kennedy recorded it in 1956, listing it as "Thrashing Time" (which, to modern eyes, may suggest a very different activity from the one that Harry sings about). It's a mix of nostalgia for the old farming ways, disdain for the new generation of farmers, and a hint of concern for the environment. Although Harry was both its composer and singer, "Threshing Time" didn't capture the imagination of his fellow folk performers and Kennedy's recording remains the only example of the song to be found in the Roud Index. Of course, it doesn't fit any of the definitions noted above so it's not a folk song – yet.[20]

Harry took pride in his memory for song lyrics and tunes but he wasn't always sure about the history or meaning of songs. He was clear about the genesis of "Barton Broad Babbing Ballad," as well as the story behind the song. Talking about "The Farmer's Servant," a tale of infidelity, he remembered a local example where a farmer was caught in the act with a servant and forced to pay hush money to keep the affair secret. But in other cases he could offer little explanation.[21] Lomax asked Harry about many of his songs when they spoke in the 1950s; Harry's responses reveal his lack of awareness of historical events, but also his lack of concern. Harry enjoyed the songs as independent creations; their origins were unimportant, if the tune and words appealed. What's the story behind "Bonny Bunch of Roses"? It's something to do with the Russians, thinks Harry, but "I can't make it out."[22] As for "The Good Luck Ship," which tells of an English ship defeating ten French men o' war, Harry can't expand on the tale and tells Lomax that he doesn't know any French people – although "I had a cousin, his wife's French." He still feels able to offer an opinion on the nation: "I think they're all alike, look after their own selves first."[23]

When Leslie Shepard asked Harry to name his favourite song "out of the old ones" Harry replied: "'Smuggler's Boy' I believe … That's which one I like best."[24] Broadside publishers shared his love of the song, as did many other singers: the Roud Index lists 120 versions including one by Bob Roberts of Suffolk. The song tells of a boy who is orphaned when his mother dies of a broken heart after his smuggler father is drowned at sea, despite the son's attempts to save him. A wealthy but childless woman hears the boy's pleas for employment and gives him a job: hard work and honesty pay off, he inherits the woman's wealth on her death and lives in comfort by dint of honest toil. It's a tale to make Samuel Smiles smile.

Harry's repertoire included tunes for fiddle, whistle or melodeon. None of Harry's friends talked about his playing with anything like the enthusiasm they had for his singing, but others have a higher opinion. Journalist Jim Tudor described Harry's playing as "reminiscent of the Irish caeli [sic] bands." Musician Carole Pegg acknowledges the influence of Harry's fiddle style on her own approach to the instrument.[25] Phil Heath-Coleman recognises that Harry's playing style is not readily accessible to the casual listener – and also that many people will think him "mad to suggest there may be any value in Harry's fiddle playing" – but puts forward a persuasive argument for Harry's importance as a fiddler with tunes as "finely crafted" as his songs and a playing style that is "extremely powerful and yet – in its way – precise and sophisticated." Reg Hall, who played with Harry on a few occasions, recalled that "he always played perfectly in tune. He was a harsh player, a rough player, but he always pitched dead on."[26] Harry's friend Peter Coleman has another explanation for Harry's signature sound: "The fiddle was put up on a shelf and when he got it down he'd just go plunk, plunk on the strings and start playing. How long it might have been up there I don't know, but he expected it to work."[27]

Sam and Harry may never have met, but they did share some songs including "Butter and Cheese and All," "Blackberry Fold" (recorded by Sam as "Betsy the Milkmaid"), and "The Bold Fisherman." At least four of these songs are common to Harry, Sam, and Walter Pardon: "Bold Fisherman," "The Transports" (as Harry called it; Sam recorded it as "The Robber," Walter as "The Rambling Blade"), "The Ramillies," and "The Bonny Bunch of Roses" (with or without the final -O).[28] "The Maid of Australia" is in the repertoires of Harry, Sam, Walter, and Peter Bellamy: a leading singer from a younger generation who grew up in Norfolk, befriended Pardon and became a staunch supporter of Harry and Sam.

"The Bold Princess Royal" is another song to be found in both Harry and Sam's repertoires. The lyrics of both versions are almost identical, although Harry sets sail on 14 February while Sam leaves a day later. When Bob Thomson mentioned Sam's version to Harry during an interview, Harry replied that Sam sang a different tune to his own. Thomson corrected him, telling Harry that their tunes are "pretty much the same." Harry replies, "Oh," at which point the tape stops.[29] It's the only example I have found of Harry talking about Sam. Harry's response suggests that he was aware of Sam's singing, but not in any great depth; of course, by the time of this interview Sam had not sung in public for some years.

Despite the decades Harry and Sam spent in hard, physical jobs for low wages, their repertoires lack songs of protest about the social and economic problems they faced. When they do sing about hard times or injustice, the songs are narrative rather than critical – they tell the story without taking sides, so to speak. Harry did record "The Rigs of the Times," which is a protest against rising food prices, dishonest traders and the outrageous price of beer, but the lyric's reference to a French war suggests the times were in the early nineteenth century. "What Will Become of England?" is a bleak song about the troubles of the poor workers and their starving families. It puts Harry squarely on the side of the worker, but it's a rarity in his repertoire.

If Harry wanted to protest about more recent events there was no shortage of songs in support of the unionisation of farm workers (especially in the years following the establishment of Joseph Arch's National Agricultural

Labourers' Union in 1872). "The Agricultural Labourers' Union Song," published on an anonymous broadside around 1872, promised:

> The chain of oppression is broken,
> And a freedom for serfs stand [sic] in view,
> And now is the time lads, or never,
> To stand to the Union so true."

The Caxton Press – based in Maddermarket, Norwich – printed the *National Agricultural Labourers' and Rural Workers' Union Song Book*, probably around 1906. This songbook contains two dozen pro-union anthems, most of which could be sung to the tunes of well-known hymns. None of these songs caught the ear of Harry or Sam, at least not sufficiently well to become part of their known repertoires. Perhaps Harry's memories of the 1923 strike made him reluctant to sing pro-union songs: for Sam, they were perhaps too dour and worthy to appeal to his love of a good story and a danceable tune.

Although Harry's repertoire doesn't contain much in the way of political songs, that doesn't mean he was politically unconcerned or unengaged. His granddaughter Jenny recalls that he would always use his vote in elections, although she doesn't believe he was an active union man. Initially a Liberal voter, he switched allegiance to the Labour party.[30] He held strong views about the inequalities of the English class system:

> Them what ha' got it, they are still grabbing for more, and they want to keep you down. Like when you do a job: I've been to these little people what ain't got a lot. You'll get jugs o' tea, cocoa during the time. But go out to a big one and you'll get nothing, and they'll try and cut you off a shilling when you finish. Give me the lower classes ... You won't get nothing out of a man that has got a lot ... The lower class are the ones.[31]

Sam, by contrast, kept his political opinions close to his chest. Peggy Seeger was adamant that he expressed no political opinions that she could remember, during his many conversations with her and Ewan MacColl.[32]

Harry and Sam took different approaches to song gathering. Sam happened upon songs – at home, at school, at work or in the pub – and if he came across one that he liked then he would learn it and keep it in his memory. He claimed to have learnt "Mignonette" from sheet music but learnt the rest of his songs by ear.[33] Peggy Seeger said: "Sam was a social singer ... I wouldn't think Sam was concerned about what would happen to the songs in the future."[34] But he did indicate a wish that the songs would be kept alive for future generations, telling Ewan MacColl that he wasn't concerned about making money from the songs "as long as they keep 'em a-goin.'"[35]

Harry was a more active collector, willing to go to some lengths to add a song to his repertoire. He took after his father Bob, in this regard:

> When [Bob] heard a song he liked he got them to learn him it, asked 'em to keep singing them over to him till he got it. Sometimes he'd give people a couple of shillings to keep reading over a new one, keep reading till he'd picked it up.[36]

A couple of shillings seems like a high price to pay for a man who often struggled to make ten shillings a week. Either Harry is exaggerating, or Bob was a serious collector of songs. Harry was willing to walk up to fifteen miles to collect a new song to which he'd taken a fancy – and to pay for it as well. But his financial limit was much lower, just sixpence.[37] He told Bob Thomson his method for learning a new song: "If you want to learn a song, get the tune. Once you get the tune … you can get the rest."[38]

Harry's ability to learn, memorise, and reproduce a song became the stuff of legend: according to Paul Marsh it was "a gift, a natural-born talent … the ability to pick up a song after only hearing it through a few times … coupled with a phenomenal memory [and] near-perfect recall." Leslie Shepard wrote: "If he had a rare slip or loss of memory, he would always retrieve the song in perfect rhythm. But his memory was phenomenal."[39] The truth was more mixed, at least in Harry's later years. Harry estimated that he took a week or two to learn a song well enough to sing it in public.[40] Marsh's own annotations of the recordings he studied for inclusion in *The Bonny Labouring Boy*, the two-CD collection of Harry's performances released in 2000, contain comments such as "well sung" or "strong and swinging," but there are also plenty of instances of "fumbles, mistakes," "hesitant," and "mistakes – carries on."[41]

Did Harry learn songs directly from printed sources? Roy Palmer claimed that Harry possessed "a large collection of original broadsides from which he and his father had learned their words or refreshed their memories."[42] MacColl thought that Harry learnt from broadsides and presented as evidence the way Harry pronounced the middle *w* in Warwick and pronounced gaol as goal when singing "Van Diemen's Land." Harry said he learned the song from his mother's broadsheet copy and MacColl takes this as further support for his idea that Harry read the broadsheet, but didn't consider it "print" because for Harry print meant books.[43] Harry, however, said: "I never see the sheets; my mother learnt them, and I learnt them off her." In other words, he learnt by listening to his mother and not by reading from her ballad sheets – so if she sang "War-wick" and "goal" then Harry would have learnt the same pronunciations. His father took a similar approach: learning by listening because, as Harry explained, Bob could neither write nor read.[44] Leslie Shepard, who recorded Harry in the 1960s, wrote that Harry's collection of written material consisted of handwritten texts, newspaper cuttings, and a few pamphlets – rather than a large collection of broadsides – and that Harry

Harry at Sunnyside, c.1953. (Courtesy of Jenny Barker, photographer unknown)

was "a singer with a gifted ear for a good song [who] possessed a unique memory and instinctive taste for words, melody and rhythm."[45] Of course, for the stalwart supporter of the oral tradition the idea that an iconic singer like Harry might have recourse to written lyrics is something to be avoided. Harry's friend Cliff Godbold claimed that Harry learnt "The Bold Grenadier" from "one hearing of the Ian Campbell Folk Group on the old television programme *Hootenanny*" – an approach that might cause such traditionalists to break into a cold sweat, even though this tale reinforces Harry's reputation as a quick learner.[46]

Surviving materials from Harry's collection include a dozen four-page songsters, dating from around 1900–1920 and containing the lyrics of many songs which are not known to be part of his repertoire. *The Pierrot Song Book*, for example, contains gems such as "Take Me on the Flip Flap" and "My Word, If I Catch You Bending"; a handwritten note on this collection reads: "dear H have sent you the latest," which suggests that someone (possibly one of his sisters) was keeping Harry supplied.[47] Harry also kept cuttings of songs printed in Norfolk's *Eastern Evening News*. "Sprite's" Article appeared in the paper around 1928–1930, telling tales of past times and printing the lyrics of popular songs. The column's readers often requested lyrics which "Sprite," or another reader, provided a week or two later. "The Old Rustic Bridge by the Mill" is one example, the words requested by a reader who heard a street violinist playing it each night on Norwich's Earlham Road and provided by another reader the following week.[48]

A few handwritten sheets of paper filled with song lyrics also exist, along with three exercise books containing thirty-four songs (the originals are now in Steve Roud's collection). Had it not been for Francis Collinson, there may have been at least one more. According to Harry, "There's little bits of paper, little bit here, little bit there. Collinson, he took one away; that was, for to do a programme, when he was on *Sunday Magazine*. And he never did send the bugger back no more."[49]

Whoever transcribed songs onto scraps of paper or into exercise books, it wasn't Harry: "I never wrote those out … I couldn't write much. It might be I got them to write some out at home there – my sister. That's how I used to do it."[50] Harry's daughter Myrtle wrote out some songs and recalled that Harry's sister Laura and his friend Gunner Blaxell also copied some out, but was adamant that Rosa was the main transcriber.[51] Although each exercise book is dated, this is not proof that the songs were added on that date: it's possible that these books were lying around for many years before being used and the hand of more than one author suggests that entries were made over a period of weeks, months or possibly years. Other singers did not commit their songs to paper until old age. Bullards Miller wrote down twelve of his songs in a red exercise book, but not until he was in his mid-sixties. They included traditional songs such as "The Watercress Girl" and "The Old Miser," two music hall ditties called "Strolling Round the Town" and "Root the Toot," and "That One Little Room of My Own" – a sentimental Victorian song.[52] Down in Sussex, Brasser Copper didn't commit any of his repertoire to paper until a local farmer's daughter persuaded him to do so and – at about seventy-six years of age – he painstakingly wrote down the words to over thirty songs.[53]

According to its front cover, Harry's first lyric book belonged to "Laura Cox, 52 St. George's Terrace, Jan 6 1905," but it's unclear where St. George's Terrace was. This book contains twelve songs, all written down by the person who wrote on the cover, suggesting that Laura is responsible. They include versions of "Barbara Allen" and "The Spotted Cow," but most of the songs are not part of Harry's known repertoire. Some of them are popular, such as "Loch Lomond" or Stephen Foster's "Old Folks at Home"; others are rarer, at least in the folk world. Theodore F. Morse and Edward Madden wrote "Blue Bell," a tragic tale of a soldier's sweetheart whose lover does not return from war, in 1904. Canadian singer Harry Macdonough recorded it on cylinder the same year. Noel Coward sang it and it also turns up briefly in the 1946 movie *The Jolson Story*, but the version in Laura's exercise book is the only one recorded in the Roud Index. If Laura did write it down in early 1905, she clearly had her finger on the pulse of popular American song.

The second and third books were Harry's own. One book is labelled "Mr Harry Cox July 27 1913 Catfield" and is written in two different hands; the other is labelled "Harry Cox Sept 5th/13 Levels Catfield" and looks as if it was completed by three or four different people. The Roud Index lists all of the songs in this book as having been collected on 5 September 1913, the date on the front page. But "Princess Royal or Fourteenth of February" (Harry's version of "The Bold Princess Royal") is clearly dated "6/1/46", indicating that the book was added to at different times over three decades. Harry sang and recorded "The Bold Princess Royal," "The Bonny Bunch of Roses O," "The Transports," "Butter and Cheese and All," and "Jack Tar on Shore," but once again songs appear in the books that he's not known to have sung – including a version of "The Old Rustic Bridge." "The Manx Cat" is another example of a song with a single appearance in the Roud Index: it's a mildly humorous ditty about the cat without a tail, its singalong chorus bemoaning the appendage's absence:

Manx cat, Manx cat why have you got no tail,
You seem all wrong, with nothing behind to steer you along,
Manx cat, Manx cat something you seem to lack,
Without your tail we really can't tell if you're going or coming back.

A rare topical song opens the second songbook, in "The Ship That Will Never Return" (as "Titanic"). F. V. St. Clair wrote the song soon after the liner sank in April 1912: a jingoistic tribute to those who drowned that assumes everyone on board was British and behaved in a heroically British fashion, with the rich and the poor equally at risk of death and equally willing to save others. Once again, if the songbook was completed soon after the date on the cover this suggests that someone in the Cox family was familiar with up-to-the-minute popular songs and sufficiently interested in them to make a note of their lyrics.

Another of the entries in Harry's second songbook is a perfect illustration of the way in which a song can undergo accidental alteration, to the confusion of all concerned. The Roud Index calls it "The Birmingham Boy," but in Harry's book it's clearly titled "The Burmingham Boy" and this spelling is repeated throughout the song. It's possibly nothing more than a simple spelling error but the song is sung by a stereotypical Irish lad in praise of his fellow country folk, which suggests something more – as does the fact that whenever Burmingham appears in the lyric it's prefaced by an *i*. The hero is a Hibernian boy, with no connection to Birmingham at all.

Unfamiliarity with the geography of the South Atlantic may explain Harry's alteration to one of the folk world's classic songs, "The Bonny Bunch of Roses." The lyrics refer to the burial place of Napoleon Bonaparte but, rather than singing of St. Helena, Harry brings Napoleon's grave much closer to home and buries him in St. Helens.[54] Altering place names from the exotic to the familiar can also give a singer and their listeners a more personal connection with a story, so such changes can be deliberate.

Another of Harry's songs brings to mind a variant of the chicken and egg question: What comes first – lyrics written down or lyrics sung? Collectors have found "Colin and Phoebe" in Cheshire, Yorkshire, Sussex, Dorset and Oxfordshire as well as Norfolk. Thomas Arne, the musical director at Vauxhall Gardens, wrote "Colin and Phoebe A Pastoral," which appeared in a 1745 book of song titled *Lyric Harmony, Consisting of eighteen entire New Ballads with Colin and Phæbe, in Score. As Perform'd at Vaux Hall Gardens by Mrs. Arne and Mr. Lowe compos'd by Thomas Augustine Arne.* Versions appeared in broadsides, songsters, and in the repertoires of singers such as Pop Maynard. Harry recorded "Colin and Phoebe" for Charles Parker and Ewan MacColl in the mid-1960s. Listening to this recording it sounds as if Harry is singing of Colleen and Phoebe, which puts a different perspective on the two lovers. It may be his strong Norfolk accent, or it may be deliberate. Among Harry's belongings is an undated and unsigned loose sheet of paper containing the lyrics to the song, headed "Colleen and Phoebe." Did the writer transcribe what they thought they heard when Harry sang it, or did someone teach Harry the words from this sheet of paper?

Accidental or deliberate alterations impact strongly on "The Maid of Australia," with versions displaying a bewildering array of variations in title and first line. Variations in a later line shift the song between mild titillation, eroticism, bawdiness, and sexual assault: the difference between a song that's acceptable to sing in mixed company and one that became, in Walter Pardon's words, "a banned song."[55] Harry thought "The Maid of Australia" was a true song, but he wasn't sure where it originated: "It must have come from foreign here," he suggested.[56] It appears on broadsides from publishers including Such of London, but is based on an older song. When Rev. Sabine Baring-Gould – the lyricist of "Onward Christian Soldiers" – collected a version from George Doidge in Devon in 1898, he noted that it was "a recomposition by one Geo. Harris, abt. 1860 from 'The Swimming Lady.'"[57]

"The Swimming Lady" is as bawdy as its successor, although the fact that it features a rape gives it a darker edge. The song has been around for over three hundred years – well before Captain Cook's first voyage to Australia. It appears as "The Surpris'd Nymph" in volume three of Thomas D'Urfey's *Wit and Mirth: or Pills to Purge Melancholy*, first published in 1719.[58] A young woman finds what she believes to be a secluded spot by a river where she decides to swim, strips naked and dives into the water. She's beautiful, of course, and pale-skinned – "all was white, but that which should be black." The male fish are taken aback by her appearance – each one wishes it were human and at the sight of her they "spread abroad their spawn." A young man whose advances she has previously rebuffed creeps up undetected, drags her from the water and forces her to have sex. As she recovers from the assault her rapist agrees to marry her and "save" her reputation.

"The Maid of Australia" tells a similar story, except that the young woman hails from Australia and the degree of coercion involved in the sexual relationship varies from version to version. A young man walks along the side of a river, aware that it's the place where the young maids of Australia play "their wild pranks." One of the maids appears, strips naked and goes for a swim, fully aware that the young man is watching. She gets tired, he helps her out, she falls over – perhaps by accident, perhaps deliberately, perhaps he trips her up – and they "sport and play," as folk vernacular puts it. It gets late and they part, having both enjoyed the day and each other. Harry sang a final verse in which the young man has disappeared, leaving the girl with a fatherless baby and shifting the mood of the song from a celebration of sex to a morality tale about its dangers.[59] In William Gaul's version, which James Madison Carpenter collected in London in 1928, the singer is the one who plays wild pranks and it's one of the local maids who initiates sex.[60] For the most part, however, the story differs little from singer to singer.

As for the title, sometimes it's "The Maids," sometimes "Maids," sometimes "Maid" in the singular. The maid may be "Gay" or "Fair"; the title can be "The Bush of Australia," "The Banks of My Native Australia," "Far Far Away in Australia," "The Streams of My Happy Australia," or – in two versions from Carpenter's collection – "Hawksbury Banks," after the river where the events of these versions took place. In most versions the maid could have travelled from Australia to England, as she tells the young man that swimming naked is what she does back in her "native Australia" – which may explain why most versions of the song come from England.

It's the river that brings so much variety to the first line, as the singers mishear or reinterpret or adapt. In Gaul's version, the river is the Hawksbury. As the Hawkesbury is a river in New South Wales this is often taken as the original waterway of the story, thus planting it firmly on Australian soil. However, Hawksbury Junction is the point at which the Oxford and Coventry canals meet, close to Hawkesbury village in Oxfordshire – so the action may originate in the English midlands. Other versions of the song offer many more possible locations. In a Such broadside it's the Arbourer's banks, Jim Cargill sang of the Hoxbury banks, Winterton's Bob Green sang of hieland or Hearland banks (possibly a mishearing of highland), Tuddy Rudd sang of Erin's green banks, Lew Pile of Arizona walked out on the Oxbury Branch – most likely a railway line – and Everett Bennett of Newfoundland roved over raspberry banks. John Crane, another Newfoundland singer, found walking rather a chore and instead set himself down on green mossy banks. Harry usually walked by the Oxborough banks (Oxborough is a village in the north west of Norfolk), Sam strayed near the Airoland banks (possibly a reference to Loch Arioland in southwest Scotland), while Walter Pardon and Peter Bellamy both walked on the side of the Oxberry.[61]

As the young woman swims naked on her back she spreads her limbs. Harry tells us that her hair hung in "wrinkles" and her colour was black; Sam tells us her hair hung in ringlets and her "you know" was black. A minor change, but Sam's description adds an element of the bawdy. Bawdiness is ramped up in the next verse – at least in Sam, Walter, and Peter's versions – as the maid clambers out of the water and asks for help. Sam and Peter slip accidentally, while Walter trips her deliberately: each declares, "I entered the bush of Australia." This is the verse which Walter remembered his uncle Billy Gee cutting out, because it was considered obscene and banned from many of the local pubs, but by the time he was making records he was willing to include these contentious few lines.

Harry was more reticent than his fellow Norfolk singers when Peter Kennedy and Leslie Shepard recorded him singing "The Maid of Australia" on two different occasions.[62] His foot slips and they fall on the sand, then Harry draws a verbal veil over proceedings by simply repeating a clumsy line about being "on the native the plains of Australia." Gemma Khawaja, a singer whose repertoire includes many songs learnt from Harry's singing, prefers this version: "I just think that it's a lovely song, it almost makes you want to cry, it doesn't come across as slightly sordid, it comes across as quite romantic." However, she is less enamoured of the bawdier version when it's performed by singers in club sessions, as most of them lay too great a stress on the line, "I entered the bush of Australia."[63]

Harry's singing for Shepard is an unusually nervous, unconfident performance and he stumbles over the lyrics throughout the song: he may have been concentrating so hard on censoring the fourth verse that he lost focus on the others. Harry owned a transcript of "The Maids of Australia," dated July 1942 and written down by the mysterious A. W. R., which lacks the closing verse about the maid's pregnancy and abandonment but includes the lines about entering the bush.[64] The transcript's survival suggests that Harry took care of it during his life and was happy to sing this bawdier but less moralistic version in the right circumstances.

Harry and Sam expanded their repertoires by including a few spoken word verses. Sam proudly told Philip Donnellan of his ability to "say all my poetries, what I learned at school."[65] He recited *Christmas Day in the Workhouse* on stage and his recordings feature rhymes and toasts on a variety of subjects: characteristics of Norfolk coastal settlements (the rhyme which opens chapter one), weather lore, fishing practice, and an impressively complex rhyme on boxing the compass. Sam took pride in his ability to recite poems and tales; a reflection, perhaps, of the importance attached to these narratives as entertainments both on and offshore. Harry's known repertoire of spoken word pieces is smaller than Sam's, just three or four in all. Two of these toasts are brief and humorous. Harry recorded *There's Luck to the Man who Wears a Raggedy Coat* and *Luck to the Bee* (in its entirety: "There's luck to the bee that stung Adam's arse and set the world a-joggin'") at Alan Lomax's flat.

The recitations caused him to break into such uncontrollable laughter that he struggled to speak for some seconds afterwards.[66]

Another toast, shared by Harry and Sam, reflects on the inevitability of death and could be adapted by the performer to reflect personal experience or thoughts. Untitled and uncredited, it's often known by first line *The World is Round as a Wheel*; it crops up across the country, the first two lines changing hardly at all and the final lines altering each time. This is Harry's version on *Harry Cox, English Folk Singer*:

> So although the world is as round as a wheel,
> The sting of death we all must feel,
> Here's health to the livin' and peace to the dead,
> May no-one in Sutton ever want for bread.

Sam's version is nine lines long, reminding the rich that money can't buy immortality.[67] It's almost identical to the version which Brasser Copper, born in Sussex in 1845, was fond of reciting.[68] Recovering in the Royal Cornwall Infirmary in 1916, Private F. Harding left his own version in the hospital's autograph book: a six-line adaptation bemoaning the peacetime treatment of soldiers. In Kent, Joe and Lena Jones recited the toast as the final few lines of a longer piece about the importance of hard work, but repeated the first four lines of Sam's version almost exactly.[69] A Stafford churchyard played host to another variation:

> The world is a city full of many crooked streets,
> Death is the market place where each one meets,
> If life were merchandise that men could buy,
> The rich would live – only the poor would die.[70]

9 "All We Had for Entertainment"

The idea of hardy labourers or fishermen singing for pleasure in local pubs sounds simple, but hides the complex behaviours that might be involved in the successful organisation of pub sessions – the nights filled with songs and dances which Sam and Harry loved. Turn up, tune up and sing up seems straightforward but, in practice, the failure to adhere to certain customs and expectations could turn a pleasant evening's fun into something fraught with the potential for social embarrassment or worse. The pub was not, of course, the only place to sing. For most of their lives Harry and Sam sang in one of three spheres of activity: in private; in a limited personal, social or work setting; or in public spaces such as pubs. The professional sphere – when contracts were signed, tickets were sold and singers were expected to turn up and sing up for money – was confined to a few years towards the end of their lives.

Harry and Sam both enjoyed singing in private, but Sam's opportunities to do so were limited. His tiny Winterton cottage didn't have room for a private space and work on the fishing vessels was a team activity – except, perhaps, for early hours periods on watch. That was a favoured time for a song, a vital way of relieving boredom and taking your mind off the long distance to home:

> Sing to pass the time away … When you stood in the wheelhouse, if you didn't sing a little song you'd be a-meditatin' about something, thinking about home, boy, yes … break the monotony, you see. And that took all your thoughts away from everything, all troubles.[1]

Harry often worked alone, out of sight and hearing of other people, which gave him plenty of time to himself. These were "nice jobs," as he called them, when he could sing to his heart's content.[2] Alone on farms, on his smallholding, in his garden, or in "yon ind" at home in Sunnyside, Harry could spend hours working and singing to himself. If anyone did happen to wander past Sunnyside when Harry was in full flow he would happily carry on, giving the passer-by some free entertainment. Charger Salmons and Bullards Miller shared Harry's love of singing in the garden and were equally unconcerned if someone wandered past. A wanderer was fine as long as they kept wandering, but Harry was not so keen on the ones that stopped and began chatting: "If you're left all alone, you were all right, you were happy. Then if someone come then, of course, they buggered you up. You left off then, you'd stop."[3] Private singing was attractive because the singer could choose what to sing and how to sing it without having to respond to an audience. Alone on watch or in the field there was no-one to take offence if you chose to sing your bawdiest songs, no-one to laugh if you messed up a new song that you were practising, no-one to tunelessly join in with a chorus.

Singing in small, closed groups of friends or family was a regular activity at work, at home, or perhaps at family celebrations such as Christmas or birthdays. Audiences would be limited in number, strangers absent except by invitation. In many cases there would be no division between performers and audience, for every member of the group would join in with choruses or take turns to deliver a "party piece" song or dance. On board ship, Sam and his crewmates used song to help them in their work. Sam told Charles Parker that the crew would sing when hauling in the nets, explaining that "Windy Old Weather" described how the rolling of the boat helped with the job. He recalled singing "Green Broom" as they hauled, Sam leading the way with his mates joining in on the chorus.[4] Harry spoke about "getting in a gang" for work such as hoeing, but he doesn't appear to have sung any work songs aimed at making a particular activity more efficient or less wearying.

Harry and Sam grew up in large families, with parents who took delight in singing, and it's easy to imagine various family members gathering around at night and taking turns to choose a song. Married life was not the same: neither Harry or Sam spoke of these much smaller households as places filled with song every day, despite their own talents. Francis Collinson noted that Harry, "for his own good reasons ... preferred not to sing folk songs in his own house," and chose instead to sing to him in yon ind.[5] Over in Winterton, Dorcas disapproved of Sam's bawdier songs and so he preferred to sing in the Fishermans Return when Philip Donnellan came to record him (although when MacColl and Seeger recorded him in his cottage Dorcas was often present).

Harry did not like to sing traditional songs on Sundays. He was not alone in this, as E. J. Moeran discovered when he started collecting songs: "I never could persuade anybody ... even some hard-boiled reprobate, to perform for me on a Sunday, at least not in Norfolk and Suffolk."[6] Harry kept a special repertoire for that day of the week – a repertoire of hymns. Harry's mother regularly attended church in her younger days but stopped after getting married and, although the Cox family wasn't religious, she brought up her children to respect Sunday. As Harry told Bob Thomson: "We never were allowed to sing a song on Sundays when we were young, none at all. Hymns we kept for Sundays, that's what we used to sing."[7] Few song collectors were interested in songs of worship, although Peter Kennedy did record Harry singing an untitled hymn.[8]

Harry and Elsie were married for twenty-four years, but their quiet family life came to an end in 1951 when Elsie died of "dropsy" at the age of fifty-nine.[9] Shortly before Elsie died, their daughter Myrtle married Lennie Helsdon. Harry invited the young couple to join him at Sunnyside, they took up his invitation and lived with him for the rest of his life: Lenny described him as "one of the best old father-in-laws I ever should know … one of the best old boys I ever knew."[10] Harry's only grandchild, Jenny, was born the year after the Helsdons moved in and lived at Sunnyside for eighteen years, forming a strong attachment to her grandfather. They spent many hours on long country walks as Harry passed on his knowledge of birdsong and country flora. Jenny would also help with jobs in the garden or allotment and the pair would play cards and board games in the evenings.[11]

When Jenny was growing up, Harry enjoyed celebrating Christmas with his family at Sunnyside. He would cut down a small holly bush in local woodland and bring it back to serve as a Christmas tree, decorating it with tinsel, baubles, and small candles in brass holders. On Christmas Day friends would call in the morning, joining Harry for a drink before the family sat down to a traditional Christmas dinner. In the evening Harry would sing, Myrtle would play piano, and sometimes Harry would play his melodeon. Jenny often bought white grapes as a present for her grandfather: in deference to the holiday season, Harry would drink rum as well as his usual glass of mild.[12]

After Elsie's death Harry carried on visiting his favourite pubs, where he was still a welcome regular at the singing sessions, and continued to work on the land. He was a man of routine in much of his day-to-day life. Breakfast was usually a simple one of bread and milk, although in later years he would have cornflakes instead – sprinkled with salt, not sugar, and eaten with a teaspoon. He read the local morning paper (the *Eastern Daily Press*) after breakfast, although he sometimes encountered words he did not know: "hard wads," as he called them. Harry's typical working day lunch was bread and cheese, while a favourite evening meal might be herrings fried in flour, kippers, or beef pudding – always eaten with a broad-bladed knife but no fork – followed by a pie made with his home-grown seasonal fruit. Like Sam, Harry enjoyed herrings as often as he could get them: whenever they travelled to Yarmouth, Myrtle or Lenny would buy some and Harry would eat them as fast as they could be cooked.[13]

Sometimes, Harry would attach a trailer to his bicycle and collect wood from a friend's land, using the wood for activities such as making scythe handles, firewood, or frames on which to grow peas. In the evenings Harry liked to listen to the news, shipping forecasts, and boxing matches on the radio. By the 1960s Sunnyside had a television and Harry watched the news, boxing, and Saturday afternoon wrestling. Occasionally he would bring out his old portable gramophone and the family would listen to some of his 78 rpm discs or he would sing, play his fiddle or melodeon, blow a tune on his tin whistle, or dance his jig doll. Jenny enjoyed the doll: "With the hard wood shoes it sounded terrific," she remembered. "It was hypnotic."[14]

Although Myrtle could play the piano, she did not inherit her father's talent for singing – nor his love of traditional song. She openly acknowledged her dislike of traditional music, writing to friends: "I hope the Folk Singing is going well for you, although I'm not keen. I don't grudge other people's pleasures." Sheila Park, one of Harry's friends, remembered Myrtle having a voice "like a foghorn." Myrtle acknowledged her lack of vocal talent, telling a visiting song collector: "I can't sing." When he tried to persuade her to give him a song she gave him a friendly warning: "I tell you, if I start singing you'd clear your gear and be out of that door."[15]

Modern music could be heard in Sunnyside, despite Harry's avowed belief that most of it was "squit."[16] Lennie remembered Harry singing along with "Amazing Grace," "Red Sails in the Sunset," and even Lonnie Donegan's version of "Battle of New Orleans."[17] Harry and Myrtle both enjoyed Slim Dusty's "A Pub With No Beer" and "took a fancy," as Myrtle put it, to the songs of one-man-band Don Partridge. These included his 1968 top-ten hit "Rosie" and a song Myrtle remembered as about going to the moon (probably "Breakfast on Pluto") – they bought second-hand records, often taken from juke boxes.[18]

Sam reached retirement age in 1943. There are no recollections from family members of him doing anything connected with fishing once he left the fleet; no memories of him gardening, woodworking, or keeping an allotment. After he was forced by ill health to leave fishing, his later jobs required hard work but without the glamour and adventure of a life at sea. Such jobs brought in much-needed wages but were physically demanding, repetitive, and low paid: once he could live without such tasks, he left them behind. In retirement Sam lived quietly with Dorcas, spent time in the Fishermans Return, or walked up to a bench near the church to sit and talk with friends. Harry Hession, who was stationed at Winterton during the war, remembered Sam in the Fishermans Return, regaling off-duty servicemen with songs and stories.[19] Sam sang at village events, but greater fame eluded him and the press ignored him. In one of his few appearances in the media between 1908 and his "discovery" he was noted in the late-1940s as the leader of one of Winterton's bands of singers – in his case, the group that gathered in the Fishermans Return.[20] A few years later he played a supporting role to his fellow villager George Beck, when the *Yarmouth Mercury* noted that the eighty-two-year-old Beck "had given much public service to Winterton and district" and pictured him sitting on the bench underneath the village sign with his faithful black Labrador and two friends – Ephraim Hodds and Sam.[21]

Over in Catfield, Harry kept busy with a range of different activities long after he reached pension age, just as he had done since his early teens. Harry loved animals and filled the house, garden, and outbuildings at Sunnyside with an array of pets and other creatures. Harry usually kept a cat: various felines including Smoky, Tuppence, Joey, and (a particular favourite) Gay Cat lived with him over the years. Rabbits and guinea pigs stayed in hutches at the back of the house. Injured wild animals would be taken in and cared for – a gull with a broken wing was a notable example and the inspiration for Georgia Shackleton's tune "Harry's Seagull" – and Harry kept chickens and ducks for their eggs. Lenny Helsdon bought a young Labrador named Trixie to train as a gun dog, but she soon attached herself to Harry and the two became inseparable.[22]

Harry may have loved animals but he was a pragmatic man, both willing and able to hunt or fish. He was a friend of Bertie High, the local eel catcher, and would keep him company in his hut at Candle Dyke during the night, helping to lay the nets then chatting quietly with his friend before it was time to haul them in.[23] He acted as a beater at shoots, including the coot shoots on Hickling Broad. These were large-scale events: J. Wentworth Day was an enthusiastic participant and claimed in 1951: "I have been at a coot shoot on Hickling Broad where more than six hundred birds have been killed in a day."[24]

At the start of the 1960s Harry took on the job of coypu control in local marshland. Coypu, South American rodents weighing up to nine kilograms and sometimes reaching almost a metre from nose to tail, were introduced to Norfolk in the late 1920s for fur farming but soon escaped and became established in the wild. By the 1950s there were estimated to be as many as two hundred thousand in the east of England, with the Broads home to many of them. Concerns about crop damage and predation led to demands to eliminate them, hence the government's establishment of a clearance campaign and the recruitment of trappers like Harry, whose job it was to remove the unwanted invaders.[25]

Harry spent many hours growing vegetables and plants. He worked his allotment at Potter Heigham all year round, renting it from Norfolk County Council for less than three pounds per year and growing corn or sugar beets.[26] He took most pride in his tobacco, devoting about a quarter of his large garden to it and experimenting with the drying process: mixing the leaves with a range of substances including brown sugar, molasses, and rum to give his pipe tobacco different flavours. On Thursdays Harry cycled into Catfield to collect his pension and visit his friend and fellow tobacco grower George "Gunner" Blaxell, who lived near the post office and the Crown pub. Gunner and Harry were close friends for many years, sharing not only a love of music – Gunner played melodeon – but also of boxing. Both pastimes come together in another exercise book, titled "George Blaxell, Writing Book," which was part of Harry's belongings at the time of his death. The opening pages are devoted to the thorny subject of "How to learn boxing without a master," and are full of instructions about stance, movement, taking and throwing punches, and

Jenny, Myrtle and Harry: three generations of the Cox family, at Sunnyside, c.1966-7. (Courtesy of Jenny Barker, photographer unknown)

– for the boxer without a sparring partner – how to make a dummy opponent out of sacking and stuffing. The handwriting is clear, the spelling is usually correct, but punctuation is lacking. A few pages later, in what looks like the same hand, are the lyrics to "The Bonny Labouring Boy," with each verse written as one continuous sentence.[27]

Many of Harry's activities gave him plenty of time to sing. Singing alone had its pleasures, singing with the family around the fireside helped to while away the winter nights, but the pub session was at the heart of the singer's life. In Bob Copper's words: "a song sung alone on the hillside under the wide blue sky helps the day along, a song with good companions in the hot smoky atmosphere of the tap-room is something altogether more cheery and satisfying."[28]

Norfolk and Suffolk pub sessions were characterised by a mix of singing and dancing. Suffolk sessions were often in the charge of a "chairman" whose job it was to invite singers to take their turns, control unruly or uninterested customers, keep general order, and call a halt to proceedings at the end of the night. At the Ship in Blaxhall – the name derived from "sheep" rather than from any nautical connection – Harry "Wickets" Richardson was the chairman and at the Eel's Foot it was Philip Lumpkin, both men replacing the usual chairman's gavel with a cribbage board, thwacking it against the edge of a table to gain attention.[29] Norfolk pub sessions usually coped without a chairman leaving the landlord or landlady, the singers, and their supporters to police the evenings themselves.[30]

A successful pub session depended on a series of factors and, if all were in place, a great night of song was more or less guaranteed. A welcoming licensee was crucial: if the person in charge was not keen on traditional song, then it was unlikely they would be amenable to evenings filled with the stuff. Enthusiastic locals happy to hear their workmates or neighbours were important, as was another room where locals who wanted a quiet drink or chat and those who considered themselves a bit above a common sing-song could drink in peace (a singing session was supposed to bring custom into the pub, not send it up the road to a rival inn). A decent fiddler or melodeon-player would be welcome, bringing a bit of variety to the evening and providing music for stepdancing or jig dolls – even if they were expected to keep quiet when singers such as Harry were centre-stage.

Sam Howard, an east Norfolk singer from the same generation as Walter Pardon, felt that a Saturday night was the best night, with most locals having a day off to look forward to and some spare cash in their pockets. A festival or fair day was even better. To bring business in on a quiet weeknight, some licensees might provide a popular singer with a free beer or two to persuade them to sing and, hopefully, attract a little more business. In most cases singers probably sang no more than a few songs each evening – in a popular session, with a large number of singers ready to do their turns, an individual might sing no more than one or two songs. Harry sang seventeen songs in one session at the King's Arms in Ludham, but Howard referred to this number as a "record."[31]

Peter Kennedy's seventeen-minute film *Here's a Health to the Barley Mow* gives something of the flavour of a Saturday night pub session in 1950s Suffolk.[32] Set in the Ship Inn the film features singers, stepdancers, Wickets Richardson in his cribbage board-wielding role as chairman, and a variety of locals joining in on the choruses or sitting quietly and enjoy the songs. Two well-known Suffolk characters take part: Cyril Poacher sings "The Nutting Girl" and Bob Roberts plays melodeon. Wickets sings "Fagan the Cobbler," complete with actions: he sits down, grabs a pair of shoes (his own, one assumes) and mimes various shoemaking activities as he sings. When the stepdancing begins, two of the four dancers are women and they are shown joining in with enthusiasm – though no female singer leads a song.

Kennedy's film is far from being a fly-on-the-wall documentary: the presence of filmmaker and equipment is obvious, with Wickets and others taking regular glances at the camera. The bar clock shows a quarter past seven when the session is in full swing, which seems rather early for a Saturday night, even when the pub would have been closing at half past ten or eleven. The number of women in the bar is unusually high, possibly because Kennedy encouraged them to come in from their usual spots in the pub's other room – although they clearly knew the choruses and stepdances. Kennedy took two attempts at shooting part of the film: With barely time to take a breath between verses, Poacher sings the second half of "The Nutting Girl" wearing an overcoat and scarf on top of the jacket he was sporting during the first half of the song. He's also managed to change his woolly jumper.

Luckily for Sam and Harry, the Broads and the Norfolk coast held a few places where a successful session could be found. Sam boasted that he'd sung in every port on the British coast, sometimes in competitions but more usually informally in pubs. Back home in Winterton he would drink and sing in the Fishermans Return or the Three Mariners. When the latter pub closed in the mid-1950s and a local lodging house, Bulmer House, rebranded as The Mariners, Sam and his cronies stayed loyal to the Fishermans Return.[33] If Sam joined sessions at pubs in other villages, he never mentioned this to his interviewers – although he was happy to boast of his impact on customers: "Oh, you'd hear a pin drop when I used to sing. If them young 'uns made a noise when I started to sing, well, they'd throw them out the pub."[34]

Harry and his friends frequented a range of pubs, all within an easy bicycle ride on quiet lanes from Sunnyside. The Crown at Catfield, the Windmill and the Catherine Wheel at Sutton, the King's Arms and the Baker's Arms in Ludham, and the Falgate Inn and the Railway Tavern in Potter Heigham all played host to Harry.[35] He made two of his final appearances in the Pleasure Boat at Hickling Broad. When Shirley Collins performed in Norwich in 2006, the concert organiser suggested a trip to the Pleasure Boat the following day, perhaps expecting Harry's presence to still impact on the pub's atmosphere. It didn't go well, as Shirley recalled:

> I'm sorry to say it was an utter disappointment. It was a weekday lunch time and there was no feeling that Harry had ever been there. It was unwelcoming, brash, plastic and desolate, and we couldn't wait to get away. Before you asked about it, I had erased it from my memory![36]

Over the decades licensees, customers and expectations of a good night out changed. Harry avoided the Falgate at one point because he didn't see eye to eye with the landlord – whether it was a new landlord or a new disagreement with an old landlord isn't known. "Young 'uns" could be problematic. One night in the King's Arms during the 1930s a group of young men were noisy and refused to stay quiet during the singing. Harry and his friends walked out and avoided the pub for some time afterwards.[37] By the 1950s singing sessions faced competition from radio, television, and juke boxes in some of the more forward-looking Broadland pubs. Rock 'n' roll, the skiffle craze, and growing interest in trad and modern jazz gave the younger generation an excitement and glamour that elderly men singing about poaching and transportation couldn't match even if they threw in a few rude 'uns. Harry was dismissive of these new entertainment technologies, nostalgic for the days when music in pubs was made by the locals: "Now these young blokes come in here, they can shove the wireless on, they're singing all this 'ere squit. They like to hear that." Harry was equally dismissive of the rock 'n' rollers' performance style: "Keep wrigglin' theirself about ... You can sing as well without that ... they make me sick."[38] He seems to have forgotten the part he played in bringing entertainment technology to the local pub circuit when he cycled around with his portable gramophone.

One contentious aspect of the pub singing session resulted from the insular nature of rural communities, but was no less important to the singers because of that. The issue of "song ownership" could cause arguments between friends, threats to strangers and breakdowns in the usually convivial atmosphere of the pub. The idea of song ownership is a simple one: a song becomes associated with an individual singer, who claims "ownership" of that song and precedence over any other singer who may wish to sing it when the "owner" is present. A composer in London, New York, or Manchester may have written the song, but this was of little account to the locals of Catfield or Winterton.

"Singers did not sing each other's songs," said Bullards Miller's son Leslie. It's a concise summation of the idea of song ownership in Harry Cox's community. Close relatives were not exempt from conforming to the rule: Leslie would not sing his father's songs in his father's presence and on one occasion, when George Riseborough joined his father in singing but made a mistake with the words, Jack promptly hit him over the head with his stick. When family members could be subject to violence, strangers were even more at risk: one man made the mistake of singing one of Bullards Miller's songs in the Crown at Catfield and the locals had to hold Miller back to prevent him attacking the unfortunate.[39] It was acceptable to learn a song from its "owner" – Harry and his father both did so and paid for the privilege – but to sing it in their presence was frowned upon.

According to Chris Heppa, Charlie Chettleburgh could lay claim to "The Lost Lady Found," even though Harry Cox recorded it a number of times. Chettleburgh was the singer chosen to record it for *East Anglia Sings*, which suggests that it was "his" song rather than Harry's, possibly by virtue of age as Chettleburgh was fifteen years older.[40] However, Harry sang four songs on the album and it may be that E. J. Moeran and his production team decided to give another singer a chance rather than allowing Harry to claim too many credits. Despite the apparent strength of the idea of song ownership, there's no record of Harry or Sam claiming ownership of any particular songs: possibly their repertoires were so extensive that they felt no need to claim one or two songs as their personal property.

Walter Pardon was respectful of song ownership. In his younger days he sang few of the old traditional songs in deference to the older singers, describing the idea of ownership as the older singers' "perk." He explained, "They always sung their own songs, you see. Uncle Bob Gee would sing 'Jones's Ale'

... Tom Gee always sung 'The Bonny Bunch of Roses' – no-one else would sing that or dare." It sounds like Tom would be as ready as Bullards Miller to react violently to such effrontery. Pardon picked through the rest of the songs, developing a repertoire from "what was left":

> "The Dark-Eyed Sailor," I was allowed to sing that – no-one else wanted to and I always liked the song so that went all right with me. "When the Fields are White with Daisies," that sort of thing ... they were more modern songs what they never bothered much about.[41]

Pardon and his uncles lived in Knapton, a mere twelve miles from Catfield and twenty from Winterton; in those communities Harry and Sam happily sang "The Bonny Bunch of Roses" without fear of Tom's retribution. In South Walsham, Ralph Vaughan Williams collected a version of "Jones's Ale" from a Mr. Hilton in 1908, but South Walsham was twenty miles to the south: too far to adversely affect Bob Gee's claim to the song. Although Pardon was active in the 1960s and 1970s, he showed little awareness of singers outside his corner of Norfolk – even Harry and Sam:

> Now Harry Cox, he used to sing up the Catfield Crown, I believe, but I never did meet him. I heard him on the sound radio, and I did see him on television ... I know Sam Larner was singing well, too, but I never did meet him either. They were the only two I knew about; I don't think there was a great lot in my time, not in this area.[42]

This lack of awareness of other singers might be explained by Pardon's isolation as a singer. Despite developing a large repertoire from his family, as a young man he sang alone or at family gatherings, rather than in local pubs. He never married, lived alone after his parents died, and apart from army service during World War II he rarely left his home village until he found his own degree of fame in the second folk revival.[43]

For most Norfolk singers the pub was the place to shine. Bob Pegg went to the Sutton Windmill in 1968 to hear Harry sing as an invited guest and found another, unnamed singer already singing in the public bar: "Country singers, like tom-cats, can be jealous of their territory," he wrote.[44] Hard-won reputations needed defending as well. Harry and Sam are open to scrutiny because they were extensively recorded. But many of their contemporaries made no more than one or two recordings and in some cases didn't record at all, so we will never be able to judge if Larpin Sutton was a better singer than Bredler Larner, if one or both was a better singer than Sam, if Fred Cox was a better singer than Harry, or if Bob Cox could out-sing both his sons. Of course, the idea of one artist being "better" than another is fraught with difficulties. Nevertheless, partisan opinions in favour of one singer or another were expressed.

Bob Cox, Harry's father, was wise enough not to ruin his reputation as a fine singer, refusing to sing for E. J. Moeran despite repeated requests. Moeran wrote: "I think he regarded himself as a maestro whose day was done, and he did not wish to sully his reputation as an artist by singing with a cracked voice in old age."[45] Sam Howard believed Bob was a better singer than Harry or Fred. Billy Riseborough thought that his father Jack was a better singer than Harry. Billy's brother Eddie described Harry as a "cart shed singer," far less talented than Jack.[46]

Reg Reeve was a staunch supporter of his grandad, Fred Cox. According to Reg, Fred was "a brilliant musician" who could play piano, organ, fiddle, Jew's harp, and concertina. As far as singing was concerned, "Harry was a good old Norfolk singer, [Fred] was more musical. He was more [of a] singin' in tune type person." Fred was a better singer than Harry, knew as many songs as Harry, and was a more talented musician – in the opinion of his grandson. However, he was not comfortable singing in public – "he hasn't got the bottle to do it," Reeve said, summing up Harry and Fred's talents succinctly, if crudely:

> I would've said anything Harry could do, he could do better, to be truthful. Probably Harry wouldn't like to hear me saying that. [Fred] was definitely a better singer, but I mean Harry had the bullshit and the drivel in the middle.[47]

Harry could be scathing in his opinions about other singers. Ted Goffin was reputedly a fine singer – Harry learnt "The Foggy Dew" from him – but when Peter Coleman asked Harry if he knew of "a singer called Ted Goffin" Harry responded in all seriousness, "Well, I wouldn't call him a singer." One day towards the end of his life Harry shared a taxi with fellow singer Mate Nudd – a Hickling Broad marshman and contemporary of Harry's who sang at the Pleasure Boat Inn but wasn't recorded until 1970, when Tony Singleton collected four songs from him. Harry asked Mate, "What are you goin' to do?" and Mate told him, "I'm goin' to sing, like you." Harry replied, "You won't sing like me."[48]

Harry's tendency to avoid first names could make him sound brusque even when speaking about his own family. In 1953 Harry told Alan Lomax: "I got four sisters living now," adding, "as far as I know." But he didn't name them. He never referred to his granddaughter Jenny by name, calling her "Gal," or "the gal" when speaking to others. Pauline Godbold, Harry's friend, once asked him, "What's your son-in-law's name?" He replied "Helsdon, I think, but he ain't nothin.'"[49]

Sam was fond of reminding interviewers of his competition victories, of his ability to command his pub audience and of his vocal prowess. He'd been judged by strangers and awarded prizes; he was a talented chorister with a tenor voice.[50] First-hand evidence of young Sam's abilities is missing, however: even the *Shetland Times* reports tell us little or nothing about the finer points of his performances, so it's impossible to compare or contrast him with his competitors in the Shetland singing contests, and his Winterton friends left a mere handful of recordings. When Harry and Sam's contemporaries made recordings they were approaching, or already in, old age. As Peggy Seeger noted, "They knew how the songs should be sung but most of their vocal ability was gone." Writing as early as 1934, Whiffler had been harsher, declaring that almost all traditional singers were now so aged – their voices so feeble – that "they have had to be passed over as impossible for recording purposes."[51]

We are not hearing these singers at the height of their powers or in the most sympathetic of settings – we have two short examples of Harry in his late forties, but we will never know how he, Sam, Waxy, Bob Green, or Jack Riseborough sounded in their twenties. Would Harry's dismissal of Mate and Ted have been accurate when they were in their prime? Audio recordings of these old men were never undertaken in the best of environments and when TV cameras turned up at the pub they created an artificial environment, at a time when televisions were still a recent and alien intruder in people's homes. Singers and customers reacted in different ways: some relishing the chance to appear on TV; others nervous and unsure; few, if any, behaving as they would usually behave at a pub session.

By the beginning of the second folk revival Harry's style had shifted from the outgoing, melodeon-wielding, dancing performances that Billy Durrants recalled. He took little account of his audience or, indeed, whether or not he had an audience. He sang with his eyes closed or staring into the distance beyond the heads of his listeners, immersed in the story of the song. Such a style, Peter Kennedy claimed, lent itself to repeated listening whereas the concert singer's approach to folk song – full of "tricks and dramatic effects" – soon became tiresome. Francis Collinson felt that Harry was in command of the greatest range of "techniques and artistic devices" of any English traditional singer, able to vary the melody of a song from verse to verse in keeping with the lyrics' meaning and emotional quality. Such skills had no equal, Collinson wrote, except among "the older Gaelic singers of the Hebrides."[52]

Ethnic, a new magazine devoted to traditional music, appeared in January 1959. The first issue featured an article titled *Harry Cox – The Catfield Wonder*. The anonymous author (probably Mervyn Plunkett) was impressed by Harry's technical skill and praised the simplicity of his style: "Like that of every other great country singer his style sounds deceptively simple and has little decoration. He makes little use of the shake and decorates sparingly." More curiously, the writer commented: "While he does not slur to any marked extent, a noticeable feature of Harry's style is the quite artificial quality of many of his vowels and most of his consonants."[53]

When Bob Pegg saw Harry at the Windmill in 1968 he discovered that – despite advanced age, poor health and nervousness – "it was still the same Harry we had heard on record. The songs were steadily and tunefully sung, and each one delivered as if it was a matter of personal experience."[54] T. J. Macfarlane also saw Harry at the Windmill, possibly on the same evening. Harry's voice was "sturdy … not a quaver or a crack in it, and taking phrasing, rhythm and grace-notes with perfect precision."[55]

Sam Larner kept his eyes open, the better to watch over his audience. Sam was an outgoing performer, judging his audience's reactions and responding accordingly, usually in a "vigorous and exuberant" way.[56] He was there to engage with an audience, to entertain its members – to impress the crowd. Harry was content to sing for his own pleasure because he loved the songs and their stories; if others enjoyed his singing too, then all well and good. Sam's pleasure stemmed as much, if not more, from the enthusiastic response of his listeners as it did from his love of the songs. Harry was in service to the song; the song was in service to Sam.

As transport links improved and people began to afford their own cars the folk revival of the 1950s brought more and more tourists – and new collectors armed with tape recorders – to the increasingly accessible Broads and Norfolk coast. Record labels began to sniff out potential (small) profits. The idea of song ownership at a local level should have become untenable: twelve or twenty miles was no longer a sufficient distance for two different singers to claim ownership of the same song. A singer's reputation could no longer be defended against nothing more than a few locals, as comparisons could now be made with singers from across the country and even overseas. And yet, speaking in 2019, Mike and Damien Barber explained that song ownership was alive and well:

> That's still very strong in Norfolk, people do not like other people singing "their" song. That song could be something really famous, like "Streets of London," [Ralph McTell's top-ten hit from 1974] but if you're known for singing it locally then it's "your" song – no-one would dream of singing it in the pub in front of you. If they did, people would get very snooty about it.[57]

As old certainties faded away, a few singers would embrace and be embraced by the new entertainment technologies. Harry and Sam would gain fame well beyond the bounds of the Fishermans Return, the Windmill, or the Crown, but they would discover that song ownership could take many forms – not necessarily to the benefit of the old singers who had cherished the songs over the generations.

10 Sam is "Discovered"

The story has been repeated over and over: Sam Larner was discovered in a Winterton pub in the 1950s. Who knew he existed? No-one of note, it seems. He lived in a far-flung corner of Norfolk – in splendid isolation from the city-dwelling arbiters of culture and taste – amusing himself and his friends in the Fishermans Return, immune to entertainment's march of progress. Then a BBC producer "discovered" Sam and brought him fame in his twilight years.

Philip Donnellan did find Sam in Winterton, but the details of this event are rather hazy. It was probably in 1956; he was most likely seeking out new singers for the BBC and a now-anonymous Winterton villager could well have recommended Sam. When he was eighty-five, Sam explained:

> A man from the BBC who was doing a tour went into the local pub and asked if there was anybody in the village who could sing folk songs. Someone told him about me and he asked me to go over. I went, and this chap asked me if I would have a pint. I said I would, and then he asked me if I would sing.[1]

What did Sam sing? Of course, he sang "a rude 'un." Next evening, Donnellan came to Sam's house and recorded him singing more songs. According to Sam, the BBC man told him that he "could make a packet" with his singing. Sam added: "I've been making a packet and they haven't let me alone since."

Philip Donnellan worked for the BBC in Birmingham, firstly as an announcer and newsreader then as a radio journalist. He was an early adopter of portable tape recording, which enabled him to gather interviews from people in their own surroundings – Charles Parker was using a similar approach at the time.[2] By 1956 Donnellan was already familiar with Norfolk, even if he was not familiar with Sam: during the BBC's *East Anglia Week* in June 1949, Donnellan presented the BBC Midland Light Orchestra in concert at Yarmouth Town Hall.[3] In July 1956 the BBC Home Service broadcast episode five of *The Coast*, which featured the East Anglian coast from Happisburgh to Great Yarmouth and which Donnellan edited and produced. It's possible that he was researching for this programme when he met Sam.[4]

Sam's first known appearance on radio was on Coast and Country episode "The Wash." was a well-established Home Service series, visiting communities around Britain and recording locals. The *Radio Times* advertised it, honestly but plainly, as "a programme of people talking." The programme devoted to the Wash was broadcast on Sunday 15 September 1957 at 1:10 p.m. The *Radio Times* credited Donnellan as having devised, recorded, and edited the show, but none of the people who took part were listed and the programme no longer exists – so it's impossible to establish what contribution Sam made to justify his fee of one guinea.[5]

Sam waited for over a year before his next radio appearance. *Down to the Sea* was broadcast on 27 February 1959 and Sam was paid the substantial fee of eight guineas for his contribution.[6] *Down to the Sea* was a successful Midland Home Service series, broadcast since mid-1953 when it was advertised as "a nautical miscellany." As its title suggests, the programme was recorded in various coastal towns and villages including Cromer, Lowestoft, and Gorleston. Sam attended an afternoon rehearsal and an evening recording session, both in a house called Thatchers, in Happisburgh. Some previous episodes of *Down to the Sea* were recorded in Happisburgh, at the home of retired seaman Captain Arthur Reddish, so Thatchers was probably Captain Reddish's house. Sam's contribution to this programme is also unknown. However, his copy of his contract refers to "Anecdote and Sea Songs" – "anecdote" is a handwritten addition – so Sam is likely to have talked and sung, two activities he enjoyed. One possible piece of evidence about Sam's participation exists: a sheet of paper on which are written the lyrics to "The White Squall." The lyrics are written in a clear, legible style but below them is a list of seven songs written in pencil by someone with much poorer penmanship and spelling. The list includes "Napolen [*sic*] Dream," "A Salor [*sic*] Gay," and "The Wingt [*sic*] Squall," and Sam's family believe that he wrote these titles down in preparation for a radio broadcast.[7]

Whenever Sam speaks, his rich and distinctive Norfolk accent and his use of local dialect add to the pleasure of hearing what he has to say. He was aware that he didn't sound like the BBC's usual on-air voices, telling one interviewer: "I never thought I was gonna come on the wireless. I shoulda refined my tongue." The prospect amused him and he's soon laughing heartily, until a coughing fit takes over.[8]

Later in 1959 Philip Donnellan edited and presented a series of four programmes devoted solely to Sam, usually referred to as *Sweet Lives and Lawless Billows*. The *Eastern Daily Press* devoted a few column inches to previewing the series, illustrated by a photograph of Sam stepping out of a convertible and waving to the camera. The anonymous journalist repeated the story of Sam's "discovery," gave a brief history of Sam's life on the fishing boats and

Sam, Dorcas and friend at the door of Bulmer Cottage, c.1956. The gentleman in the middle is probably Philip Donnellan. (Courtesy of Jane Roberts, photographer unknown)

noted that Sam had been singing for some years at Winterton concerts, parties, and dinners. The story ended with Donnellan's comment: "It isn't a question of encouraging Sam to sing. You can't stop him."[9]

In each fifteen-minute programme Donnellan gave listeners some background information about Sam and his Winterton fishing community, Sam and Donnellan talked, and Sam told stories and sang songs. The BBC Midland Home Service broadcast the series on 22 and 26 October and on 5 and 11 November, tucking each programme away in a late evening slot, usually 10:30 p.m. The title by which the series is known is only used by the announcer in the introductions to the first two programmes. The *Radio Times* billed the first, third and fourth parts as *Traditional English Songs remembered and sung by Sam Larner* while part two – for no obvious reason – was titled *Traditional English Songs sung by Sam Larner*.

Sam opened each programme with a verse or two of "Green Broom," before talking to Donnellan – who the announcer referred to as "the introducer." The conversation is informal, the two men enjoying each other's company, and the interactions suggest that all four parts were recorded at a single session before

Donnellan inserted additional speech of his own during the editing process. Dorcas was present for at least some of the time. After he'd sung "Old Bob Ridley-O," Sam told Donnellan of his success in the Shetland singing competitions and asked Dorcas: "I got the first prize, didn't I Mother?" Dorcas replied concisely, but with no particular enthusiasm, "Yes."[10]

Sam sings energetically, but the programmes don't always show him in the best light – he sounds as if he's trying a bit too hard, his singing lacking the effortless flow of other recordings. Donnellan may have edited his own speech, but no time or money was wasted editing Sam's conversation or singing. Sam begins "Will Watch" strongly enough (the words differing markedly from the version he recorded for MacColl, Seeger and Parker) but barely six or seven lines into the song he forgets the lyrics and resorts to "la-da-da-da" for another line or two before declaring "I can't do it," telling the story as a narrative and then complaining "oh, if I could only bring that to memory ... I can't memorise it, I can't. Ain't that funny."[11] Donnellan follows with: "Well, if you consider the number he does remember, it doesn't seem funny at all, not to me anyway." It's flippant, a throwaway comment, but it would have been better to cut the song, or give Sam another chance to sing it through.

Donnellan was happy for Sam to sing a favourite bawdy song, but spared listeners' blushes by steering them away from the sexual metaphors. He introduces one song by announcing that he calls it "The Portuguese Card Sharp" (he seems to be unique in doing so) and then briefly explains the rules of the card game which is supposedly the song's subject, before Sam sings "Game of All Fours." Neither Sam or Donnellan make any comment about the song's true subject matter. Sam closes episode two with "The Maid of Australia" – "or a bit of it," Donnellan declares, with a knowing inflection in his voice that hints at the reason why the BBC won't play it all. Sam barely gets into verse two before the programme ends. Two years later the Midland Home Service broadcast four programmes over successive nights from Sunday 28 to Wednesday 31 May, billing them simply as *Sam Larner: Traditional Songs*.[12] There's no evidence that Sam had recorded any new programmes, so it's likely that these were repeats of *Sweet Lives and Lawless Billows*.

Sam's major contribution to BBC radio came through the *Radio Ballads*, a series of programmes developed by MacColl, Seeger and Parker. Seeger wrote:

> The *Radio Ballads* were woven together by a master dramatist and songwriter (Ewan MacColl); a seasoned BBC radio producer (Charles Parker); and a classically-trained folk musician (Peggy Seeger), tripling as instrumentalist, amateur music arranger and director.[13]

The team had a clear aim for the *Radio Ballads*: as Seeger put it, "they were originally meant to narrate the impact of work on those who perform it." The first of them, 1958's *The Ballad of John Axon* told the story of an English rail-wayman who, in the previous year, had refused to abandon a runaway train, saving many lives but sacrificing his own. Others in the series explored the lives of coal miners, road builders, teenagers, travelling people, boxers and people with polio, but *Singing the Fishing* is the best known of all.

Singing the Fishing was the third of the Ballads. It was first broadcast on 16 August 1960 and won the Prix d'Italia for radio documentary later that year. MacColl, Seeger, and Parker collected 250 recordings from men and women of the herring fishing industry, ensuring that the programme was based on a wealth of first-hand experience. Sam was just one of these people, but his recollections were central to the narrative and to MacColl's songs, written specially for the programme. Sam's is the first name spoken by the announcer and he's the first singer to be heard, singing "Up Jumped the Herring." He's featured across the programme, singing more songs and talking of his life at sea, the vessels on which he sailed and his talent for cooking dumplings.[14]

Peggy Seeger travelled to Winterton with MacColl and Parker to record Sam. She remembered how this "little pudding of a man ... always had a cap on, even in the house." The trio of interviewers stayed at the Mariner's, Seeger remembered, and visited Sam in his "little tiny cottage" several times. The small house was soon full with Sam, Dorcas, the three programme makers and their equipment taking up much of the space:

His wife Dorcas was there. She was very quiet, sitting in the background. She was blind. I don't remember her ever walking about. He was a sweet man. He was delighted to have us – he loved talking. He positioned himself as close to me as possible, shall we say. He would wink at me now and again. He was a flirtatious bugger.[15]

Seeger used another word to describe Sam when we first discussed him – "randy."[16]

The best-known song from *Singing the Fishing* is MacColl's "The Shoals of Herring". MacColl took inspiration from Sam's memories when creating the song and Sam's voice comes across strongly in MacColl's lyrics. The success of MacColl's interpretation can be measured by Sam's comment when he first heard the song: as Seeger remembered, "when Sam Larner first heard 'The Shoals of Herring', made out of his own recorded speech, he declared 'I known that song all my life.'"[17] Music journalist Ken Hunt called the song a lynchpin moment:

People can't believe that "Shoals of Herring" is [MacColl's] composition: it's too buffed and rounded, edges knocked off by the passage of time, for it to be his composition – but it is. It's a phenomenal song and I don't use the word phenomenal lightly.[18]

Some of MacColl, Seeger and Parker's recordings formed the basis for Sam's 1961 debut album, *Now is the Time for Fishing*, and MacColl and Seeger published a selection of Sam's songs in *The Singing Island: a collection of English and Scots Folksongs*. MacColl outlined his plans to Sam during one of their discussions, telling Sam that he was planning on sending a recording to Folkways and Riverside (both American record labels) to see if they wanted to produce an album of English traditional singers and that the Mills Music Corporation would be publishing the book. On the book, MacColl told Sam:

> On each of the songs it will say "Taken down from the singing of Sam Larner." And I'll get in touch with the publishers and ask them if they'll give you a lump sum as well, just a token fee, for the use of these songs, but also you'll get a percentage of the royalties every time these songs are sung. That is, if you're agreeable to that.[19]

Sam's exact words in response to MacColl's proposals are often unclear, but his final response is unambiguous: "If they'd like to give me a little something they can have the rights o' them altogether ... Cos I'm old now ... I don't care, as long as they keep 'em a'goin." When *The Singing Island* was published in 1960 it included a dozen of Sam's best-known songs, including "The Wild Rover," "The Dogger Bank," and "The Ghost Ship," as well as "The Black Velvet Band"

A rare photo of Sam in formal attire, dated November 1951. Top row, l-r: Sam, Edward Powles and (possibly) George Larner. Bottom row, l-r: Dorcas, Thirza Powles (née Larner), Jane Green (née Larner). (Courtesy of Jane Roberts, photographer unknown)

and "Van Diemen's Land" from Harry's singing. As MacColl promised, each of Sam's entries were identified as "From the singing of Sam Larner of Winterton, Norfolk, 1958." MacColl and Seeger presented Sam with a copy, inscribed with "Sam: a book in which your songs are not 'written wrong.' Many thanks for your songs and your friendship. Peggy and Ewan 1960."[20]

Thanks to the growing interest in traditional music in the 1950s, BBC television called on Harry for *Song Hunter* – a series of six broadcasts presented by Alan Lomax and featuring British and Irish traditional performers. It was the first programme in the charge of a young producer called David Attenborough.[21] Harry appeared live on the fifth edition of the show, subtitled *Songs from an English Inn*. During his trip to London he visited Alan Lomax, who recorded him singing and in conversation.[22]

Song Hunter benefitted from a BBC initiative known as the Folk Music and Dialect Recording Scheme, a project devoted to the collection of songs and stories spoken and sung in dialects from across the British Isles. Collectors included Peter Kennedy, Bob Copper, Seamus Ennis, and Hamish Henderson and between them the team gathered material from seven hundred people – from primary school children to nonagenarians. The BBC issued guidance to the scheme's collectors, to ensure that song collection would progress smoothly and at minimal cost. Its policy regarding copyright as it applied to traditional song, based on the Copyright Act 1911, was clear: "When traditional music is first reduced to writing or any other tangible form of permanent representation such as recording that particular version of it becomes the copyright property of the person who so writes it down or records it."[23] The law was on the side of the collectors, who were doing nothing illegal by reproducing recordings and claiming copyright. Legally, the BBC and independent collectors were on solid ground, but the guidelines noted that some source performers might pose problems.

Additional guidance made it plain that singers must give the BBC permission in writing to broadcast any recording made of them. It advised that such permission would be best obtained after the recording session has started, "for psychological reasons" – singers were presumably less likely to ask awkward questions or deny permission if they were already in full flow. As for financial reward, this should not be offered routinely, as a singer might not consider themselves to be a performer and "would perhaps be insulted if offered a fee." A gift, or free food and drink, might be more appropriate, but if a collector felt that a financial reward was in order this should be no more than two pounds for each recording.[24] Of course, if collectors were employed by the BBC then the corporation would be paying the fees and gaining the copyrights, but the corporation's policy gave independent collectors the green light to operate in the same way.

Kennedy visited Norfolk on a few occasions during the early and mid-1950s, recording singers and instrumentalists from Morston and Blakeney on the north coast, Burgh-next-Aylsham in the centre of the county, and the

Broads. On his first collecting trip, in November 1952, Kennedy recorded long-forgotten performers including Herbert Smith (who would only perform once Kennedy agreed to buy him a new A string for his fiddle), Anne Mary Bullamore, Major Philip Hamond (who eventually performed after a lengthy diatribe about how the BBC was ignoring Norfolk), and Alfred Barker, whose diction was poor "owing to a hole in the side of his mouth." Kennedy was impressed by the elderly and blind Major Hamond, who was an unusual source singer in terms of his social rank and education. (He noted that Hamond was "bilingual," being able to speak the Queen's English and to converse with the locals in a broad Norfolk dialect.) The performers may be forgotten, but they shared some songs with Harry and Sam: Barker sang "The Bold Fisherman"; Hamond sang "The Foggy Dew" and "Up Jumped the Herring."[25]

A year later – on 10 October, according to Kennedy's report – he recorded Harry Cox at the Windmill in Sutton before going to the Ship at Blaxhall to record an evening session. It was a fruitful day's work: Harry sang a dozen songs including an unnamed hymn, "Betsy the Servant Maid," "Newlyn Town," "The Foggy Dew," and "Up to the Rigs" as well as playing "tap dance tunes" on an "accordian" [sic] and talking about his life.[26] Kennedy and Harry met again in July 1956, when they spent two days together: Harry's daughter Myrtle had recently written to Kennedy, he claimed, saying that Harry looked forward to seeing him. Kennedy collected twenty-four songs from Harry over the two days.[27]

As I Roved Out, a programme dedicated to "the folk songs and music still sung and played in the British Isles," was broadcast over four series between 1953 and 1958 and used recordings from the recording scheme.[28] The series featured leading members of the traditional music scene including MacColl, Ennis, the Coppers, Maud Karpeles, Kennedy, and Francis Collinson, showcasing singers and players from across the United Kingdom. Kennedy believed that much of the show's success was due to the "emerging personalities of the singers":

> To give variety to the presentation of the songs, we gave a brief description of the singers and our meeting with them, and before they sang we let the tape run on with some of their conversation and talk. They told us about themselves, their domestic lives and their work as well as what the songs meant to them … they gave us much of their own character and the background struggles from which it had developed.[29]

The programmes were broadcast on Sunday mornings on the Light Programme, giving fans of the BBC's light entertainment station a rare peak-time chance to hear British traditional song. Kennedy and others would go on to use this successful mix of talk and song frequently on record albums.

Harry appeared on *As I Roved Out* on 7 February 1954, an episode that also featured Ewan MacColl. Spike Hughes – a writer on opera and travel, former jazz musician, and son of song collector and composer Herbert Hughes – introduced the show and also arranged its theme tune.[30] Six weeks later Harry was back on air, on a Midland Home Service programme called *Folk Music of the Midlands* with singer Isla Cameron, pipe and tabor player Robert Kenworthy Schofield, and others.[31]

Harry appeared on BBC radio intermittently over the next ten or twelve years, often in programmes involving Lomax, Kennedy, or MacColl. Lomax's eight-part series *A Ballad Hunter Looks at Britain*, broadcast in late 1957, featured Harry in its fourth episode. Lomax described him as a "tall, lean, old farm labourer" with a repertoire of 250 songs and played a recording of "Jack Tar on Shore." On 30 October 1958 Harry recorded songs and interviews with Charles Parker, at an unnamed Norfolk location, for a Midland Home Service programme noted in his contract as "East Anglian Feature" – he was paid three guineas.[32] Another Midland programme made use of Harry's talent and repertoire to help tell the story of a life at sea. *A First Taste of Sail*, in which speakers talked of their early nautical experiences, was broadcast on 27 January 1961. The title suggests that this was a programme tailor-made for Sam Larner, but Harry got the gig. Three weeks before the broadcast, Harry recorded his contribution in Catfield, singing "The Apprentice Boy" and another, unidentified, "traditional sea song" for three guineas plus repeat fees. At the end of the year he sang "The Foggy Dew" on *Counterpoint*, a radio magazine programme devoted to events in East Anglia. The song came from the January recording session, the unnamed "traditional sea song" mentioned in his contract, even though it is by no stretch of the imagination a song about the sea.[33]

In early 1965, MacColl presented a radio series about the traditional songs of Britain and Ireland, *The Song Carriers*. He used recordings of Harry and Sam in five of the ten episodes, although Sam appeared only once while Harry made five appearances. MacColl praised the singers but recognised their failings, commenting about Sam's performance of "Butter and Cheese" that "though his breathing is not what it was, and his voice has lost a lot of its flexibility he still has the ability to involve us in his own sense of the absurd."[34]

In the early 1960s, someone came up with the inspired idea of producing a television programme devoted solely to Harry and Sam. Charles Parker, from BBC Birmingham, travelled to Norfolk in 1963 to record the show, which became *The Singer and the Song*. Two of Harry's contracts from that year survive. Both give the title of a proposed TV programme as "SCAN – 'Folk Singers,'" name Edmund Marshall as the producer, and give Catfield as the place where Harry recorded. In both sessions Harry was interviewed and sang an unspecified number of songs, receiving ten guineas for the first recording session and substantially more (twenty-five pounds) for the second session.[35] *Scan* was a midweek magazine show on BBC One Midlands, usually scheduled on a Wednesday evening at half past ten and broadcast only to televisions receiving signals from the Oxford, Peterborough, or Manningtree transmitters. When *The Singer and the Song* was eventually broadcast it appeared in another regional the slot titled *Choice*, on Friday 3 July 1964. It was still tucked away, however – just before the late-night news, weather, and closedown.

It was the end of a busy day's broadcasting for the BBC, which had launched BBC Two only three months earlier. Most of BBC One's airtime was devoted to the Wimbledon tennis championships and to the third cricket test between England and Australia. Evening shows included episode two of Charles Dickens's *Martin Chuzzlewit*, the *Graham Stark Show* written by Johnny Speight, and *Club Night* from the Palace Theatre Club, Stockport. A late-night feature described as "Sam Larner and Harry Cox, both of Norfolk, sing the songs they learned as boys and talk to Charles Parker" was unlikely to be the entertainment highlight of the day for anyone yet to be converted to traditional music.[36]

The Singer and the Song is a fascinating half hour, a rare chance to hear and see two fine traditional singers. There is one question that begs to be answered: Why, when Harry and Sam lived barely ten miles apart, did Parker not bring them together in one place? It makes economic and logistical sense if nothing else. Why drive the BBC's recording equipment along the road between Winterton and Catfield, unload, set up and take down the equipment twice when it would have been easier to park at one venue (Harry's house afforded more space inside and out than Sam's little cottage) and bring the other singer along by car?

Perhaps neither man wanted to give up his home comforts, perhaps one or both were feeling too unwell to travel, perhaps they were reluctant to meet or even actively wished to avoid meeting. Myrtle laid the blame at Sam's door:

> But that Sam Larner's a mystery man ain't he, because my father never did meet him, you know … I didn't know anything about him 'til I saw this film … there was never any mention of him meeting my father and he never seemed to be wanting to … I mean he weren't many miles from him and they could've got together.[37]

Whatever the reason, the best chance of recording the two men side by side and hearing them singing together was lost.

Even without a duo performance or two, *The Singer and the Song* is worth seeing – Peggy Seeger wrote a "fan letter" to Parker, praising its beauty and telling him how moved she and MacColl were by it.[38] Each man sits in his own home; Harry's in yon ind, while Sam's in what looks like his living room. The camera concentrates on their faces, close up for most of the time, the only exception being when Harry dances his jig doll and the camera pans down to the puppet. Parker's voice-over introduces Sam as the camera lingers on a painting on the living room wall: it's a Yarmouth drifter, YH709, the *Thirty-Two* – an obvious visual counterpoint to Parker's description of Sam as a man "still able in his song to recapture the tang of life as a herring fisherman." For Harry's introduction we move outside, to see him scything tall grasses in another heavy-handed visual link, this time with Parker's description of Harry as "a man of the land ... he works and sings to the rhythms of life before the combine harvester." The introduction may have been intended to invoke feelings of nostalgia, but it also creates a sense of two men of the past, out of tune with the modern world.

Sam is dressed in a dark jacket and a light-coloured shirt, buttoned up to the neck. He's bare-headed, rather than wearing the hat which Peggy Seeger remembered as a permanent fixture. He's the first to sing and talk, opening with "Windy Old Weather" before Parker asks him about going to sea. Parker then asks for "The Dewy Morning" and Sam obliges, smiling broadly when he sings the line about espying a "pretty, fair maid." We hear Harry before we see him: the legs of his jig doll appear in close-up as Harry diddles a tune and makes the doll dance. The camera pans upwards to his face as the doll stops dancing and Parker declares, "I've never seen a thing like this before in my life." Harry sits next to a brick fireplace, his tobacco tin and matches are on the mantlepiece, his jacket lies over the back of the chair and he's wearing a gansey. He begins by talking about his father and life on the land, then sings "Seventeen Come Sunday." The programme alternates between Sam and Harry, each man taking his turn to speak about his life and sing a song or two. Parker asks questions but keeps them brief and gives his subjects as much screen time as he can – it's only when Sam talks about and sings "Mignonette" that he sounds irritable, annoyed that Sam isn't concentrating exclusively on the "old songs."

Sam and Harry avoid the bawdiest songs of their repertoires. Harry sings "The Bold Drover" – a tale of adultery, prostitution, cuckolding and accidental revenge – but that's as near-the-knuckle as it gets. Sam steers clear of all his rude 'uns, although after a short section of "Mignonette" he goes on to break into a fragment of an unidentified song from the minstrel tradition: another song that doesn't fit with Parker's ideas about the sort of old, traditional songs that Sam and Harry should be singing, but luckily Sam only remembers one verse. He ends the programme with "The Wild Rover."

Harry and Sam may be due some credit from across the sea in Ireland. Every night, in the pubs and bars of Dublin, Belfast, Cork, Kerry, and more, bands and solo performers launch into "The Black Velvet Band" and "The Wild Rover" as tourists from around the world happily sing along to these two archetypal "Irish" songs. No-one suggests that Harry or Sam originated these songs, simply that the well-known versions sung widely today are based on the versions they sang. The evidence is mixed, but there is a school of thought which gives Harry and Sam a leading role in popularising these singalong favourites.

Ewan MacColl's 1955 recording of Harry singing "The Black Velvet Band" was released on *The Bonny Labouring Boy*. It's a familiar tale of woe. A naïve and inebriated young apprentice is caught in possession of a stolen pocket watch, pickpocketed from a passing gentleman by the "pretty colleen" who ties up her hair in a black velvet band. He takes the rap for her crime and sails off to Van Diemen's Land to serve seven years. The Roud Index has versions by Cyril Poacher and Percy Webb from Suffolk, John Stickle from the Shetlands, and Mrs. Terry of Sussex as well as from Canada, Maine, and New South Wales. It was also a favourite song of Harry's friend and fellow singer Jack Riseborough. Print versions date back to the first half of the nineteenth century, often setting the story in the Essex town of Barking, which suggests that the song has English origins. In 1907 George Gardiner collected a version from Alfred Goodyear, a Hampshire singer who placed the events in Bedfordshire. Mrs. Terry, from whom Clive Carey collected the song in 1911, sets it in the "sweet little town" of Belfast, as does Harry.[39]

Sam sang "The Wild Rover" for many a year. MacColl and Seeger recorded him and it appears on *Now is the Time for Fishing*. Harry reportedly sang it, too.[40] The lyrics could almost be Sam's autobiography: a tale of a free-spending, hard-drinking, worldly-wise traveller who eventually returns home to live a quiet life but is still willing to play a trick or two. In the final verse he swears he'll never again be a wild rover, a reflection of Sam's promise regarding whoring in "The Reckless Young Fellow." Like "The Black Velvet Band," "The Wild Rover" appears in a number of nineteenth-century printed publications: it may go as far back as the late seventeenth century. There's no place name to change, but there's variation in the rover's length of time away – seven years, twelve years, many years – and in the singer's favourite tipples. Sam sang of wine, ale, and beer; Pop Maynard enjoyed brandy and beer, while the Dubliners downed whiskey and beer.

Seeger and MacColl suggest that "The Wild Rover" derives from an older song, "The Green Bed."[41] Harry sang this song, although there's no evidence of Sam having done so. There's certainly a similarity in the stories. In "The Green Bed" a sailor home from sea tries to get lodgings in "an alehouse where he had been before," but he still owes the landlady forty-five shillings so she's about to turn him out when – surprise! – he reveals his pockets filled with gold. Of course, this changes everything: the sailor is given the green bed to sleep in and the landlady's daughter to sleep with. He's a man of principle, however, and spurns both.

The Dubliners took "The Black Velvet Band" into the UK top twenty in 1967.[42] Writing in 1948, E. J. Moeran noted that the song was East Anglian, but popular in County Kerry – in 1967 Norfolk's press was in no doubt of the debt the Dubliners owed to Harry.[43] When the band's recording hit the charts, the *Evening News* declared that "The version of the old song which the bearded Irishmen sing was taken down from Harry's repertoire many years ago."[44] The band also made it to number forty-three later in the year with "Maids When

You're Young Never Wed an Old Man," and regularly performed a version of "The Wild Rover" that, with the exception of the foot stamping in the chorus and the words of the third verse, stays close to Sam's interpretation.

Speaking in 1987, MacColl was clear about the origin of the Dubliners' version of "The Black Velvet Band." He claimed that he first heard Harry sing the song in 1950 or 1951 and that Luke Kelly, a member of The Critics Group and a founder-member of the Dubliners, took this version with him when he returned to Dublin to form the band. According to MacColl, when the Dubliners' version became a hit he wrote to Kelly and asked that Harry be given a share of the royalties:

> I wrote to Luke and said, "Luke, this song is Harry Cox's and Harry's old now, he needs the dough, he really needs some comforts, you know." He said, "I'll see that he gets everything," so nothing happened ... So we followed it up and then discovered that his money had been embezzled by their manager.[45]

How much did Harry lose? MacColl claimed that the song was a number one hit and grossed four hundred thousand pounds, so Harry's share of this could have been substantial.[46] A gross income of four hundred thousand pounds represents sales of around 1.2 million singles (based on a retail price of about thirty-two-and-a-half pence): however, MacColl is incorrect in claiming that the song went to number one – it reached fifteen in the UK and four in Ireland – so his estimate of four hundred thousand pounds is likely to be an exaggeration.

Frankie Armstrong was a member of The Critics Group, which MacColl and Seeger formed to explore folk song and performance. She remembers that MacColl used *The Singer and the Song* as an educational tool in Critics Group discussions:

> I have very strong recollections. Part of the film was Harry and his dancing doll ... and then we saw Sam singing a kind of vaudeville song called "Mignonette" and talking about being on the herring boats. It's funny, because I don't always have a clear visual memory going back that far, but those films I really do have a very strong recollection of. Most of the time we only had [audio] recordings, so this was a wonderful opportunity to explore what they looked like, aspects of their lives. How life, body types, temperament, impacted on how they sang. All those things fascinated me at the time.[47]

As Armstrong says, *The Singer and the Song* affords a unique opportunity to compare Harry and Sam's physical approaches to singing and talking. Sam's facial expressions constantly vary; his hand movements accentuate phrases. He holds a handkerchief in his hand, speaks directly to the interviewer rather than to the camera, and prefers singing to the people in the room rather than the unseen audience through the camera lens – except for occasional glances forward. When talking, Harry looks directly at the interviewer too, with occasional brief glances to the others. He's chatty, but he's uncomfortable. From time to time he smiles or laughs, glancing self-consciously towards Parker and the crew. When singing he keeps his eyes open, but they're unfocussed or looking to the ceiling – as if he doesn't want to see the BBC staff, but is too polite to show it. He appears most comfortable when he operates his jig doll, when the camera spends most of the time looking at the doll rather than Harry.

Harry was not overjoyed at the presence of the BBC crew and equipment: to prepare for the recording he had to stop all of his collection of American wall clocks, then restart them after the event – something he complained about to his granddaughter.[48] Lenny Helsdon remembered the recording sessions at Catfield as chaotic: Engineers took power from the mains electric supply, because the household supply wasn't powerful enough for the recording equipment. Seven BBC vehicles blocked the road outside Sunnyside. The session took about ten hours from start to finish (Harry's contract indicates that it was planned to last for four-and-a-half hours). Between them the BBC staff, the singer, and others drank a total of sixteen crates of beer. As a result, said Helsdon, "Harry didn't care too hoots because he was so drunk he didn't know what was happening at all."[49]

"Monitor," the media critic of the *Coventry Evening Telegraph*, previewed the show.[50] After opening with the declaration that the folk revival was largely the result of increasing interest in blues and country and western music, they wrote enthusiastically of Harry and Sam as men who knew "hundreds" of songs whose origins are "lost in antiquity and foreign places." The Cox family gathered round to watch *The Singer and the Song* but because of reception problems they weren't able to see the show clearly. No-one knows if Sam and Dorcas saw it – if they tried, it's likely that poor reception would have thwarted their attempt just as it did Harry's.[51]

Anglia TV, East Anglia's commercial station, gave Harry his next TV appearance. Myrtle wrote to the Stricklands to let them know of the programme, which was due to go out on 28 June 1965 at 10:50 p.m., but she was not too excited at the prospect of seeing her father on the television. She was working hard, picking fruit on local farms so, she told her friends, "I don't know if I'll be able to keep awake long enough to see it."[52] The programme was "Where the Whale Fish Blow", the first of a series called *Heritage*.[53] Harry's contribution to this exploration of the whaling ships of Yarmouth and King's Lynn is long forgotten, whether or not Myrtle stayed up to watch it.

The developing interest in singing, as well as listening to, traditional songs led to the publication of numerous songbooks along the lines of *The Singing Island*. One of the most popular was *The Penguin Book of English Folk Songs*, first published in 1959 and edited by Ralph Vaughan Williams and A. L. Lloyd. This slim volume gathered seventy songs, all originally published in the

Journal of the Folk-Song Society or the *Journal of the English Folk Dance and Song Society*. The majority had been collected before World War I and none came from Harry or Sam, even though many would have been familiar to them. When Steve Roud and Julia Bishop produced their updated and much larger *New Penguin Book of English Folk Songs* fifty years later, they included five songs from Harry and two from Sam.[54] But the early 1960s saw far more of Harry and Sam's songs appearing on record rather than in print.

When Harry started his recording career in 1934 the 78 rpm disc was the home entertainment medium of choice, enjoying a mutually beneficial relationship with BBC radio. Compared to stars like Al Bowlly, Gracie Fields, or George Formby, Harry Cox wasn't even a flicker in the entertainment firmament – but at least his voice was fixed on shellac. When Harry next appeared on record, yet another giant technological leap meant that vinyl was now pre-eminent as a 45 rpm single, a 33⅓ rpm LP and, occasionally, in the form of an EP. During the 1950s Harry appeared on a few compilation records, featuring various artists who each contributed one or two songs. *Folk Song Today: Songs and Ballads of England and Scotland* was the first of these, released as a ten-inch album in 1955 using Peter Kennedy's recordings made under the auspices of the EFDSS.[55] Artists included Bob Roberts, Shirley Collins, Bob and Ron Copper, and Harry, who sang "The Foggy Dew." Kennedy's sleeve notes tugged at the heartstrings, not altogether accurately: "The singer is a retired farm labourer now living alone and remembering the hard times of his youth," he wrote, conjuring up images of a lonely and isolated old man stuck in his rural retreat rather than the active head of a three-generation household.

Harry next appeared on an HMV EP titled *The Barley Mow: Songs from the Village Inn*, a collection of Kennedy's recordings that features Cyril Poacher, Bob Roberts, Jack French, and Edgar Button. Harry's photograph adorns the cover – a serious, thoughtful-looking Harry complete with his distinctive trousers and the string that keeps his braces from slipping off his shoulders. Harry sings "The Foggy Dew," recorded at the Windmill pub in Sutton – the same recording that appears on *Folk Song Today*, unless Harry made a habit of always coughing at the same point in the song. It's remarkably free of background noise for a pub recording and there's no audience response at the end of Harry's performance, supporting the idea that Harry was singing before the pub opened for business.

The EP's release date is unclear, but it was on sale by June 1958 when *Tape Recording and High Fidelity Reproduction Magazine* published Kennedy's article on his tape-recording technique. For readers eager to follow in his footsteps, Kennedy revealed the equipment he was using at the time: a *Wearite* tape deck, running at fifteen or seven-and-a-half inches per second, with a separate amplifier running off mains electricity or, if no mains supply was available, with power from Kennedy's car battery.[56] Sadly, the sound quality of many recordings of traditional singers suggests that few collectors took

Kennedy's advice about recording techniques, or could afford to buy his recommended equipment.

The EFDSS celebrated its diamond jubilee in 1958, dating the jubilee from the establishment of the Folk-Song Society. *The Tatler* – a magazine popular with Britain's establishment – deemed the anniversary worthy of note. Sydney Carter, the writer of "Lord of the Dance," took on the job of explaining to the magazine's readers how the old songs were finding a new audience among young fans who were following the path from skiffle to rock 'n' roll to English folk song. Seeger and MacColl loom large, Carter namechecks Shirley Collins and the Coppers, and refers to "rude old sailors from the Norfolk shore" for good measure. As for Harry, he's featured in a photomontage titled "Folk Music Faces," alongside Sheila Gallagher from Donegal, singer and banjo player Margaret Barry, and Northumberland shepherd Jimmy White.[57]

Harry appeared regularly on compilation albums over the next few years. *The Unfortunate Rake*, released by Folkways, is an intriguing disc consisting of twenty songs with the theme of the young man (or sometimes woman) whose dissolute lifestyle and bad company leads to their early death – from sexually transmitted infection in the earlier ballads to a gunfight or an industrial accident in later versions. The album includes songs by A. L. Lloyd, Alan Lomax, Dave Van Ronk, Pete Seeger, and Harry, who sings "The Young Sailor Cut Down in his Prime."[58]

In 1961 the Caedmon label released its ten-album series *The Folksongs of Britain*, which featured a variety of tracks by Harry and Sam. Peter Kennedy and Alan Lomax edited the series, but the tracks originated from many different song collectors. Seven of Harry's recordings appear in the series. Sam appeared twice, both times from Philip Donnellan's recordings: "The Smacksman" (a.k.a. "Coil Away the Trawl Warp") on volume six and "Napoleon's Dream" on volume eight. More importantly for Sam, 1961 saw the release of his debut album *Now is the Time for Fishing* on Folkways Records, making him the first English traditional singer to release a full-length LP devoted solely to one artist.[59]

Moses Asch and Marian Distler established Folkways Records and Service Co. in New York in 1948, with the ambitious aim of recording "the entire world of sound." In the years up to Asch's death in 1986 the label released 2,168 albums – around one per week throughout the period – featuring poetry, spoken word, and traditional song from across the globe by artists including Seeger, MacColl, and Lloyd.[60] *Now is the Time for Fishing* contains songs, rhymes, and conversation collected and edited by MacColl and Seeger between 1958 and 1960, as their sleeve notes explained:

> The songs presented in this album were recorded at different times, on different machines, under different acoustical conditions and there is, naturally, a considerable variation of level and quality. The

editors, however, consider ... that this collection is one of the most important to have been made in England in recent years.

MacColl and Seeger selected the material from a total of sixty-five pieces Sam recorded for them and which they described as "traditional ballads, broadsides, sea songs, music hall pieces, and various miscellanea." Despite their self-effacing reference to "defects" the album's sound quality is impressively clear; Sam sings and talks beautifully throughout, the songs are strong, and MacColl and Seeger's notes are detailed.

Sam was eighty years old or more when he made the recordings that form *Now is the Time for Fishing* but, despite advancing years, his voice is full of character. Sometimes the story makes him laugh, even though he's sung the song hundreds of times before. Sometimes a song retrieves memories from decades past. Once or twice he pauses mid-song to ask a question of

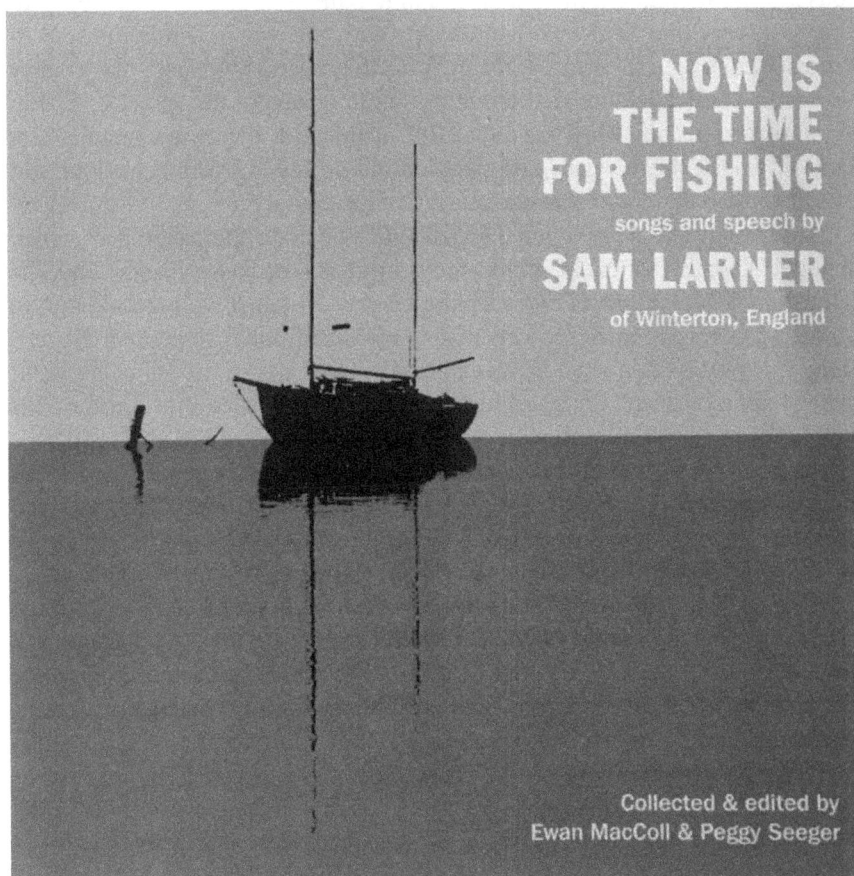

NOW IS THE TIME FOR FISHING

songs and speech by

SAM LARNER

of Winterton, England

Collected & edited by
Ewan MacColl & Peggy Seeger

The cover of the Topic Records re-release of *Now is the Time for Fishing*, Sam's first album. (By kind permission of Topic Records) his listeners – "You can box a compass, can't ya?" he asks before reciting a compass-boxing rhyme – or to make a comment. He's always aware of the drama of the song, of where to pause for best effect. On "The Dogger Bank," singing of the ship's hard-drinking captain who likes a drop of good ale, he divides the line into two – half-singing "he likes a drop," then speaking "of good ale." It's as if he's suddenly decided to take the audience into his confidence, to tell them a secret with an intimacy that implies "this is just between us."

The anonymous gramophone correspondent of *The Times* was impressed. Sam gave "a lively solo performance" and proved himself to be "a genuine entertainer with a rich, devil-may-care personality." Who might find Sam's record appealing? The reviewer was happy to recommend the album to "those unconverted to folk song." Sam might have been pleased with another comment, but folk purists may have spluttered over their morning marmalade, for the reviewer described Sam's vocal style as "music-hall, or possibly public-house."[61] Who might find it unappealing? Sam himself, as it turned out. There's a story that Sam wasn't too happy with the way in which the spoken word sections were presented, feeling that they made him seem like a "dirty old man." Roger Digby related the story in his review of the cassette version of the record in the 1990s and found it plausible. But there's no denying that Sam did speak those words and people's memories of Sam's behaviour add weight to the veracity of this description of his character.

Sam's debut release never challenged 1961's chart-topping albums – which included Elvis Presley's *G.I. Blues*, the soundtrack to *South Pacific*, and *The Black and White Minstrel Show* by the George Mitchell Minstrels – but he claimed impressive sales for a recording by a traditional singer. An *Eastern Daily Press* article reported Sam's claim of sales of eleven thousand copies in the last six months of 1963 and his claim that he recorded the album on his eightieth birthday, rather than on various dates between 1958 and 1960.[62]

Harry's first solo album appeared in 1964 and once again an American label was responsible. Folk-Legacy Records of Sharon, Connecticut, released *Traditional English Love Songs* using recordings by Peter Kennedy and sleeve notes from Kennedy and Francis Collinson taken from the 1958 *Journal of the English Folk Dance and Song Society*. Harry sang fourteen songs, most if not all of which would have been familiar to his friends in the pubs of east Norfolk. Collinson declared him to be "possessed of a more complete range of the traditional singer's technique and artistic devices than anyone in England today." Kennedy painted a less romantic portrait than the portrayal of the lonely artist he gave on *Folk Song Today*. Harry was now "a widower and a retired farm worker [who] lives with his married daughter at Catfield": a more honest but still not wholly accurate description of Harry's household arrangements.[63]

The British release, renamed *Harry Cox sings English Love Songs*, also appeared in 1964 courtesy of Davies Transcription Services Records.[64]

Collinson's notes were missing from this version, but Kennedy provided a short paragraph of information for each of the songs and noted that he made the recordings between 1953 and 1956. The note on "The Birmingham Man" is instructive, suggesting that Kennedy's grasp of Norfolk geography was as tenuous as Harry's knowledge of Napoleon's island of exile. Harry sings "Burningham" rather than Birmingham and Kennedy notes that Harry wonders if the place should actually be "a local place called Burnham (i.e. Burnham on Crouch)." Kennedy's choice of "local place" – an Essex town over one hundred miles to the south of Catfield rather than Burnham Thorpe, Burnham Market, Burnham Norton, or Burnham Overy Staithe, all less than half that distance away on the north Norfolk coast – is unlikely to be Harry's.

Davies Transcription Services was a curiosity, far removed from the leading labels of the day such as HMV or Decca. The Sheffield company was active in the early-to-mid-1960s as the go-to label for anyone keen to buy a record of the sound of Sheffield tramways – including the ever-popular "Mr. C. C. Hall checks the manual brakes of car number 46" – and recordings made on the last day of the Ecclesall and Middlewood routes. ("The quality of recording is not very good," the sleeve notes boasted.)[65] The company further enticed train lovers of Britain with EPs of the iconic *Flying Scotsman* locomotive and the trains of London's Metropolitan Line, and supported local music by releasing records by the Sheaf River Jazz Band and the Sheffield University Big Band – an eclectic discography, made even more so by the addition of a folk song collection or two.

Harry Cox wasn't the first folk artist on the Davies Transcription Services label. That honour goes to Cyril Tawney, a leading revival singer and songwriter who released his debut album, *Between Decks* – recorded by the ubiquitous Peter Kennedy – on DTS Records in 1963. The album contained "The Sailor Cut Down in His Prime" and two of Tawney's best-known compositions, destined to become folk club standards: "Sally Free and Easy" and "The Grey Funnel Line."[66]

Harry's second album, *Harry Cox English Folk Singer*, appeared in 1965 as an eightieth birthday tribute from the EFDSS.[67] It was available solely to EFDSS members and associates, so commercial success was never an objective. The seventeen tracks – which Kennedy recorded and edited – include Harry talking about his life and his music, an untitled waltz played on melodeon, a couple of fiddle tunes, and the by now over-familiar "The Foggy Dew" (although on this version Harry doesn't cough). Kennedy's sleeve notes mix a few facts about Harry's appearances on radio, TV, and record with a description of Harry the singer which chimes with descriptions from his friends and family:

> Each time you hear him the songs grow on you, for he presents them with complete selflessness and sincerity. To watch him, with his eyes closed or looking into the distance beyond the company,

you realise that he is living the story of each song … he is, in fact, giving an artistic performance into which he pours as much, if not more nervous energy than the best stage singers.[68]

Three albums and a handful of compilation discs, none of which required Harry or Sam's presence in a professional recording studio, make up the sum total of their 1960s discography. Apart from singing and talking, there's no evidence to suggest that Harry or Sam played an active role in any these records – no involvement in song selection, editing, cover design or any other aspect of production. More albums would appear, but they would be posthumous releases.

11 On the Road

As increasing car ownership, affordable and reliable portable tape record-ers and a desire to explore England's musical traditions converged, "weekend collectors" emerged: amateur enthusiasts with access to a car and a recorder, travelling round the country on their days off work. Far more numerous than the professional collectors such as Kennedy or MacColl, this group was crucial in recording a wide range of singers. They missed Sam but found Harry, turn-ing up at Sunnyside to grab their own recordings of the master in much the same way as folk fans with mobile phones might be bothering source singers in the twenty-first century. An expanding record industry slowly brought out collections of English folk songs, with the new long-playing records making it possible to have twelve, fourteen or more songs on one disc. BBC programmes like *Song Hunter* brought folk songs to a mass audience – and some of them liked what they heard.

The collectors of the first revival were convinced that English folk song was dying out and the collectors of the second revival felt the same way. Singers who learnt wholly or mainly by face-to-face transmission were ageing and younger singers were drawing on a variety of sources including records and radio programmes. The potential source of material was not a small group of singers from the same locality – it was international. Even more threateningly, the new breed of performer played instruments that were alien to English song, notably the acoustic guitar, brought along by the fans of skiffle.

Skiffle isn't usually given much credit for the success of the folk revival, but there's a case to be made for its importance. The term originated in 1920s USA as a slang word for a rent party, but skiffle was a peculiarly British form of popular music: a mix of simple songs using instruments that were easy to play, at least at a basic level. The UK first heard this vibrant new sound thanks to bandleader Chris Barber and singer/guitarist Lonnie Donegan. Barber (on bass) and Donegan played blues numbers by artists such as Lead Belly in "blues sessions," when the rest of the band was taking a break. When Barber decided to name these sessions he took inspiration from a 1929 Paramount Records disc called "Hometown Skiffle" and articles in *Jazz Information* which referred to pianist Dan Burley as playing "skiffle music."[1] Enthusiasts eager to make their own music found that a professional level of proficiency was unnecessary: acoustic guitars (usually played as rhythm rather than lead instruments) a tea chest bass, and a simple drum kit (or maybe a washboard) were all that was needed – although a kazoo or harmonica might be drafted in from time to time. A singer (whose most notable characteristic might be enthusiasm) would join in, perhaps doubling on guitar. The songs came from America – stories of freight trains, engine drivers, battles in southern states and cotton picking formed the set lists for teenage bands whose members were yet to leave the British Isles.

Lonnie Donegan is the musician most often associated with the genre today but Chris Barber, Chas McDevitt, Beryl Bryden, Ken Colyer, and others were crucial in popularising it. There was plenty of crossover between skiffle, jazz, and folk as the decade progressed. Scottish traditional singer Anne Wilson took her stage name of Nancy Whiskey from the lyrics of "The Calton Weaver." Martin Carthy gives Ken Colyer, born in Great Yarmouth and a leading British exponent of New Orleans-style jazz, an honourable mention for helping the revival by supporting influential folk acts including Margaret Barry and Michael Gorman.[2] Carthy played skiffle, Frankie Armstrong sang it, Led Zeppelin's Jimmy Page began his career in a skiffle band, and in Liverpool Paul McCartney and John Lennon joined the Quarrymen skiffle group. Even Alan Lomax was seduced by the sound of skiffle, forming the Ramblers to record songs in the skiffle style.

Harry was unimpressed by skiffle – as he was by the other musical styles beloved by teenagers:

> I wouldn't listen to a song like they make today … 'cause there ain't one worth it … they're out of my line, and they can do what they like but they can't sing a song not where there's sense in it, not like I can.[3]

Britain's hip young music fans didn't stay in love with skiffle for too long either, and as the craze faded many skifflers turned to folk music, bringing their guitars with them. The folk scene they joined was still small and yet to gain any real momentum. The struggling revival found itself with a new influx of performers and audience members; in the words of music journalist Robin Denselow, "As skiffle faded out, the folk clubs faded in."[4] Frankie Armstrong was typical of the young skifflers who moved into the revival. She was happy singing the usual skiffle repertoire, until she "found the Weavers … Woody Guthrie, Pete Seeger." Thereafter, "the music took on a more serious, political tone." The group changed its name to the Ceilidh Singers and started listening to British folk performers: "the Spinners and the Campbells and some early Ewan MacColl, I guess. Then we moved entirely to British material," said Armstrong.[5]

Back in Norfolk, skiffle caught the teenage Peter Bellamy's imagination. As skiffle waned and Bellamy found rock 'n' roll he also started looking for skiffle's roots, exploring the music of Lead Belly, Pete Seeger, and other American musicians. Then, at the age of seventeen, he "discovered that England had folk music too."[6] The discovery led him to Harry and Sam and he remained a dedicated fan of the two men for the rest of his life, drawing inspiration from them in his solo career and as a member of the Young Tradition, an *a cappella* trio and one of the leading folk revival groups.[7] Harry and Sam would find many familiar songs on Bellamy's 1968 debut solo album, *Mainly Norfolk*: six of the twelve songs came from their repertoires, including "The German Musicianer," "Georgie," and "Lofty Tall Ship." Bellamy was clear about Harry and Sam's stature as singers, writing that they "stand supreme, unrivalled not only for the quantity of their songs, but also the quality."[8]

Bellamy was keen to promote Harry and Sam to his audiences and to the younger generation of singers – a talented artist, he also painted a notably lifelike portrait of Harry in pensive mood. Tony Baylis remembered him "in full flow," talking about Harry on stage during a Young Tradition gig.[9] Bellamy befriended Damien Barber when Barber was eighteen and sent the teenage singer what he described as a "Norfolk singers beginner's kit … [with] all of Walter [Pardon]'s stuff, all Sam Larner's and all of Harry Cox's."[10] The Jimi Hendrix and Rolling Stones-loving Bellamy was rumoured to listen to Harry and Sam's records "in a cloud of hashish" – a rumour substantiated by Damien Barber. "Yeh, yeh," he said, "the last time I saw Peter was heavily influenced by whisky and smoking. Peter was definitely a party man."[11]

The revival's emphasis on live performance was crucial in giving folk fans a sense of community, providing places where like-minded enthusiasts could gather to hear their idols. For many of them, their most enduring memories of favourite performers are those from live performance – often in the professional sphere that goes beyond singing at home, with workmates or down at the pub. It's a sphere of activity that's neatly summed up by Frankie Armstrong: "Come and sing at our festival or folk club – and what's your fee?"[12]

The prospect of being paid for singing might be an appealing one, but it brings with it a set of responsibilities that were alien to Harry and Sam as singers. For most of their lives they sang for their own pleasure, to their own timetable. If a singing session down at the White Horse or the Fishermans Return didn't appeal then they didn't go to it. If they did go to a session they chose the songs they would sing; requests could be accommodated, refused, or ignored. The landlord might expect a few songs in exchange for a pint or two, or they might sing a little longer if the hat was being passed round, but there was little pressure on either man. Certainly, when collectors arrived with a tape recorder or paper and pencil Sam or Harry might have felt honour-bound to give them a few songs, but these visits were few before the second revival. Sam sang at local events but these, too, were informal.[13] The folk clubs of the 1950s and 1960s wanted more.

Folk clubs offered payment, however small, but this was part of a two-way arrangement. To raise the fee, the clubs charged for entrance and to attract an audience they advertised in advance, putting the singer's name on posters and advertisements weeks or even months ahead of the promised event. Contracts were signed, diaries were filled in and plans were made to sing to a paying audience, possibly a few hundred strong. In Fred Woods's words, "at one fell swoop, came the complete distortion of everything a traditional singer stands for." The intimacy of the home, the pub, or the field – singing alone or for a handful of people – was replaced by the strange, new environments of the folk club or the folk festival. Folk music was "wrenched into a false context and will never be quite the same again," said Woods.[14]

Some of the older generation of singers embraced the new context and its opportunities. Walter Pardon, who spent most of his life singing at home in Knapton and rarely set foot in a pub until he was in his sixties, was a folk club and festival regular in his old age and sang at the United States Bicentennial celebrations in Washington, DC.[15] Shropshire's Fred Jordan was one of the earliest of the traditional singers to join in the club and festival circuit – the first, according to Woods. Jordan was constantly on the search for new songs, happy to take them from the younger generation. Ken Hunt spoke of Jordan's "keen-eared attitude to songs. He actually picked up songs from the folk revival. If he heard a good song, he'd learn it."[16] The Copper Family took successfully to the circuit too, the original line-up changing over the years to the present day when the younger generations are still performing.

Harry and Sam were obvious candidates for the revival's expanding audience: source singers whose lives began in the nineteenth century and overlapped with legendary figures of the first revival, and who were blessed with extensive repertoires of "authentic" English songs. Yes, Harry and Sam were old men by this time and their voices were fading, but such things hadn't prevented the Gramophone Company from believing that Joseph Taylor could make commercially viable recordings. Appearances on the live circuit promised a financially and artistically rewarding few years for both men. Unfortunately, time had moved on a little too far. The folk revival arrived too late for Harry and Sam to become regular performers on the club and festival circuit and their appearances are notably few in number. They never embarked on organised tours, and their occasional appearances in the clubs were confined primarily to London venues and to a period of no more than five or six years.

Sam's relationship with MacColl and Seeger led to appearances at London's Ballads and Blues club, where MacColl and A. L. Lloyd were regular performers. The club opened in the Princess Louise pub on High Holborn in central London – previously a skiffle club.[17] Peggy Seeger remembers the upstairs room, holding about one hundred people, was often full to bursting: "We did cram them in," she said. She still remembers Sam Larner singing at the club and enjoying himself hugely, adapting his singing style to suit the large audience:

> He just loved being on that little stage, flirting with all the girls in the front row. He was a right showman. In front of an audience he sang differently ... He would act out "Henry Martin," he would act out the waves, someone spying from the crow's nest.[18]

Sunday nights at the Ballads and Blues were special, as they were hootenanny nights. Held every week, "The Hootennany" [sic] featured a combination of some of the Ballads and Blues resident performers – MacColl, Lloyd, Bruce Turner, Fitzroy Coleman, Dominic Behan, and others. Some nights had themes: for example, one hootenanny was devoted to songs from the Radio Ballad, *The Ballad of John Axon* and promised "many new songs about railway workers."[19] Harry sang on at least one occasion, probably in the latter part of 1958. *Ethnic* magazine reported that Harry had visited "the heart of Revisionist Revivalism – the Hootingnanny [sic]." It was, Harry reported, "The rummest do I bin to lately."[20] Earlier that year, on 23 March, the hootenanny's guests all came from East Anglia: Bob Roberts from Suffolk, who sang "Still I Love Him" on the *Barley Mow* EP; Arthur Weems, who seems to have slipped through the net of history; and Sam.[21]

Sam sang at a number of events organised by MacColl and Seeger, who also remembered Sam singing at the Ballads and Blues successor, the Singers Club.[22] Memories being the unreliable things they are, the precise chronology of events isn't always clear. In his notes to *Now is the Time for Fishing*, MacColl wrote that he first brought Sam to a hootenanny in 1957, at the Princess Louise, then brought him back two months later for an eightieth birthday celebration. However, Sam's eightieth birthday was in October 1958, not 1957. Whatever the precise timeline may have been, the birthday concert did take place, this time at the Horseshoe on Tottenham Court Road – a venue capable of holding five hundred people. It was sold out, wrote MacColl, "and it is doubtful whether many among those present will easily forget the picture of this stockily built eighty-year-old fisherman leading five hundred teenagers in the chorus of 'Maids When You're Young Never Wed An Old Man.'"[23]

A young Martin Carthy was in the audience for one of Sam's London concerts, which he remembers as taking place in a pub on or near the Edgware Road, and the experience had such a profound effect on him that he would still affirm over sixty years later that Sam changed his life. Carthy, aged about seventeen, went along with a friend who was booked to play the support slot:

He asked me to go along to what was then called the Ballads and Blues, to see this Yarmouth fisherman. So I said yeah, alright, I'll come along. He'd told Ewan MacColl that he'd been in Canada collecting folk songs for five years. Unfortunately, he was a complete fraud ... He played four or five songs in each half, but he was totally ignored. I have the feeling that he was taking me along to stand in the way of the right hooks that would inevitably follow when he was unmasked. There were no right hooks in the end, he just got ignored, because Ewan MacColl was a massive fan of Sam Larner, he was the real deal if you like. My impression is that Ewan got Sam to come down and stay with him so they could talk and Ewan choreographed the whole evening.

Ewan MacColl didn't sing a single note, he just talked to Sam and Sam sang songs. The last song he sang was very carefully and deliberately chosen by Ewan. It was this astonishing version of the Henry Martin story, which Sam called "Lofty Tall Ship." That was the thing that completely blew me away. I'd never, never heard a tune like that in my life. There was one version that everybody sang. It told the story well enough but it wasn't an astonishing tune. Sam's tune had a sophistication and a colossal amount of variation. This is the 1950s we are talking about and pop music – to call it simple doesn't even begin to describe it. The thing that strikes me when I look back on that evening is that it really illustrated to perfection that just because I'm English, I still didn't know what English folk music is. That was the thunderbolt.

Carthy found Sam to be an engaging on-stage presence:

He was a fabulous performer, with an energy about him that was astounding for someone pushing eighty ... He engaged the audience all the time, he engaged Ewan MacColl. When he was singing a song that was a bit rude, really, "No John," I remember him turning round to Ewan and saying "Am I to go on?" which of course caused great hilarity. He was just playing with the audience, he was used to audiences, he knew what he was doing.[24]

Sam did indeed change Carthy's life, bringing him a career as a leading singer that still continues.

When two young American singers arrived in England in the early 1960s, eager to develop as performers through floor spots and guest appearances in the burgeoning folk revival scene, Carthy was at hand to offer support. Young Bob Dylan arrived in October 1962. He was already a recording artist and came to London to act in a BBC television play called *The Madness on Castle Street*. Within days he started playing in local folk clubs, and befriended and learned from Carthy. A couple of years later it was Paul Simon's turn to bene-fit from Carthy's knowledge and skill, learning how to play "Scarborough Fair," with its famous refrain naming four herbs. Simon and Art Garfunkel turned it into an international hit.[25] "Scarborough Fair" was a popular song well before Simon's successful recording: there are over three hundred instances of the song from the UK and it was collected across the United States well before Simon heard it in London. Neither Harry or Sam is known to have sung it, but a song called simply "Old Norfolk Song" is almost identical to Carthy's version of "Scarborough Fair," a notable difference being the first of the herbs – savory replacing parsley to join sage, rosemary and thyme.[26]

Harry made his own impact on the performers emerging from the revival. MacColl might have spent more time with Sam, but Seeger remembers that Harry's singing left a bigger impression:

> Ewan was very moved by Harry in a way he wasn't moved by Sam. Sam was a jolly guy, he was a performer on stage and he loved being the performer everybody listened to. Ewan described Harry Cox as almost like out of a Norse saga: craggy, never smiling ... Ewan spoke very movingly about Harry Cox.[27]

MacColl summed up his feelings about Harry as a singer in the first episode of *The Song Carriers* in 1965, when he introduced a recording of Harry sing-ing *The Barley Straw*:

> Perhaps the best living representative of English traditional singing style is Harry Cox ... [he] has carried in his head more than two hundred songs – an important part of the musical heritage of the English people. His memory is prodigious, his metrical sense highly developed, his feeling for pitch still extremely accurate. He uses very little decoration, but that little is used with considerable skill. His dramatic sense is sharp and mature and is always contained within the structure of the song he is singing.[28]

MacColl's praise wasn't reciprocated. According to Myrtle, although her father liked MacColl he was not a fan of his singing style.[29]

There's plenty of evidence for a cheery, good-humoured Harry, but MacColl's impression of a never-smiling, focussed and thoughtful singer is supported by others who saw him perform in his later years. Seeger com-pared Harry's tendency to close his eyes or stare into space when performing to the singers she knew in her native America: "That's an American thing, too. Appalachian singers sit and stare into space. They don't check on how you're responding ... it's involvement."[30] Harry explained this tendency in his own way:

When I sing a song my mind is on it – 'til I've done. I don't let nothing else come into my mind. I let everything go. Keep your, keep your way clear, so you know you're going right. Nothing don't trouble me.[31]

Shirley Collins was another singer to be deeply affected by Harry, first hearing him on Alan Lomax's 1953 recordings, which she transcribed for Lomax when she was living and working with him:

Although I was young, I recognised in Harry the same qualities that I knew my grandad had, and the Sussex singer George [Pop] Maynard. Yes, they were old men, but their singing was full of grace, understanding, compassion, and humour. Grandad had sung to my sister Dolly and me when we were young children at nights during bombing raids over Hastings in the Second World War, so I was used to hearing old people singing unaccompanied, whereas lots of young singers found that quite hard to take.

As I listened to those reel-to-reel tapes of 1953, I grew more and more aware of what a remarkable singer Harry was, how well he inhabited the songs and sang them with a rare conviction and grace, always beautifully paced; it was far more than a mere performance. Like the finest traditional singers, he gave the songs what I can only describe as the knowledge of time and an understanding of life; there was never a superficial performance. I sometimes struggled with Harry's strong Norfolk accent, and occasionally had to ask Alan what certain words were – embarrassingly so once or twice, as they were sexual euphemisms I hadn't heard before![32]

Collins heard Pop Maynard and Harry Cox at Cecil Sharp House, when she was nineteen. Pop and Harry "both stole my heart," Collins wrote. These two "modest, courteous men" sang on the same night: "Their voices were perhaps not as strong or melodious as they once had been, but there was a gentle dignity about them both that felt heroic."[33] She met Harry before he went on stage, but was too shy to speak to him – except to tell him how much she enjoyed his singing on the Lomax recordings. Nevertheless, she describes hearing him sing in the flesh as "a privilege and a highlight of my early life."[34]

Harry performed at the third English Folk Music Festival at Cecil Sharp House in October 1959. On the night before the festival he went to a party at Reg Hall's house, where he was joined by Pop Maynard, Fred Jordan, Scan Tester, and others. At the festival, Harry joined in on an informal session in the basement room. This was the first time Hall had the chance to play with Harry: "we clicked musically," he recalled. Karl Dallas remembered Harry at the session, "sawing away at his fiddle while people all around him strummed guitars, rattled spoons, bashed drums."[35] Harry's opinion of this gaggle of informal accompanists wasn't recorded.

Harry may not have taken to the folk club circuit, but Mervyn Plunkett did drive him to south Norfolk to join sessions at the home of musicians Walter and Daisy Bulwer. The first visit was in January 1960 and Plunkett wrote fifteen years later: "I only know that I shall never again experience the excitement and elation of the first tune we ever played together – 'The Jenny Lind Polka.'" Two years later, Bill Leader of Topic Records was on hand to record another session at the Bulwers' home. Harry asked to try Walter Bulwer's viola – the first time he had attempted to play this instrument – and played four or five tunes, which Leader recorded. Later that day the tape was inadvertently recorded over, so his one and only session on viola was lost forever. Harry's voice was not at its best, and what Plunkett described as "full-tuned fiddle strings" proved rather too tense for his fingers: attempts to record him singing "Ekefield Town" were unsuccessful and, Plunkett wrote enigmatically, "by this time tensions of a different kind prevented a satisfactory performance being achieved." "There was tension," remembered Reg Hall, who also took part in the session, "because Mervyn created it. He did this all the time." Hall believes that an attempt to get Harry to play "The Foggy Dew" on fiddle may have contributed to the mood, as Bulwer, Hall and Plunkett wanted to play the tune in waltz time but Harry could not adapt from his usual 4/4 rhythm.[36]

On two occasions, Harry's visits to London were cut short when he fell ill. In around 1956, Harry was urgently admitted to St. Mary's Hospital with severe abdominal pain caused by an acute retention of urine. He remained there for six weeks following surgery – a visit to see Harry in hospital was Myrtle's first trip to London.[37] Harry's professional singing career came to an end after one performance at Cecil Sharp House (Myrtle dated it to April 1964).[38] He was suddenly taken ill, rushed home to Catfield in agony and sent immediately to the Norfolk and Norwich Hospital with what sounds once again like acute retention of urine, an indication of prostate problems. The performance was to be his last concert engagement and his final visit to the capital: "Last time I came up to London to sing at Cecil Sharp House I was in hospital for weeks after," he told *Melody Maker*, "so I'd rather stay at home now."[39]

As the Swinging Sixties slowly emerged and England began to resemble a pendulum, Harry and Sam retreated to their homes in rural Norfolk. Old age and poor health meant that their brief flirtations with the revival circuit were drawing to an end: from now on, fans would have to visit Norfolk if they wanted to hear their heroes singing live. *Melody Maker* journalist Karl Dallas wasn't sorry to see an end to Harry's London performances, preferring to hear him in a pub session. For Dallas, these performances presented him "rather like a museum exhibit, which he wasn't."[40]

Harry and Sam were established as source singers for the folk revival, their songs firmly set in the repertoires of numerous revivalist performers, but outside the revival – at least for a short while – another Norfolk singer eclipsed their fame. Ask the mythical Man on the mid-sixties Clapham Omnibus to name Norfolk's most famous singer and he would likely respond, if at all, with the *nom-de-chanson* of Alan Smethurst – the Singing Postman – and perhaps indulge himself in a few bars of Smethurst's pop favourite, "Hev Yew Gotta Loight Boy?" The Singing Postman never actually made the top twenty, but he did appear on *Top of the Pops* and the song won an Ivor Novello Award for best novelty song. Smethurst grew up in Norfolk but he wasn't born there and, even worse, his postal career took place in Grimsby. Still, he sang his songs in a strong Norfolk dialect and accompanied himself with a jaunty acoustic guitar, so it was folky enough for most people. Sam might well have enjoyed the song, joining in and laughing along at the lame jokes, but Harry would most likely have one word to describe it – squit.[41]

The Singing Postman soon faded from public view. Although Harry and Sam were no longer singing outside their Catfield and Winterton social circles, occasional radio or TV appearances and record releases meant that they still generated interest among folk fans and the local media. *The Singer and the Song* was the pinnacle of their radio and TV careers, but there was more to come in their final few years.

Sam was popular enough in Norfolk to make his diamond wedding anniversary worth a story in the local press. The article, "Octogenarian Fame," mentioned Dorcas briefly but focussed on Sam, perpetuating the myth of his "discovery" by Philip Donnellan and making the unfounded claim that Sam had spent time in the London Fire Brigade – perhaps inspired by Tuskin Hodds's letter of fifty years previously, which was reprinted in the month the article appeared. It also noted that Sam had survived a lengthy period of ill-health, but was now enjoying a new lease of life. "How many men," the writer mused, "have achieved singing fame when they were octogenarians?"[42]

Sam's broadcasts and London appearances proved popular, but despite his niece Annie George's claim that "people were always at his house, getting him to sing on tape," no recordings of him are known to exist beyond those by Donnellan, and MacColl, Seeger and Parker.[43] On the positive side, this means that his commercially available recordings were made to a high standard and Sam's discography is unsullied by tracks filled with the background noise of clocks ticking, dogs barking or children chattering – unlike some of Harry's. Sam had stopped singing in the London clubs by the middle of 1964, when *The Singer and the Song* was broadcast, and this may partly explain the absence of amateur recordings, as he'd ceased performing before most enthusiasts had access to portable tape recorders. Perhaps the old sailors at the Fishermans Return were an intimidating and unwelcoming bunch, discouraging song collectors from taking out their tape recorders and asking for a few songs. Perhaps Sam had quickly faded from the revival's memory. Damien Barber sees this explanation as indicative of an emphasis on songs, rather than on the people singing them:

Everyone's obsessed with the ... songs and music and not so interested in the person. Everyone wants to know you when you're singing songs and being involved with the scene but when you've stopped they're not interested in you anymore ... That's all wrapped up in this whole collecting thing.[44]

Eager collectors often visited Harry and as a result there are many recordings of his singing. During research for *The Bonny Labouring Boy*, the two-CD set of Harry's singing released in 2000, Paul Marsh found over seven hundred recordings of individual songs and toasts; some were recorded on many occasions, others only once or twice.[45] The fifty-four tracks on the album range from the BBC's 1945 Windmill recordings through Mervyn Plunkett's 1958 recordings of "Betsy the Servant Maid" and "Miss Doxy" to Bob Thomson and Michael Grosvenor Myer's November 1970 recording of "The Poacher's Fate."

Harry would usually give these enthusiastic collectors what they wanted, singing a few songs and talking about his life, but he was not always happy about it. Peter Coleman remembers two young folk singers turning up at Sunnyside on a Sunday afternoon, much to Harry's disgust. "Come at four o'clock on Sunday afternoon when you're gonna have your grub, who wants to start singing then?" Harry told Coleman, who shared Harry's opinion. "You don't do that," Coleman told me, "I know who they were but no names, no pack drill." Nevertheless, Harry gave them a couple of songs and they, in turn, sang a couple to him. Harry was not impressed, telling Coleman, "I wish they hadn't bothered."[46]

Other collectors and enthusiasts were more welcome. Harry's granddaughter Jenny has fond memories of Frank Purslow coming to hear Harry sing; of Mervyn Plunkett visiting on a few occasions, often with his wife and daughters; and of Reg Hall bringing his reel-to-reel tape recorder to the house. Leslie Shepard visited on a couple of occasions between 1959 and 1965, recording songs and conversations – and noting that Harry's drink of choice to relieve a dry throat was Tizer, the popular fizzy soft drink.[47] Lewis and Isobel Strickland came to Sunnyside on more than one occasion, always arranging their visits in advance by contacting Myrtle. They were welcome guests: "Of course it will be alright for you to come so long as we know, the day before, at least," Myrtle wrote in response to one of their requests, while after an earlier visit she wrote, "I'm glad you enjoyed yourselves here. Of course you can come again."[48]

If Harry liked you, accepted you and thought you were sincere in your love of his songs – and you arranged your visits in advance through Myrtle – he was generous with his time and with his singing.[49] Myrtle was happy to organise these visits, but uninterested in what went on down in yon ind. She usually left Harry and his visitors alone once a tape recorder appeared:

Sometimes I think it is better if my father is alone on occasions like this especially if anyone is trying to record. I tend to get in the way as I'm not very interested and get bored with the whole thing although I mustn't tell my father that.[50]

Shepard thought Harry was "relaxed and friendly, but slightly reserved." He was impressed with the singer's calmness and the way he seemed absorbed in a song every time he sang:

> There was not the slightest trace of egoism in him. His manner was almost shy, but with a certain dignity. He did not have much to say unless I asked him questions, when he responded with simplicity and directness. His Norfolk accent had a certain charm, particularly in the lilting lift at the end of sentences, making a response almost a tentative question.[51]

Four Norwich singers and collectors visited Sunnyside regularly in the late 1960s. Cliff and Pauline Godbold, who ran the Norwich Folk Workshop, knew Harry well and introduced him to Peter Coleman and his niece-by-marriage, Sheila Park. Visits often took place on a Sunday: "We were honoured," said Coleman. Park agrees that these Sunday sessions were a rare privilege, aware that Harry "didn't entertain just anybody … [I] didn't realise at the time."[52] When the Godbolds visited, their two young boys often came along. Myrtle took the lads for walks in the neighbouring fields while Cliff and Pauline spent time with her dad. On a couple of occasions, Cliff and Pauline arrived with two young revival performers – Johnny Moynihan and Anne Briggs. At Sunnyside, Moynihan played fiddle as Harry danced his jig doll.[53] Harry shared songs, displaying a prodigious memory for their lyrics. During one visit Coleman, having learnt one verse of a song, was eager to learn more:

> I told him, "I'm looking for a song, Harry." "What one is that?" he said. So I told him I thought it was called "The Rigs O' London." He said "Oh, you mean this one" and he sung it, right out … Sheila was tape recording at the time so I could listen from that.[54]

Singer and club organiser Tony Baylis was another welcome visitor, meeting Harry four times and recording him twice. When he first arrived in the Broads to record Harry, Baylis found the locals "suspicious" of his motives: "I don't think they knew of him. I think his singing had been in earlier years." The revival may have been gathering strength in towns and cities such as Norwich, but Baylis felt that it had yet to reach the isolated villages of Broadland. Luckily, Baylis met Cliff Godbold, who introduced the men to each other, and Baylis arranged his recording sessions through Myrtle. Baylis believes that Godbold's introduction was crucial in gaining Harry's trust: "I think that it broke down any barriers ... I didn't find Harry difficult to talk to at all. He wasn't reticent in any way." Baylis and Harry met in yon ind, where Harry sat down in an old armchair with Trixie the Labrador at his side (and at least one of his American clocks in close proximity to the microphone).[55]

By the middle of the 1960s many of Harry's friends and fellow singers from his younger days were gone. His best friend Gunner Blaxell died in October 1965 aged ninety. Myrtle wrote of his death a few days later:

> I don't know if you see in the paper that George Blaxell has died he was buried on Friday. That was my father's last pal, gone. It must be terrible when you grow old and lose all your old friends.[56]

The next couple of years were hard for Harry. Myrtle wrote to Reg Hall in mid-1967, saddened by the fact that Harry's old friends were all dead, and that they no longer saw Hall, Frank Purslow or Mervyn Plunkett:

> No-one comes these days, haven't seen Mervyn for 2 yrs now. My father gets very lonely. I suppose one does at his age 82 yrs. We never have any visitors which doesn't bother me ... but as he can't do too much now he needs company when he is sitting down a lot.[57]

By this time, most of Harry's siblings had died. When Bob Thomson asked Harry if he kept in touch with his brothers and sisters he replied: "Got one brother in Gorleston, one sister in Catfield, that's the whole lot out o' thirteen." According to Jenny they were Fred and Anna; Harry didn't name them and gave no indication that they were in regular contact.[58]

By the mid-1960s Harry's health was deteriorating and he was no longer singing outside the comfort of his home, so friends and fans organised occasional pub sessions to keep him in touch with the music he loved. Cliff and Pauline Godbold arranged at least two sessions at the Sutton Windmill in Harry's honour and invited him along to perform. The first of these sessions, on 1 June 1966, gained a review in that autumn's *English Dance and Song* magazine.[59] Sixty or seventy people crammed into the room to hear Harry in a session that also featured songs from other local singers – most of these were no doubt fans and supportive of the guest of honour, but there was an exception. At some point in the evening, wrote the reviewer, "the meeting was graced with the singing of 'Jimmy', the local Sutton singer come to reclaim his territory." Jimmy – his identity has not been further established – was clearly put out by Harry's presence on his turf. Harry's days as the Windmill's star turn were long gone. Harry was surprised by the size of the audience, as he was expecting no more than a dozen or so to turn up, and he was troubled by a bout of catarrh but he managed to sing ten songs over the course of the night, starting with "The Dolphin" and ending with the trio of "Betsy the Serving Maid," "The Wild Rover," and "Geordie."

The Godbolds, numerous Norfolk and Suffolk singers, the Young Tradition (Peter Bellamy, Royston Wood and Heather Wood), and others crammed into the Windmill once again, on an autumn night in 1968. While Jenny Barker remembers it as a "lovely evening," another audience member was more critical of the event. Musician and academic Bob Pegg wrote about his experience of this Windmill session twice. Soon after the event he wrote a lengthy report in *Abe's Folk Music*, the Leeds University Ballads and Blues Society magazine, which he edited. He revised and shortened this report for inclusion in his 1976 book *Folk: A Portrait of Traditional Music, Musicians and Customs*, which is, as he said, "rather less generous (and a bit less informative)" than the original.[60]

Bob and Carole Pegg were committed folk fans who would go on to form Mr. Fox, one of the revival's more intriguing bands. They hitchhiked from Leeds in order to hear Harry, who impressed Bob with his repertoire of songs.[61] Other aspects of the evening gave Bob cause for concern. Before Harry arrived, the Windmill's regular singer was already there, performing for a small group in another of the pub's rooms – probably this was Jimmy, the unwelcome floor singer from the 1966 session. Harry opened with "The Green Bed" but looked nervous from the start, his hands shaking and his voice troubled by a constant rattle in his throat. A few songs later he took a break and when asked if he was ready to sing again he replied: "I wish I could play you like I used to play, I'd sing you 'til tomorrow morn." Some in the audience took this as a joke, but Bob noticed a touch of bitterness in Harry's voice.[62]

Harry seemed to enjoy things more when he danced his jig doll, reprising the dance after the audience's enthusiastic response. Packie Byrne, the Irish singer and whistle player, was in the room and after he sang a couple of songs someone suggested that he should play a tune for Harry's doll to dance to. Bob noted that Packie and Harry seemed to have little shared musical terminology – as he put it, their "terms of reference" were "diffuse" – so Byrne started a reel and Harry's doll joined in. Byrne suggested a jig, but Harry didn't seem to understand what he meant and so Byrne played another reel. The combination of whistle and doll was a great success, the two men began to interact more confidently and the audience cheered.[63]

By the end of the evening Harry was showing more confidence, singing "The Old German Musicianer," "The Bonny Labouring Boy," and "The Seven Jolly Gipsies" unerringly, but many of the audience were drunk and no longer paying attention:

> Some of the locals, in another room … decided to take the rise out of the strangers who packed the public bar. The sense of uneasy awe with which the evening had started had become a feeling of

Harry and Packie Byrne at the Windmill, Sutton, 1968. (Courtesy of Pauline Godbold, photographer unknown)

strange indifference. For some there, Harry Cox was little more than a curiosity, a musical dinosaur miraculously preserved long after ceasing to operate as a function of his environment.[64]

A woman with a portable recorder taped the event without asking Harry if he minded. A young singer told Bob, "it doesn't really matter. Old Harry doesn't know what's going on anyway." Bob disagreed, writing in *Abe's Folk Music* that Harry knew what was happening: "He may not have been well-informed as to the latest machinations on the scene, but people have been filching songs from him for many decades now."[65]

Bob and Carole Pegg knew of Harry from his recordings and radio appearances and were aware of his reputation as a singer of English song. They attended one of MacColl and Seeger's workshops, at the Royal Sovereign in Leeds, where they heard and discussed a selection of Harry's records. Bob believes that "by 1968, an awareness of Harry's eminence, and of his recorded performances, was widespread among people who were engaged with the 'traditional' side of the folk revival," and he and Carole were so excited at the prospect of hearing him live that they were happy to hitchhike for two days to reach Harry's stamping ground. Bob and Carole visited Harry at Sunnyside the day after the Windmill session: "He was a bit of a hero to us ... He was at

home with his daughter, who was very friendly and hospitable, as was Harry."
As singers themselves, Bob and Carole were well aware that beneath Harry's
deceptively simple approach to singing there was real skill:

> Harry was a consummate storyteller in song. Though he was
> unmistakable when you heard him sing, the narrative was always
> paramount. It was an easy-sounding style, and it was only when
> you tried to sing one of his songs yourself that you became aware
> of the technical skill that went into his performances.[66]

Harry must have taken to the young couple: he gave them one of his jig dolls,
which they called Harry in his honour, and they in turn sent him presents of
tobacco, unaware that he was growing his own.

Bob Pegg's comments about the Windmill session support the idea that
Harry was becoming something of a forgotten man in his Broads homeland,
but he still commanded respect in the wider folk community. Soon after that
session, Harry's status within the folk revival was confirmed when the EFDSS
honoured him with its Gold Badge, celebrating "those who have made unique
or outstanding contributions to the art or science of folk dance, music or
song." From its inception in 1922 it has been awarded to around 150 individuals: Sharp gained his badge in 1923, Maud Karpeles got hers in 1928, Vaughan
Williams waited until 1943 for his, Shirley Collins received hers in 2003, and
Peter Kennedy finally gained his badge in 2004. Martin Carthy was awarded
his badge as part of the Watersons in 1982, Ewan MacColl and Peggy Seeger
gained theirs in 1987, and Frankie Armstrong was a 2018 recipient. Grainger
and Moeran are still waiting for theirs – as is Sam.[67]

Harry was too ill to travel to Cecil Sharp House, so Myrtle received the
badge on his behalf. Then, in early 1970, Peter Kennedy travelled to Norfolk
and gave a presentation during another Windmill session. Kennedy found
Harry in fine voice, especially on a rendition of "Betsy the Serving Maid."[68]
Harry was unimpressed by the honour bestowed on him by the EFDSS:
"Harry had something to say about that," remembered Peter Coleman. Ever
the pragmatist, Harry declared: "That badge, I don't know what good that is
to me. If they'd give me five shilling a week with it." Someone made up a song
for the occasion and Harry was happy enough with the song and its performance to offer mild praise that "it wasn't done bad."[69] The lyrics survive, on a
typewritten sheet headed "'Harry Cox' (to the tune of 'The Bold Fisherman')."
The final verse makes it clear that this was a celebratory composition:

> In Folksong books his name we'll place,
> His songs will linger on.
> So fill to us the Parting Glass,
> God bless us every one.[70]

Harry Cox by Peter Bellamy. Bellamy clearly modelled this portrait on the photo of Harry and Packie Byrne. (From a photocopy of the painting owned by Chris Holderness)

The Gold Badge brought Harry a new, brief, period of fame. Anglia Television was the first to come knocking, inviting Harry onto its early evening magazine show *About Anglia* less than a week after the EFDSS announced the award. Harry was paid five guineas and was at the studios for three hours. The BBC took its time in planning its own feature, eventually bringing Harry back to

Norwich for an appearance on its eastern region magazine show *Look East* on 6 January 1970, the day after Peter Kennedy presented the badge at the Windmill. The BBC paid Harry five guineas "For talking about English Folk Song & Dance Society."[71] Myrtle recalled this appearance with enthusiasm, telling of a day on which she and her father were treated royally by the production team:

> That was the best place I'd ever been to. BBC treated us very well … Pot o' tea, cakes and all that. Anything you wanted in the drink line … We went up another deck … and we were surrounded by televisions. Twenty or thirty televisions all going in this great big room. And this bar, where the stars come.[72]

Harry gave another interview while he was at the BBC studio, recording a short piece with reporter Tony Scase for the following day's edition of the BBC's national early morning radio news programme *Today*. The title of the piece, as listed on the contract, was factually accurate if lacking in glamour: "Int. by Tony Scase with Harry Cox 84 y. o. folk singer."[73]

By the end of the 1960s, folk music was fragmenting into a diverse and often puzzling array of styles and approaches – the music press was applying labels like folk-rock, psychedelic folk, acid folk and folk-baroque to acts such as Fairport Convention, Steeleye Span, Davy Graham, Pentangle, Mr. Fox, and Dando Shaft.[74] Plain old folk was becoming overshadowed by these genres and subgenres and plain old folk singers found themselves pushed back towards anonymity by an array of guitar-playing songwriters and crumhorn-wielding youths. Back in the Broads, friends and family organised one more session for Harry: in celebration of his eighty-fifth birthday he went to the Pleasure Boat at Hickling Broad. The pub was packed, with invited guests in one room and locals and tourists listening in from the garden and the rest of the pub. There was plenty of singing and drinking, all leading Lenny Helsdon to remember it as "a lovely old do."[75] It was something of a swansong, however.

12 The Road Goes on Forever?

Roads do not go on forever. Walk east through Winterton and you'll soon run out of road, as the land meets the rough and unforgiving North Sea; live a long life and you'll eventually come to the end of that road as well. As the second folk revival got into its swing, Harry and Sam were reaching the end of their roads and it would not be too long before both men would pass on. Their final years were spent quietly in their home villages, but there would be some controversy even as their legacy to future generations of singers was becoming established.

Harry's granddaughter Jenny was used to the frequent visits of song collectors and fans, many of which she recalled with pleasure. But some of Harry and Sam's friends and relatives were less enamoured of the attentions of journalists, broadcasters, and song collectors. Sam welcomed his meetings with collectors and fans; Harry, who had far more of these visits, enjoyed some (the Godbolds, Peter Coleman, Sheila Park, for example) and tolerated others. But a few relatives and friends saw many of these visitors as nuisances – and some of them as little more than rip-off artists.

Even before the emergence of the tape-recording amateur collector, Elsie Cox disliked many aspects of Harry's singing life and worried that her husband was being exploited. Harry's daughter Myrtle believed that Elsie disliked all of the palaver associated with song collectors' visits because she was convinced they were taking Harry's songs and stories without giving anything back:

> Somewhere along the line she got the feeling that they were picking his brains ... and there was no return for it. You know, they'll take all your best knowledge away and you'll know no more about it ... they're gonna use these old songs which have been handed on through your father and your grandfather ... and you'll have nothing at the end of the day.[1]

Elsie died before the bulk of the collectors reached Sunnyside, but had a point. Beliefs about money and the use of "their" songs would badly affect Harry and Sam's families in later years.

Myrtle was sure that Harry's fame as a singer led to ill feeling among his brothers and sisters:

> That weren't the type of thing that went down very well … They might have thought there was something involved in it. They might think there was some money in it. They might not [have] liked the idea that he was getting their father's songs. Because they were his father's songs weren't they. You see, the others had no part in it whatever. No part at all. No, they didn't get on very well over it.[2]

Over in Winterton, Annie George felt that Sam had been exploited by song collectors and folk club organisers alike. For one performance, she told the *Eastern Daily Press* in 1994, Sam sang eighty songs for a fee of just two guineas.[3] A letter to Sam from Peter Kennedy refers to such an event during the weekend of Sam's eightieth birthday. The letter invited Sam to perform at an unspecified event (possibly at the Horseshoe on Tottenham Court Road) on Monday 20 October 1958, two days after his birthday, and offered him a two-guinea fee. Kennedy also offered to arrange accommodation, invited Sam to lunch on the Monday, and hoped that he could attend the "Hootenany" [*sic* – everybody seemed to struggle with spelling the word] on the Sunday night.[4]

Annie's figure of eighty songs seems like an exaggeration, far in excess of Harry's "record" of seventeen songs in one session and a larger number than Sam's known repertoire. A conservative estimate of three minutes per song to include introductions, general chat, and applause – as well as singing – would suggest that Sam was on stage for at least four hours. Even Bruce Springsteen in his prime might baulk at such a night's work, but in 1960 a typical manual worker was earning about fourteen pounds per week, so two guineas (possibly with free accommodation and lunch) for four hours' work was more than double the average pay – earned by doing what Sam loved to do.[5] Other events attracted Annie's ire. In the 1994 *Eastern Daily Press* article she said that, after this London appearance, "people were always at his house, getting him to sing on tape and taking him a can of beer. They thought they were giving him the world – I got very angry about it." The article didn't name the "people" who so angered Annie George, but very few collectors were known to have recorded Sam and none of them have a reputation for fleecing their sources.

Jane Roberts remembered that her father Jack "Brindy" Hodds tried to offer Sam some advice, but to no avail. She recalled hearing how song collectors

> would come along with a recorder … and bring him a bottle of whisky and he'd sit there and he'd get slowly drunk and "Oh, Sam,

can you just sign this please?" Dad said to him: "Don't do that, because you're signing away everything to these people. Think about the family, think about Annie [George]." "No, they're my friends." Couldn't tell him. So consequently everything got signed away.[6]

Over fifty years after Sam's death, it's impossible to accurately assess the nature or extent of "everything." Sam's claim that he'd been "making a packet" suggests that he was happy with the money paid for his appearances and recordings, but there's no reliable surviving evidence of how much money was changing hands. Annie George (and others) clearly felt that it wasn't enough. When the Great Yarmouth and District Archaeological Society was publicising its decision to award Sam a blue plaque, Andrew J. Fakes sent out a publicity letter which highlighted the story:

> It would be safe to say that there is some ill feeling in Winterton because Sam sold his interests in his music very cheaply at the end of his life and others have benefited. Sam loved singing and was flattered by the interest taken in his songs and was perhaps gullible of people he trusted. He was taken to London and put up in a hotel and was given twenty pounds signing away the rights to his own music.[7]

Speaking in 2019, Fakes emphasised that the ill-feeling remained, but was unable to corroborate the story of the London hotel and the twenty-pound payment.[8]

The problem of artists failing to receive their "rightful" financial rewards is not limited to Harry and Sam, or to folk song. Composer and Harry Cox fan Philip Heseltine, writing in 1926, complained that for "'Captain Stratton's Fancy,' my most popular song, an absolute potboiler which has been published in three keys, gramophoned, and continually broadcasted [sic], I have had less than three pounds in four years."[9] In 1979, Fred Woods summarised the copyright situation during the period when Harry and Sam were being recorded:

> Thanks to some disgraceful drafting in the 1911 Copyright Act – even more shamefully retained in the 1956 Act – all copyright in collected traditional music belongs to the collector who first "fixes" (i.e. either writes down or records) the tune, or to the editor who may merely add a few phrase marks ... singers were thus deprived of royalties on recordings and public performances to which they should have been entitled.[10]

Amateur enthusiasts, collecting for their own pleasure with no intention of making money, might not be expected to offer payment beyond a pint or two – but professional collectors could legally take a similar approach. After all, hadn't the BBC advised its Folk Music and Dialect Recording Scheme staff to give singers free food and drink rather than money?

Sam may have been partly to blame for the anger about lost income. He was prone to exaggeration and known to his family as a braggart. As Brindy Hodds put it: "Everything Sam had was the best, until he had a boil on his bum – that was the worst."[11] Writer and broadcaster Keith Skipper was a junior reporter when he met Sam:

> He had a rare twinkle but I can understand why some found him a bit overpowering. He tended to assume you knew a fair bit about him! I felt as a late developer on the scene he was out to make the most of his fame. That may have jarred with some.[12]

Such a tendency to exaggerate the extent of his fame and success may explain Sam's claim that *Now is the Time for Fishing* sold eleven thousand copies in the last half of 1963. As the sole performer on the album, Sam could have expected a sizeable royalty payment from those eleven thousand copies – substantially more than twenty pounds.[13] However, this claim was met with varying degrees of incredulity and disbelief from members of the current folk scene. Such a figure is an unattainable dream for the folk record labels of the twenty-first century, when sales of a few hundred copies of a source singer's album are celebrated and sales in double figures are not uncommon. It's likely that Folkways founder Moses Asch would be similarly surprised at the number: sales figures show that in the last six months of 1963 the label's best selling album sold 3,912 copies – a far higher figure than for most six-month periods, but barely one third of Sam's claimed sales. The average sale per title was a mere 171. In the first six months of the year the label's best selling album sold 780 copies and the average was fifty-eight sales per title.[14] Folkways released albums by Pete Seeger and by the New Lost City Ramblers during 1963 – major American folk acts, either of whom could have achieved the top sales figures. A first release by an obscure English singer is unlikely to have challenged for the top spot; a mid-table placing might be optimistic.

English source singers were not troubling the album charts in the 1960s and they wouldn't be troubling them in later decades either. Topic Records released Sam's *Now is the Time for Fishing* and Harry's two-disc *The Bonny Labouring Boy* on CD in 2000; twenty years later, neither album has yet achieved five hundred sales in the UK.[15]

Copyright ownership is another thorny and contentious issue. Six surviving documents – each one signed in Harry's hesitant, wavering script – give an insight into the arrangements Harry made regarding his songs. In November 1955, a brief agreement between Harry on one side and Peter Kennedy and

Sam, c.1960, from the sleeve of the Topic re-release of *Now is the Time for Fishing* (By kind permission of Topic Records)

the EFDSS on the other gave the society the "right of reproduction and publication on gramophone records" of two of Harry's performances from October and December 1953 in exchange for a fee of two guineas, with no royalties. Five years later, Harry signed another agreement with Kennedy – acting on behalf of the Caedmon label's *Folksongs of Britain* album series – permitting his performances of seven songs to be included in the albums and agreeing not to record any of these songs for another commercial release for ten years. The editors, in turn, agreed to pay a royalty on sales of these songs apart from the Caedmon series – for example, through music publishing deals – none of which were guaranteed. Harry consented to a fee of fourteen guineas, without royalties, for the use of his performances on the Caedmon albums, the money to be paid only when their inclusion was approved. Two more agreements in 1963 and 1965 gave the EFDSS worldwide rights of reproduction and publication for ten years over a total of forty-two of Harry's recordings, for a total fee of eighty pounds. Harry also assigned the copyrights of these songs to the EFDSS in exchange for royalties of varying percentages dependent upon the method of reproduction.[16]

In 1966 a new company called Folktracks (later renamed Folktrax) was formed "especially for the purpose of protecting, and acting in the interests of, copyright holders of traditional music collected in Great Britain and Ireland." Peter Kennedy owned Folktracks and he asked Harry to reassign the copyrights of the seven songs earmarked for the Caedmon series from the EFDSS, in exchange for one third of the net royalties from authorised publications of the assigned songs. In 1975 Folktrax published three albums by Harry called *The Spotted Cow: English Love Songs*, *The Captain's Apprentice: English Sea Songs*, and *Widliecombe Fair: Songs, Music and a Hard Life*. The Folktrax archive website claims that "assignment of the copyright of over seventy of his song arrangements was made by Harry Cox himself to Folktracks and Soundpost Publications on 30 December 1960."[17] In 1994 Myrtle remembered that Kennedy did send royalty payments to Harry, and to her after Harry's death, but she added: "I don't hear from him now."[18]

The reassignment document mentions a "new publication" called *Folk Songs of Britain*. This is probably a reference to the Caedmon album series, but in 1975 Kennedy edited a book with a similar title, the 840-page *Folksongs of Britain and Ireland: a treasure trove for anyone interested in the traditions of the British Isles*. The collection includes 360 songs in English, Welsh, Scots Gaelic, Irish Gaelic, Manx Gaelic, and Cornish. Twenty-one come from Harry's repertoire; Sam is noted as a singer of six of the songs, but none of the versions in the book are his. Kennedy acknowledged Harry's importance, describing him as a "main source contributor" and noting that "I was always rewarded by my visits and revisits" to Catfield. Exactly how much money this "main source singer" received from these various deals is unknown.[19]

Peter Kennedy has a complicated history regarding song collection and copyright: one interviewee described him as "the elephant in the room" when these subjects are discussed. In his extensive Peter Kennedy discography, Reg Hall discusses Kennedy's work in detail and writes

> Many of the original tapes … no longer exist, and much of the other documentation is inconsistent and sometimes conflicting. Published information, including recording dates and locations, has frequently been inaccurate, the most serious being the frequent incorrect attribution of the person who made the recording. Many of the published recordings differ from issue to issue … some with different sections of associated speech, and some with instrumental accompaniment dubbed on.

The Folktrax website, Hall writes, is "not renowned for its accuracy."[20]

Kennedy also claimed the copyright to a set of Sam's songs and released *Sam Larner, The Singing Sailor of Winterton, Norfolk* on his Folktracks label.[21] At some point Kennedy changed the album's name to give it an "edgier" feel: by 1975 it was a cassette release with an identical track list, titled *Over the Dogger Bank: Sam Larner's Saucy Sea Songs* – a misleading title as most of the saucy songs don't relate to the sea, most of the sea songs aren't saucy and some of the songs are neither saucy nor sea songs. The Folktrax archive website claimed that Philip Donnellan made the recordings "just before the celebration of [Sam's] eightieth birthday on 18 October 1965." Sam would have been eighty-seven on that date, had he not died the previous month. On the same page it informs readers that Sam was forced to end his fishing career by the economic depression, rather than by ill health; that Sam's singing style is similar to Harry's; and that Harry came from "a fishing family living near Yarmouth."[22]

Although the family believe that Sam signed away his own rights, the Folktrax website claims that Edward George – Annie's husband and Sam's executor – passed the copyrights to Kennedy in 1966. It also claims that George assigned some of Sam's copyrights to the company on 1 August 1964, while Sam was still alive.[23] As for Kennedy's own reasons for acquiring copyrights, he claimed that in so doing he was protecting the songs and ensuring that the singers could receive some financial reward for their efforts, arguing that he was better placed to deal with anyone who wanted to record or publish these songs than were singers like Harry and Sam, who were not experienced in the ways and means of the music business.[24] If there is a case to be made for Harry and Sam losing out on big money – morally, if not legally – it's probably based on the successes others made of "Black Velvet Band" and "Wild Rover". But what is clear is that no-one became rich beyond the dreams of avarice by selling albums by Harry, Sam, or their fellow source singers.

Sam came to the end of the road in 1965. His health deteriorated during the early 1960s and by the time of his eightieth birthday severe arthritis was impacting on his movement.[25] As the Larners aged, Annie George began to care for them. Her granddaughter Jane helped and remembered: "Nanny used to cycle up twice a day to look after [them] because aunt Dorcas wasn't a very well lady. I would give her a hand, do the washing and prepare stuff to cook, things like that."[26] Sam spent long periods in hospital during his last year of life and even when he was at home he was not in the best of health. After a lengthy hospital stay during the spring of 1965 he was back home by early June. Dorcas felt that he was reasonably healthy and able to receive visitors, and she described their situation as "jogging along as best we can and happy at being together again."[27]

Sam and Dorcas weren't together for long, according to a letter from Myrtle Helsdon to the Stricklands, who had visited the Larners in the previous couple of weeks. "I hear Sam Larner is back in hospital," Myrtle wrote, "no wonder he wasn't feeling very good when you saw him, he must have been queer to be taken away so soon."[28] Myrtle clearly kept up with news of the Larners, even if there was no direct contact between Sunnyside and Bulmer Cottage.

On 11 September, Sam died a patient in St. Nicholas Hospital in Great Yarmouth. Annie registered Sam's death, giving his occupation as "a fisherman (retired)." Probate was granted to Edward George. Sam left £857 10s. gross, £802 10s. net: not a lot for a man who claimed he'd been making a packet for the last decade.[29] Dr. Kingsley Jones certified Sam's death as due to "Myocardial degeneration and arteriosclerosis" – heart and circulatory problems, a common cause of death for a man of Sam's age. However, the reason for his admission to St. Nicholas Hospital is more of a mystery. St. Nicholas was a psychiatric hospital for people with long-term mental health problems and Dr. Jones was not an overworked junior doctor, the sort of physician who would usually be tasked with certifying a patient's death, but a consultant psychiatrist.[30] These pieces of evidence together suggest that Sam's hospitalisation was the result of some sort of mental health problem – but which one (if any) of the many possible alternatives it may have been can no longer be established.

Sam lies buried in Winterton churchyard, his memorial stone reading: "In Loving Memory of My Dear Husband Samuel Larner." The inscription on the lower half of the stone was added four years later and reads: "Also of Dorcas, wife of the above."[31]

Harry reached his eighty-sixth birthday in 1971, but by then he was seriously ill. Harry was stoic in the face of his illness; Myrtle worried that her father "may not tell me all." During his 1964 hospital admission, doctors discovered a malignant growth and told Myrtle that Harry had about four or five years to live. A year later Myrtle wrote to friends: "My father has a growth in the bladder so one never knows with him, he doesn't know of course, I mustn't tell him, so please don't mention it at any time. I'm telling you this confidentially." Myrtle's stance seems odd today, but she was conforming to the prevailing medical opinion of the time that patients should not be told of a potentially terminal diagnosis. Writing three years later she remained optimistic but was aware that the cancer "will get him down eventually." Although he was seriously ill and no longer singing beyond his own four walls, Harry stayed well enough to work in his garden and craft his beloved jig dolls. However, he was soon forced to give up the allotment he had carefully cultivated for decades.[32]

Harry beat the doctors' prediction by three years but he deteriorated swiftly in the end. In mid-March 1971 he went into hospital after becoming acutely ill and spent his eighty-sixth birthday as an inpatient. He went home to Sunnyside after two weeks, still with a urinary catheter in place, and went straight to bed. He never regained enough strength to leave the bedroom. Myrtle learned how to clean, drain, and change the catheter bag and helped the district nurse to bathe Harry and change his bed sheets each day.[33]

Harry's friend and fellow singer Peter Coleman visited him regularly during his final weeks and remembers that Harry lay on a small cot under the eaves in his first-floor bedroom. He also remembers Harry's organised approach to enjoying mints as he lay in bed: "On his cabinet he had a row of strong mints and they were all in various stages of sucking. They varied in width. He'd say 'I keep 'em like that so I know which one to start on first.'" Coleman was the last of his friends to visit Harry before he died: "It was on a Tuesday, I think. I went upstairs, he was lying under the eaves. He said: 'I ain't got long'. He knew."[34]

After almost seven years of serious illness, Harry died on 6 May 1971 – two days after his friend's final visit and with Myrtle at his side. Dr. David Gabriel certified the primary cause of death as bronchopneumonia, with carcinomatosis and cancer of the prostate as underlying problems. Myrtle registered the death two days later. She was exhausted by this point and struggled to answer the many letters she received from Harry's friends and fans. Harry's death was something of a relief for Myrtle, who felt able to tell the Stricklands of the strain of caring for her father for twenty years: "My marriage started here and quite honestly I'm surprised it thrived," she wrote. "My husband has been very good, it is hard to always agree with our elders." Despite the difficulties, Myrtle didn't wish that things had been any different: "I feel at ease somehow," she explained. "I gave up my life for him doing my best and I have no regrets."[35]

Harry left £4,011 – a substantial sum for an agricultural labourer. The years of self-employment, and a working life that carried on well beyond retirement age, paid off – aided, to some extent, by his late-flowering fame as a singer. He lies in Potter Heigham churchyard – in an unmarked grave, at his own request – near Bob, Sarah, and Elsie.[36]

Harry and Sam garnered one or two obituaries, although not as many as might have been expected from their fame of a few years earlier. The *Eastern Daily Press* called Harry the father of Norfolk song and in Sam's obituary, titled "Old Sam Larner Has Sung His Last Song," the newspaper declared that Sam was known as "one of the country's great folk singers." It also repeated its earlier claim that Sam had spent some time in the London Fire Brigade; maybe someone remembered Tuskin Hodds's reference to carrots and fire brigade horses from that tongue-in-cheek letter of sixty years earlier and took his jokey comment too seriously.[37]

The national broadsheet newspapers hadn't celebrated Sam but Harry made it into *The Times*, sharing the 8 May obituaries with Helene Weigel – actor, co-founder of the Berliner Ensemble and wife of Bertolt Brecht – Lieutenant Colonel Sidney Lambert and Lord Portal of Hungerford. The obituary was brief, but acclaimed Harry's authentic voice and his role as "the father of East Anglian folk music." The EFDSS gave Harry two obituaries – an honour it didn't give to Sam. Peter Kennedy wrote a detailed item for *Folk Music Journal*, opening with a version of the "sting of death" verse, with Harry's hope that no-one in Sutton will ever want for bread. Tony and Diana Singleton wrote a short obituary in *English Dance and Song*, praising Harry's memory for songs and the melodic quality of his voice. The *Melody Maker* also gave Harry a detailed memorial, folk music specialist Karl Dallas calling him one of Britain's "greatest and most monumental traditional singers." Three years later, when Dallas started a column called *Folk Giants*, Harry was his first subject.[38]

Harry and Sam both have entries in the prestigious *New Grove Dictionary of Music and Musicians*. In Harry's entry, Reg Hall praised "the outstanding quality of his performances, his sense of timing and extensive repertoire." Dave Arthur was less effusive about Sam, but borrowed A. L. Lloyd's description of him as a "showman singer" and wrote of him as an endearing personality who "performed with his left hand cupped to his ear and occasionally executed a few jig steps."[39]

If Harry was less than impressed with the EFDSS Gold Badge, he might have been happier with another potential memorial to his life as a singer. A few months after his death a member of the society proposed that a Norfolk pub should be named after him. A Peter Bellamy painting of Harry smoking his pipe, with "Harry Cox" written boldly at the top of the picture, was suggested as the pub sign. The *Eastern Evening News* agreed that this was a splendid idea and invited a Norfolk brewery to come forward to offer one of its own hostelries. Sadly, the Harry Cox Arms never slaked the thirst of Broadland locals.[40]

Death, someone once said, is a great career move for a singer. Neither Harry or Sam achieved huge posthumous wealth or fame, but their appearances on record, radio, and TV continue – albeit sporadically – using archived material. The BBC repeated *Singing the Fishing* in 1967 and was able to proudly proclaim the programme's status as the winner of the 1960 Italia Prize for best documentary.[41] Five years later, Philip Donnellan produced a BBC Two programme based on the *Radio Ballads* and titled *The Shoals of Herring*. Sam is once again heard – and this time seen – talking and singing about his life at sea. His voice appears first, taken from the radio show, over a tracking shot of Winterton churchyard that gradually zeroes in on his gravestone. He appears on screen soon afterwards, in a scene taken from *The Singer and the Song* and intercut with footage of herring fleets and Scots fishermen.[42] Another of Donnellan's BBC Two programmes, *The Other Music*, appeared in 1981 and told the story of the folk revival from 1945 to 1981. It featured an extensive roster of performers and interviewees but it's especially notable for appearances from Harry, Sam, and Walter Pardon.[43]

The two singers also appear briefly in other programmes, including BBC Radio 3's *Late Junction* and its *Early Music Show*, which celebrated the two hundredth anniversary of the Battle of Trafalgar with a special broadcast from on board *HMS Victory*, Sam's recording of "The Sailor's Alphabet" appearing alongside recordings from A. L. Lloyd, Frankie Armstrong, and Cyril Poacher. Sam made it onto the BBC's iconic *Desert Island Discs* when it was Martin Carthy's turn to choose his eight favourite records. Carthy chose "Lofty Tall Ship," the song that so deeply affected him when he heard Sam sing it in the late 1950s.[44]

Local recognition of Sam's talents came in 2008, when the Great Yarmouth and District Archaeological Society (now the Great Yarmouth Local History and Archaeological Society) placed a blue plaque on Bulmer Cottage. The plaque, crowned with three fish in a shield, states that "Samuel James SAM LARNER 1878–1965 Fisherman and Folk Singer lived here" and mentions one of his achievements: "Featured in the BBC Home Service *Radio Ballad* 'Singing the Fishing' winner of the Prix d'Italia Prize 1960." The plaque was formally unveiled with due ceremony – including performances by melodeon player and East Anglian Traditional Music Trust founder Katie Howson and Cromer stepdancer Richard Davies – in the cottage's front garden. The society attempted to erect a plaque in Harry's memory in Catfield, with the support of the East Anglian Traditional Music Trust, but this attempt didn't come to fruition.[45]

Sam's second album *A Garland for Sam* appeared on Topic Records in 1974, all fifteen songs coming from Philip Donnellan's 1958 and 1959 recordings for the BBC. Russell Wortley, reviewing in *Folk Music Journal*, described Sam as a "first-rate" singer whose clear diction makes the words easy to follow, but says little more about him. He criticises the absence of an audience, firmly of the belief that the responses of listeners are an essential part of the experience of hearing folk song.[46] *Cruising Round Yarmouth* appeared in 2014, a comprehensive double CD containing sixty-seven tracks – mostly songs, but interspersed with many of Sam's oft-repeated tales, from Donnellan's recordings and from MacColl, Seeger and Parker's 1958–60 sessions. In his sleeve notes Musical Traditions label boss Rod Stradling proudly described the album as containing "the more-or-less complete recorded repertoire of this wonderful Norfolk singer." Reviewing the album for *Living Tradition*, Jim Bainbridge called Sam "one of the real source singers of England" and lauded the album for being filled with "real quality traditional English song." Christopher Heppa also celebrated the release, stating that Sam's stories and rhymes alone made

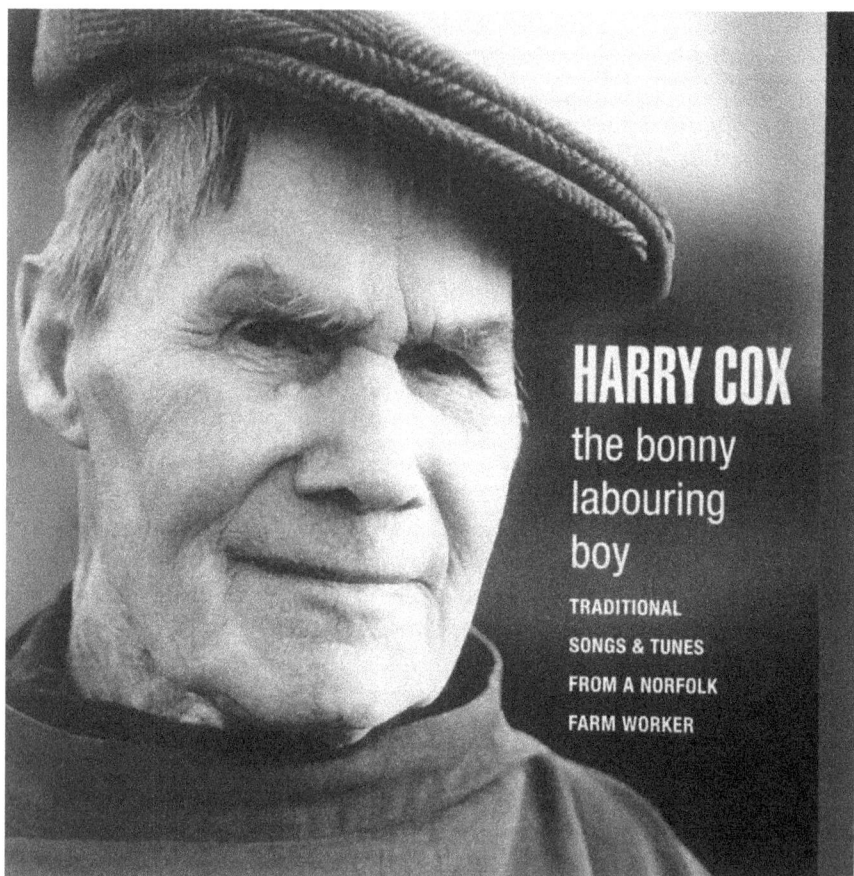

The cover of *Bonny Labouring Boy*, a two-CD collection of Harry's songs and conversation. (By kind permission of Topic Records. Photograph of Harry by Brian Shuel)

the album worth having, while Vic Smith congratulated Sam on his superb sense of timing and – on the more *risqué* songs – his "cheekiness as he chuckles his way through all the innuendos."[47]

Harry also has two comprehensive posthumous albums to his credit: *The Bonny Labouring Boy* – a Topic release from 2000 – and *What Will Become of England*, which appeared on Rounder Records in the same year and contains forty-six tracks of song, talk, and tunes from Lomax and Kennedy's recordings. Kennedy's sleeve notes to the Rounder release state inaccurately that Harry and Moeran met for the first time in 1945 and ladle on the image of a poverty-stricken rural worker who "grew up on the damp and impoverished Norfolk fens" – a phrase guaranteed to raise the inhabitants of Harry's beloved Broads into high dudgeon. Kennedy acknowledged the errors and omissions in the sleeve notes, but blamed the editing process in which "all our original notes pass through many hands and undergo a series of snips and pastings" and which was out of his control.[48] Kennedy claimed in 1971 that he had prepared another album of Harry singing sea songs that he learnt from his father, but this has never appeared.[49]

The Bonny Labouring Boy draws its fifty-four tracks from recordings made between 1945 and 1970 by a dozen different collectors including MacColl, Sheila Parks, Mervyn Plunkett, Cliff Godbold, and teams from the BBC. The reviewers were enthusiastic, with one or two notable caveats: Vic Smith described Harry's singing and repertoire as "quite breathtaking" and praised the album as an outstanding and definitive collection. Hugh Anderson's six-line review praised the record as a "model for field recordings," but still managed to devote most of the text to a discussion of the album's booklet. He gave this succinct appraisal of Harry's performances: "The singing on these two CDs is repetitive as it is by one singer, but acceptable in small amounts." Trevor King called the album "the last word on Harry Cox," but avoided any comment on the quality of Harry's singing. And though Mike Yates doubted that "we can say that he was a better or more important singer than, say, Sam Larner or Walter Pardon," he celebrated Harry as "a wonderful singer with a large and fascinating repertoire" and the album as "a highly important issue for the folk world."[50]

Paul Burgess thought the album was impressive, finding Harry's Norfolk dialect and strong, occasionally gruff, voice to be the "inauspicious exterior" of a singer with "total control over his material." Still, he recommended listening to it a bit at a time rather than all the way through. Even less favourably, John Docherty of the *Hampshire Chronicle* commented on Harry's "unremarkable voice, with its limited range." Ten years after its release, "P. R." reviewed the album for *Hi-Fi World*, praising Harry's "unique, attractive tone" and enthusing about the songs and their stories – especially "The Transports" and "The Grand Hotel" – commenting: "And you thought that gangsta rap was violent!"[51]

The reviews of *What Will Become of England* were more critical. Yates called Harry the "backbone" of the post-war English folk revival, but he was critical of Peter Kennedy – whose recordings form the majority of the tracks on the record – for shortening some of the songs: as a result, Yates wrote, "this is not the album it should have been." Matt Fink damned Harry with faint praise, calling him "a good enough singer," criticising the presence of so many tracks filled with talk rather than songs or tunes and opining that the album was "too academic" to be enjoyed by the casual listener. Most critical of all was one Chet Williamson, who was clearly not a fan of Harry Cox or of English traditional singing in general. He supports the idea of preserving the recordings, is rather more equivocal about making them commercially available, compares Harry to the handkerchief-capped character of Gumby from *Monty Python's Flying Circus* and likens listening to Harry's songs to inhabiting one of Dante's circles of Hell. Oh, and he also warns prospective listeners about Harry's "cheap accordion" and "out-of-tune violin" as well as his vocal failings and tendency to repeatedly clear his throat. The record, he concludes, is "pretty damn painful" to listen to. Harsh words, but his opinion is probably not too far removed from that of most non-fans of English traditional song.[52]

Numerous compilation albums featuring tracks from Harry or Sam have appeared over the years since their deaths. The Discogs website lists thirteen such albums for Harry and eleven for Sam, the majority on the Topic label, but there are more to be found. For example, seven of Harry's instrumentals appear on the compilation album *The Pigeon on the Gate: Melodeon players from East Anglia*.[53]

Music business machinations around contracts, royalties, and copyrights may have impacted negatively on the years surrounding Harry and Sam's deaths, but it's vital that these problems do not cloud the positive impact the two singers made on England's traditional music scene. Fifty years after Harry's death, there's still plenty of love and respect for Harry and Sam around Norfolk. Brian Gaudet is one such lover of their songs and has organised festivals in memory of Harry and Sam (as well as one for Walter Pardon). SamFest commemorated the fiftieth anniversary of Sam's death and included a performance by Peggy Seeger. In a short act of commemoration for Sam's life, festival-goers were invited to sing along to "Shoals of Herring" and "Coil Away the Trawl Warp." HarryFest included a jig doll convention in Catfield with a special appearance from one of Harry's own dolls.[54] Norfolk-based Stone Angel, one of the folk scene's longest-established bands, paid tribute to Harry and Sam on their 2004 album *Lonely Waters*, with a song written by singer and guitarist Ken Saul, who borrowed the title of one of Harry's best-loved songs, "What Will Become of England."[55] In true traditional style, the song begins with the singer walking out on a May morning.

Outside Norfolk, Harry, Sam, and their songs appear in some unlikely places. In 2014 a song inspired by Sam's life came to the big screen, thanks to two of Hollywood's most famous filmmakers. Joel and Ethan Coen's movie *Inside Llewyn Davis* tells of a failing folk singer – the Llewyn Davis of the title, played by Oscar Isaac – in the New York scene of 1961. At one point in the movie Davis visits his father, an ex-merchant seaman who now has dementia and is living in a care home. In the hope of triggering a pleasant memory or two, Davis plays his father a song which he "used to like" in his younger days. The song is Ewan MacColl's "Shoals of Herring," written no more than a year or so before the scene between father and son is supposed to take place.[56]

The development of recording technologies and methods over recent years enables long-dead performers to appear posthumously as if by magic. Harry and Sam have both appeared on new recordings, thanks to electronic sampling. Chumbawamba sampled Harry for "Jacob's Ladder," on the band's 2002 album *Readymades*: Harry's singing of a single line from "The Pretty Ploughboy" (about sending troops to the war to be slain) joins a sample of Davy Graham's guitar tune "Anji." Sam is sampled, along with Ewan MacColl, on Walking with Ghosts' "Mr. Stormalong." Sam begins with a trademark peel of laughter, then chats about shimmers of herring and scrunks of mackerel over a drum and keyboard groove – it's a groove he would probably approve of, it being the sort of insistent rhythm that's suited to a bit of net hauling or a stepdance or two. He reappears later, singing "Now is the Time for Fishing" as the song slowly draws to a close and birdsong and wave noises take over from drums, guitars, and saxophones.[57]

Since his death, Harry has inspired two classical composers who have followed in Moeran and Heseltine's footsteps by drawing on the English song tradition. Philip Underwood composed *Seven Folksong Fancies: A Tribute to Harry Cox* during the winter of 2004. Alan Waller, a Norfolk-based devotee of folk music, commissioned him to create the work – originally titled *The Potter Heigham Keyboard Book (A Tribute to Harry Cox)* – for a recital at All Saints Church in Little Melton during the summer of 2005. Underwood went on to perform the work in Lancaster Priory and in Anglican parish churches in Dronfield and Windermere.[58] Saxophonist and composer John Harle has made more extensive use of Harry's work, having first heard Harry's singing when he was working on music for the BBC series *A History of Britain by Simon Schama*. For the final episode, broadcast in 2002, Harle wanted "a quintessential English voice … to accompany aerial shots of rolling hills … grand, but rooted in the English tradition." Harle was a neighbour of Tony Engle, then the managing director of Topic Records. Engle gave him copies of the *Voice of the People* albums, which featured Harry among many others. Harry's voice "fitted a treat" and Harle chose his singing of "The Pretty Ploughboy."

Harle was so struck by Harry's songs and voice – which he described as "pulled from the roots of a plant in Norfolk" – that he went on to set some of Harry's songs in new arrangements from leading English composers including Dominic Muldowney ("Georgie"), Geoffrey Burgon ("The Bonny Labouring Boy"), and Harle himself ("The Female Drummer," "Adieu to Old England"). The project became known as The Black Velvet Band and involved musicians including pianist Steve Lodder and guitarist Neill MacColl (son of Ewan and Peggy Seeger) – plus recordings of Harry. The first concert was, appropriately enough, at the 2004 Norfolk and Norwich Festival. Christopher Smith reviewed the night favourably, giving particular praise to Harry's "deep, rich and clear" voice, Paul Clarvis's percussion and the "pungent spice" of Harle's sopranino saxophone. A performance at EFDSS headquarters in Cecil Sharp House on 9 June fared less well. Harle was forewarned that the "purists" of the EFDSS might not be keen on his reinterpretations of traditional song – the warning proved prescient. He and Engle attended with friends, including jazz and progressive rock saxophonist Dick Heckstall-Smith, but as Harle remembers it was "possibly the most badly attended gig I've ever come across." Harle remembers the project fondly and thinks that it would have made "a super album," but it was never recorded.[59]

Songs from Harry or Sam's repertoires have inspired many revival performers and folk-rockers including Steeleye Span, Frankie Armstrong, Eliza Carthy, and Fairport Convention. Bob Pegg didn't include Harry's songs in his repertoire – although Carole sang "The Female Drummer" – but he acknowledges the importance of Harry's singing in the development of his own style and includes Harry in his list of singers who "created something distinctly individual, compellingly universal, and utterly mesmerising using no other instrument apart from the human voice." Bob's list puts Harry alongside Paddy Tunney, Belle Stewart, Margaret Barry, bluegrass pioneer Bill Monroe, Judy Collins, and Lou Reed.[60]

Shirley Collins still feels Harry's influence, almost seventy years since they met for the only time:

> His repertoire was large, remarkable and varied, so many beautiful melodies. Out of his many songs, I loved best the haunting "Polly Vaughan," "The Pretty Ploughboy," "Blackberry Fold" (contains a euphemism!), "Adieu to Old England," "The Barley Straw" and the noble and mournful "Death of Nelson." I sang these on my early albums, and especially with the "Death of Nelson," tried to honour Harry's spirit.

In 2019 Shirley's singing of "Adieu to Old England" soundtracked BBC Radio 4's presentation of Jonathan Coe's novel *Middle England*, "so Harry's presence is still with us and his songs are still relevant," wrote Collins.[61]

Sam's impact on Martin Carthy is well known, but Carthy's comparison of Harry and Sam is also noteworthy: "Harry is very musical, he's got a lovely voice. Sam's voice wasn't pretty, but the passion was overwhelming. That doesn't make Harry any less passionate, but he was more contained." He's not the only person to distinguish between the two men in similar terms. Sheila Park made a similar comparison: Harry "wasn't extrovert, like Sam was," she opined. "Sam loved the limelight whereas Harry was very much aware that he was a good singer." Music critic and historian Ken Hunt reaches similar conclusions: Sam was the extrovert, the entertainer, the showman, while Harry was more studious, curious about the songs, the more active collector – in Hunt's lovely phrase, Harry "had magpie ears." Hunt loves Sam's singing because of "the saltiness in it," Harry's because of its "bucolic streak," and the breadth of the repertoire – the "cornucopia of material."[62]

As the internet draws us all ever closer and spreads variations on the truth with remarkable rapidity, Harry has become the subject of one of the folk scene's more unusual urban (or should that be rural?) legends. It's been claimed that he's the great-grandfather of Chelsea and England footballer John Terry. Like all the best urban legends, no-one can recall the story's origin – although I was told that a prankster within the EFDSS may have started it. The story is completely untrue.

Alden, Patterson and Dashwood (l-r: Noel Dashwood, Christina Alden, Alex Patterson): a trio influenced by twenty-first century artists, but approaching its repertoire in ways Harry and Sam would recognise. (Courtesy of the trio. Photograph by Jerry Tye).

What about Harry and Sam's influence on the younger members of the contemporary folk scene? Two Norfolk bands offer contrasting perspectives. Alden, Patterson and Dashwood, and the Shackleton Trio are each critically acclaimed acts whose music is influenced by traditional song, but their opinions of Harry and Sam are miles apart. When asked about the two performers, Christina Alden responded: "I'm afraid we have not heard of Harry or Sam."[63] Alden and Alex Patterson are aware of Walter Pardon and Peter Bellamy, but named contemporary singer-songwriter Johnny Flynn and folk band This is the Kit as influences, calling them both "indy folk." The trio does have something in common with Harry, though: they've taken lyrics from one source and matched them to tunes from another. As Patterson explained: "We trawl through these books looking for lyrics that look nice ... I think it's much easier to make them your own if you're not influenced by other versions." It's an approach that Harry – and Peter Bellamy – would find familiar.[64]

Singer and fiddle player Georgia Shackleton calls Harry and Sam "massive influences of mine":

> The songs [Harry] was singing and the way he was singing them made me consider my own choice of songs ... I really like the way he phrases and delivers a song, it's almost not like he's trying to perform the song for his own ego, very respectful, he's a vessel for it. ... I do love Sam's singing and style of performance. There's such a sparkle in his voice, it sounds like he's getting such joy from

the song, a joy from performing. There's always that chuckle in his voice – unless he's singing a deeply tragic ballad! I just feel it's really important to get joy from performing and singing.[65]

Harry and Sam continue to be recognised as vital sources of song. For Harry's friend and fellow singer Peter Coleman, "he was the benchmark. What more can you say?" Damien Barber draws a line from Harry Cox through Walter Pardon, Peter Bellamy, and Peter Coleman to his own career as a folk performer: "Peter Coleman's one of the biggest influences in my music, such a powerful character, a powerful singer, one of the best singers, not just in Norfolk." Barber is emphatic about where the line begins, saying: "My entire existence owes itself to Harry Cox." Brian Gaudet sees Harry as the more important singer of the two, but suggests that Sam's approach to performing makes him "Norfolk's first song-and-dance man."[66]

A song-and-dance fisherman with a public-house voice and a taciturn, respectful singer and farm worker with an extraordinary repertoire of sexualia, both from the backwaters of rural Norfolk. Not, on the surface, likely inspirations or influences for some of the finest singers, songwriters, and musicians of the last sixty years – and yet, that's what they have become. Harry and Sam have handed down a host of songs, a body of work that illuminates a world that is lost to most of us, but deserves to be remembered by all of us.

I'll leave the last word to Stone Angel and the chorus of their song, "What Will Become of England":

> "What will become of England and how should we go on,
> If ever we forget to sing the songs that Sam and Harry sung?"

Notes

Cruising Round Yarmouth: CRY
Eastern Daily Press: EDP
Harry Cox, English Folk Singer: EFS
Now is the Time for Fishing: NTTFF
Sweet Lives and Lawless Billows: SLLB
The Bonny Labouring Boy: BLB
The Singer and the Song: TSTS

Jenny Barker's collection: JB
Jim Carroll/Pat Mackenzie's collection: C/M
    Interviews are listed by catalogue number.
Alan Lomax archive material, at research.culturalequity.org: AL
    Interviews took place between October and December 1953 unless noted and are
    listed by catalogue number.
Paul Marsh collection: PM
Steve Roud collection: SR
Vaughan Williams Memorial Library resources: VWML

All websites were accessed in February 2020 and all interviews were with the author during 2019 and 2020, unless noted. Books and journals are referenced in full in the bibliography; all other sources are referenced in full in the note, on first appearance.

1 Fields and Fishing

1. "Sealore and Rhymes," *NTTFF*, Track 12.
2. Wentworth Day, J. (1951) *Broadland Adventure*, 171.
3. MacColl, E. and Seeger, P. (1961) Notes to *NTTFF*, p6.
4. Springall, L. M. (1936) *Labouring Life*, 134.
5. Around 1692, according to Defoe, a storm off Winterton Ness destroyed over two hundred vessels and killed a thousand seamen.
6. MacColl, E. and Seeger, P. (1961) Notes to *NTTFF*, 9.
7. Higgins, D. (2009) *The Winterton Story*, 39–41; *Kelly's Directory of Norfolk* (1896) 484–5.
8. *SLLB* (1959) Episode 2, BBC Radio.

9. Mansfield, N. (1986) "George Edwards," 51.
10. Myrtle Helsdon, interview by Paul Marsh, 9 September 1994, transcript, 3 (PM); Harry Cox's birth certificate.
11. The story of Nelson is in Wentworth Day, J. (1951) *Broadland Adventure*, 161.
12. *Harrod's Directory* (1877) 39–40.
13. *Kelly's Directory* (1896) 41.
14. Wentworth Day, J. (1951) *Broadland Adventure*, 161.
15. Harry Cox, *TSTS* (1964) BBC Television.
16. Barker, J. (undated) *Memories of my Grandad*. Unpublished manuscript, 4. Jenny Barker (*née* Helsdon) is Harry's granddaughter.
17. MacColl, E. and Seeger, P. (1961) Notes to *NTTFF*, 6; Kennedy (1958) "Harry Cox," 143.
18. Harry Cox, interview by Bob Thomson and Michael Grosvenor Myer, 1970, transcript, 1 (PM); (AL)T3342R02.
19. MacColl, E. and Seeger, P. (1961) Notes to *NTTFF*, 1.
20. Wentworth Day, J. (1951) *Broadland Adventure*, 23–24.
21. Harry Cox, interview by Alan Lomax, (AL)T3342R01.
22. Marsh, P. (2000) Notes to *BLB*, 25; Harry Cox, interview by Charles Parker, July 1963, transcript, 1 (PM).
23. MacColl, E. and Seeger, P. (1961) Notes to *NTTFF*, 2.
24. Sam Larner, *TSTS*.
25. Harry Cox, interview by Bob Thomson, ca.1969, C/M103.
26. MacColl, E. and Seeger, P. (1961) Notes to *NTTFF*, 2.
27. Laing, D *et al.* (1975) *The Electric Muse*, 111.
28. See "Stepdancing," East Anglia Traditional Music Trust, eatmt.org.uk; Haines, S. (2019) "East Anglian Stepdancing," 30.
29. Harry Cox, interview by Charles Parker, July 1963, transcript, 1, PM.
30. Holderness, C. (2014) Notes to *CRY*, 3; Jenny Barker, interview.
31. "Whiffler" (1934) *Eastern Evening News*, 24 February; Jenny Barker, interview.
32. Carole Pegg, email, 14 August 2019.
33. Hugh Lupton, email, 30 Oct 2019.
34. Peggy Seeger donated the doll to the VWML in 2009.
35. Myrtle Helsdon to Lewis and Isobel Strickland, 15 March 1968, 28 December 1965 (VWML).
36. Copper, B. (1975) *A Song for Every Season*, 108, 120; Thompson, F. (2008) *Lark Rise*, 63–64, 193.
37. Walter Pardon interview, undated, Reg Hall Collection, British Library C903/60.
38. Roud, S. (2017) *Folk Song in England*, 380.
39. Gressenhall Farm and Workhouse photograph archive, 1.65–1.66.
40. Lee, K. (1899) "Some Experiences of a Folk-Song Collector," 9.
41. Bennett, E. and McKay, G. (2019) *From Brass Bands to Buskers*, 4–5.
42. Thompson, F. (2008) *Lark Rise*, 128ff.
43. Gressenhall Farm and Workhouse photograph archive, 1.65–1.66.
44. Nicholson, J. (1989) *I Kept A'Troshin*, 10 and 64–65.
45. Higgins, D. (2009) *The Winterton Story*, 39–41.
46. Gressenhall Farm and Workhouse photograph archive, 1.65–1.66.

2 Two Norfolk Families

1. Higgins, D. (2009) *The Winterton Story*, 9–10. In the register his surname was spelt without the *e*, although this letter reappeared in later official records.

2. *White's* (1836) 318; *White's* (1845) 307.
3. Jane's father, Edward, was also a Winterton fisherman.
4. Anderson, J. (1964) "Sam Larner, still a singing star at 85." *EDP*, 10 January.
5. Sam Larner, interview probably by Ewan MacColl and Charles Parker, undated, C/M101; Sam Larner, interview by Ewan MacColl and Charles Parker, ca. 1958–60, C/M102.
6. It's likely given the timescale that James was Sarah's father.
7. Harry Cox, interview by Alan Lomax, (AL)T3345R01.
8. Horn, P. (1981) "Country Children," 525.
9. Harry Cox, interview by Alan Lomax, (AL)T3342R02, 1953; Moeran, E. J. (1946) "Folk Songs," 4.
10. Harry Cox, interview by Alan Lomax, (AL)T3345R01.
11. Harry Cox, interview by Alan Lomax, (AL)T3345R01.
12. Harry Cox, *TSTS*.
13. Kennedy, P. (1958) "Harry Cox," 143.
14. Marsh, P. (2000) Notes to *BLB*, 6.
15. Marsh, P. (2000) Notes to *BLB*, 6.
16. Harry Cox, interview by Bob Thomson, July 1968, transcript, 1 (PM). The fight took place in January 1894.
17. In "All Things are Quite Silent," "cave" and "nest" are used to mean home – see Vaughan Williams, R and Lloyd, A. L (1959) *Penguin Book of English Folk Songs*, 13. My thanks to Sheila Park for this information.
18. Harry Cox, interview by Alan Lomax, (AL)T3342R02; 1881 Census.
19. Reg Reeve, interview by Chris Holderness and Des Miller, 17 February 2006, transcript courtesy of Chris Holderness; 1939 National Register.
20. Winterton marriage register, 4 July 1899.
21. Census 1871, 1891.
22. 1901 census; family research by Janet Rowe of Winterton.
23. Copper, B. (1975) *A Song for Every Season*, 5 and 9.
24. Holderness, C. (2014) *CRY*, 2; *SLLB* (1959) episode 2; Heppa, C. (2005) "Harry Cox and his Friends," 570.
25. Sally Shreeve, interview.
26. Heppa, C. (2019) "Jack Riseborough," 76.
27. Holderness, C (2014) *CRY*, 2, 19–20.
28. Seeger, P. and MacColl, E. (1960) *The Singing Island*, 110–113 (their italics).
29. "Betsy the Serving Maid," *English Love Songs*, Side 1, Track 7.
30. Marsh, P. (2000) Notes to *BLB*, 35; Kennedy, P (1958) "Harry Cox," 151.
31. Harry Cox, interview by Alan Lomax, 1951, (AL)T3342R02; Kennedy, P (1958) 144.
32. Grosvenor Myer, M. and Thomson, B. (1973) "A Visit to Harry Cox," 8.
33. Jenny Barker, interview.
34. "Barton Broad Ditty," *BLB*, Disc 2, Track 8.
35. Harry Cox, interview by Alan Lomax, (AL)T3345R03.
36. "Talk About Singing," *EFS*, Side 2, Track 7.
37. MacColl, E. and Seeger, P. (1961) Notes to *NTTFF*, 2.

3 First Work, First Songs

1. Holderness, C. (2014) *CRY*, p2.
2. Sam Larner, *TSTS*. The Winterton census for 1891 and 1901 gives lower numbers: even accepting that some men were at sea on census day the numbers are more likely to be around 120 and 160.
3. Sam Larner, unknown interviewer, undated, C/M100.

4. *NTTFF*, Track 2.
5. Sam Larner, interview probably by Ewan MacColl and Charles Parker, C/M101.
6. Information from volunteer guides on board the Yarmouth drifter *Lydia Eva*.
7. "Talk," *CRY*, Disc 1, Track 33.
8. "Up Jumped the Herring," *NTTFF*, Track 3.
9. Cited by Holderness, C (2014) *CRY*, 2.
10. *Shetland Times*, 22 August 1908.
11. Anonymous (2010) *Lydia Eva*, 12.
12. Anonymous (2010) *Lydia Eva*, 10–21; Information from volunteer guides on the *Lydia Eva*.
13. Sam Larner, *TSTS*.
14. Sam Larner, interview probably by Ewan MacColl and Charles Parker, undated, C/M101.
15. Sam Larner, interview probably by Ewan MacColl and Charles Parker, undated, C/M101.
16. Anonymous (undated) *Ganseys*, 2–4.
17. Higgins, D. (2009) *The Winterton Story*, 81.
18. 1891 and 1901 census; Sophie Miller, interview.
19. Martin Warren, interview; Martin Warren, email, 18 July 2019; Sophie Miller, interview.
20. MacColl, E. and Seeger, P. (1961), *NTTFF*, 8.
21. "Sealore and Rhymes," *NTTFF*, Track 12.
22. Sam Larner, *TSTS*.
23. Cited by Holderness, C (2014) *CRY*, 2.
24. Higgins, D. (2009) *The Winterton Story*, 81.
25. Jane Roberts, interview.
26. "Sealore and Rhymes," *NTTFF*, Track 6.
27. MacColl, E. (2009) *Journeyman*, 308.
28. Sam Larner, unknown interviewer, undated, C/M101.
29. "The Dogger Bank," *NTTFF*, Track 3.
30. David Higgins, interview.
31. Samuel and Dorcas, marriage certificate.
32. Watton marriage register; Potter Heigham marriage register (in Norfolk Records Office).
33. Information from Parish registers and census returns.
34. 1891 and 1901 census; the story was told to me by Brian Gaudet.
35. Watton marriage register.
36. Anderson, J. (1964) "Sam Larner," *EDP*, 10 January.
37. Marjorie was the daughter of Thirza and Edward Powles.
38. Jane Roberts, interview; Szreter, S (2014) "The Prevalence of Syphilis," 525.
39. Sam Larner, interview by Ewan MacColl and Charles Parker, ca. 1958–60, C/M102.
40. "The Drowned Lover," *NTTFF*, Track 13.
41. Sam Larner, interview probably by Ewan MacColl and Charles Parker, undated, C/M101; *Times* (1911) 2 October; Anderson, J (1964) "Sam Larner," *EDP*, 10 January.
42. Royal Naval Reserve Force Certificate of Discharge #4079, 8 June 1910.
43. It's possible that he'd already made arrangements to do so.
44. 1911 census.
45. *SLLB* (1959) episode 2.
46. *Shetland Times* (1907) 29 June; (1908) 22 August; (1909) 10 July.
47. *Shetland Times* (1908) 25 July; 1 August. *Sentenced to Death* was composed in 1891.
48. *Shetland Times* (1908) 8 August.
49. *Shetland Times* (1908) 22 August.

50. Robert "Tuskin" Hodds, (undated) *Shetland Herring Fishing*. The letter was reproduced in January 1964, by an unknown source.
51. Cited by Marsh, P. (2000) Notes to *BLB*, 25.
52. Harry Cox, *TSTS*.
53. Harry Cox, interview by Alan Lomax (1955), transcript (PM): *Every Song a Story*, CD2 Track 19.
54. Harry Cox, interview by Alan Lomax, (AL)T3342R02
55. National School Admission Register, at findmypast.co.uk; Harry Cox, interview by Alan Lomax, (AL)T3345R01.
56. "Talk About Himself," *EFS*, Side 2, Track 2.
57. "Talk About his Father," *EFS*, Side 2, Track 4.
58. Harry Cox, interview by Alan Lomax, (AL)T3342R02.
59. Harry Cox, interview by Alan Lomax (1955), transcript (PM); Harry Cox, interview by Alan Lomax, (AL)T3347R10.
60. Harry's denial is in an interview by Bob Thomson, ca. 1969, C/M103; Barker, interview
61. Grosvenor Myer, M. and Thomson, B. (1973) "A Visit to Harry Cox," 12.
62. Yarmouth Stores 1905 catalogue.
63. "Talk About Singing," *EFS*, Side 2, Track 7.
64. 1901 census. I have been unable to trace Eleanor's address.
65. *Kelly's Directory* (1896), 79.
66. Catfield Burial Register 1881–1983 (Norfolk Records Office); Harry Cox, interview by Bob Thomson, ca. 1969, C/M103.
67. Harry Cox, interview by Bob Thomson, ca. 1969, C/M103.
68. Potter Heigham marriage register (Norfolk Records Office).
69. Springall, L. M. (1936), *Labouring Life*, 122.
70. The story of the breeding bitterns is told in the Norfolk Wildlife Trust's observation hut on Hickling Broad.
71. Harry Cox, interview by Alan Lomax, (AL)T3342R01.
72. Harry Cox, *TSTS*.
73. Harry Cox, interview by Alan Lomax, (AL)T3341R04.
74. Frankie Armstrong, interview.
75. "Talk About Himself," *EFS*, Side 2, Track 2.
76. "The Harvest," *What Will Become of England?*, Track 7.
77. Reg Reeve, interview by Chris Holderness and Des Miller, (2006).
78. Cited by Marsh, P (2000) Notes to *BLB*, 9.
79. Harry Cox, *TSTS*.
80. Harry Cox, interview by Alan Lomax, (AL)T3346R15.
81. Harry Cox, interview by Alan Lomax, (AL)T3346R07.
82. Harry Cox, interview by Alan Lomax, (AL)T3346R07.
83. Grosvenor Myer, M. and Thomson, B. (1973) "A Visit to Harry Cox," 8.
84. Harry Cox, interview by Alan Lomax, (AL)T3346R03.

4 The First Folk Revival

1. Martin Carthy, interview.
2. Winick, S. D. (1997) "Reissuing the Revival," 324.
3. Lee, K. (1899) "Some Experiences," 10.
4. Pearsall, R. (1975) *Edwardian Popular Music*, 173.
5. Lomax, A. Kennedy, P. and Collins, S. (1961) *The Folk Songs of Britain* Volume 2: *Songs of Seduction*, Caedmon TC1143.
6. Palmer, R. (2003) "Neglected Pioneer," 346.
7. Bearman, C. J. (2001) *The English Folk Movement*, 123.

8. Collins, S. (2018) *All in the Downs*, 172.
9. Hunt, K. (2006) "Peter Kennedy obituary," independent.co.uk, 16 June.
10. Lee, K. (1899) "Some Experiences," 7.
11. Sharp, C. J. (1907) *English Folk-Song*, vii.
12. Sharp, C. J. (1907) *English Folk-Song*, 119.
13. Bearman, C. J. (2001) *The English Folk Movement*, 127.
14. Lee, K. (1899) "Some Experiences," 10.
15. BBC Northern Ireland (2019) *Sam Henry, Songs of the People*, Episode 1. First broadcast 21 April.
16. Bearman, C. J. (2001) *The English Folk Movement*, 132–136.
17. Grainger, P. (1908) "Collecting with the Phonograph," 147.
18. Lee, K. (1899) "Some Experiences," 11.
19. Lee, K. (1899) "Some Experiences," 9.
20. Helsdon, A. (2014) *Vaughan Williams in Norfolk*, volume 1, Musical Traditions CD-ROM; East Anglia Traditional Music Trust (undated) *Ralph Vaughan Williams in South Norfolk*, eatmt.org.uk; Howson, J (with additional information from Alan Helsdon) (2014) *Collectors in Norfolk*, unpublished notes courtesy of Brian Gaudet.
21. Information from VWML online.
22. Roud, S. (2017) *Folk Song in England*, 153; Roud Index. The Index erroneously refers to him as "Skinny."
23. Pearsall, R. (1975) *Edwardian Popular Music*, 179.

5 A World Turned Upside Down

1. Moeran, E. J. (1946) "Folk Songs," 1–2.
2. Palmer, R. (2003) "Neglected Pioneer," 346.
3. Moeran, E. J. (1936) "Notes on Folk-Songs," 31–32.
4. See *All My Life's Buried Here: the story of George Butterworth*, georgebutterworth.co.uk; Palmer, R (2003) "Neglected Pioneer," 346.
5. Malster, R. (2015) *North Sea War*, 2, 16–21, 70, 142.
6. Higgins, D. (2009) *The Winterton Story*, p65; catfield.org.uk; Winterton Roll of Honour, in the Church of All Saints.
7. Mansfield, N. (1986) "George Edwards," 54.
8. Palmer, R. (2003) "Neglected Pioneer," 346.
9. Potter Heigham Roll of Honour, in the Church of St. Nicholas.
10. Service records for Harry Cox and Sam Larner, discovery.nationalarchives.gov.uk. Harry's online record is listed as "Henry Cox" born in Bolton (*sic*), Norfolk.
11. MacColl, E. (2009) *Journeyman*, 307; Peggy Seeger, interview.
12. Kennedy, P. (1958) "Harry Cox," 145.
13. Pegg, B. (1976) *Folk: A Portrait*, 32; Shepard, L (1995) *An Appreciation of Harry Cox*, unpublished manuscript (SR).
14. Jenny Barker, interview.
15. Harry Cox, interview by Alan Lomax, (AL)T3345R01.
16. Sam Larner's service records; Dorcas's memory of Mrs. East is on C/M100.
17. Sam Larner, unknown interviewer, possibly Philip Donnellan, undated, C/M100.
18. Sam Larner, unknown interviewer, possibly Philip Donnellan, undated, C/M100 – Sam claims the vessel sank less than a week after he left it, but naval records are unclear. Information regarding the vessels and incident is at naval-history.net.
19. Sam Larner, unknown interviewer, possibly Philip Donnellan, undated, C/M100 – Sam doesn't name the vessel.
20. Sam Larner's service records, discovery.nationalarchives.gov.uk.
21. Harry Cox's service records, discovery.nationalarchives.gov.uk.

22. Anonymous (undated) *Drill Hall Library history*, campus.medway.ac.uk/about/history.html.
23. See dreadnoughtproject.org.
24. Harry's ditty box is now in JB; Harry Cox, interview by Alan Lomax, (AL)T3341R04.
25. Marsh, P. (2000) Notes to *BLB*, 10.
26. Grosvenor Myer, M. and Thomson, B. (1973) "A Visit to Harry Cox," 12; Lenny Helsdon, interview by Paul Marsh, 24 March 1995, transcript, 1, PM.
27. Bob Thomson to Paul Marsh, email, 19 June 2000, PM.
28. BBC Television (2002) *A History of Britain*, Series 3 Episode 15.
29. Palmer, R. (2003) "Neglected Pioneer," 347.
30. Moeran, E. J. (1946) "Folk Songs," 2.
31. Harry Cox, interview by Charles Parker, July 1963, transcript (PM)
32. Moeran, E. J. (1946) "Folk Songs," 2; Moeran (1936) "Notes on Folk-Songs," 31.
33. Moeran, E. J. (1946) "Folk Songs," 3.
34. Moeran, E. J. (1946) "Folk Songs," 4.
35. Moeran, E. J. (1946) "Folk Songs," 3. Moeran doesn't identify the venue but thought it was the third session he attended.

6 Mr. Moeran Comes Collecting

1. Moeran, E. J. (1936) "Notes on Folk-Songs," 32.
2. Peter Coleman, interview.
3. Anonymous (1959) "Harry Cox," 4–5.
4. Harry Cox, interview by Bob Thomson, ca. 1969, C/M103. Moeran moved to Ireland, where he died in 1950.
5. Karpeles, M. *et al.* (1931) "Humorous and Disreputable Songs," 274.
6. Heppa, C. (2005) "Harry Cox," 575–6.
7. Jenny Barker, interview.
8. Marsh, P. (2000) Notes to *BLB*, 26.
9. Moeran, E. J. *et al.* (1922) "Songs Collected in Norfolk"; Karpeles, M. *et al.* (1931) "Humorous and Disreputable Songs"; Moeran, E. J. *et al.* (1931) "Love Songs and Ballads."
10. Moeran, E. J. *et al.* (1922) "Songs Collected in Norfolk," 22.
11. Shirley Collins (1965) *The Sweet Primeroses* (Topic Records TSDL476); The Shackleton Trio (2016) *The Dog Who Would Not Be Washed* (self-released); Karpeles, M. (1974) *Cecil Sharp's Collection*, 235–6.
12. Karpeles, M. *et al.* (1931) "Humorous and Disreputable Songs," 275–6.
13. Moeran, E. J. (1946) "Folk Songs and some Traditional Singers," 5. Harry sang "The Girl of Lowestoft" for Alan Lomax in December 1953 (as "She Was a Rum One"): see (AL)T3346R06.
14. Moeran, E. J. (1924) *Six Folk Songs from Norfolk*.
15. See Smith, B. (1994) *Peter Warlock*.
16. Smith, B. (1994) *Peter Warlock*, 212, 221ff.
17. Palmer, R. (2003) "Neglected Pioneer," 150–151.
18. For the photograph of Fred Brown, see Moeran, E. J. (1936) "Notes on Folk-Songs," 31; for the photograph of Bullards Miller, see Heppa, C. (2002) "From My Father's Songbook," 16.
19. Augustus John, cited by Smith, B. (1994) *Peter Warlock*, 130.
20. I am indebted to Sandra Laws, churchwarden at Winterton, for information about the incident.
21. The date of the incident is given at heritage.norfolk.gov.uk/home NHER#8582.

22. Heseltine, P. (1924) "Introductions XVIII: E. J. Moeran," 172; Barry Marsh attributes the remark to Harry, but he was not "old" at the time. See Barry Marsh, interview by Paul Marsh, 29 May 1995, transcript, SR.
23. *Daily Herald* (1923) 21 March.
24. *The Farm Strike* (1923) by British Pathé, youtube.com/watch?v=RrHwJL5j3KM.
25. Howkins, A. (1985) *Poor Labouring Men*, 169.
26. Mansfield, N. (1986) "George Edwards," 56.
27. *Daily Herald* (1923) 21 March.
28. *Hansard*, HC Deb 02 July 1923 vol 166 cc35–6.
29. Marsh, P. (2000) Notes to *BLB*, 9; Howkins (1985) *Poor Labouring Men*, 161.
30. Mansfield (1986) "George Edwards," 56.
31. Marsh (2000) Notes to *BLB*, 9; Palmer, R (2003) "Neglected Pioneer," 349–350.
32. Harry Cox, interview by Alan Lomax, (AL)T3345R01.
33. Potter Heigham marriage register, Norfolk Records Office.
34. Records at findmypast.co.uk.
35. Harry Cox, interview by Alan Lomax, (AL)T3345R01.
36. Barker, J. (undated) *Memories*, 7.
37. Harry Cox, interview by Alan Lomax, (AL)T3345R01; The photo is in the notes to *BLB*, 11.
38. Ethel Cox's death certificate.
39. Harry Cox, interview by Alan Lomax, (AL)T3345R01.
40. Myrtle Helsdon, interview by Paul Marsh, 9 October 1995, transcript 1–3 (PM); Dog Licence dated 8 January 1927 (PM).
41. Brett's of Yarmouth, bill dated August 1927 (JB); Barker (undated) *Memories*, 1.
42. Barker, J. (undated) *Memories*, 1, 5–6.
43. Brett's bill, now in JB.
44. Marsh, P. (2000) Notes to *BLB*, 12; Potter Heigham baptisms, Norfolk Records Office.
45. Sam Larner, unknown interviewer, possibly Philip Donnellan, undated, C/M100.
46. Higgins, D. (2009) *The Winterton Story*, 66.
47. Sam Larner, audio recording C102/8 S1, British Library; Register of Deceased Seamen, January 1929, findmypast.co.uk.
48. Sam Larner, unknown interviewer, possibly Philip Donnellan, C/M100.

7 Harry Finds Fame

1. Grieg, R. (2004) "Joseph Taylor," 388–391.
2. See, for example, Joseph Taylor (1908) "Sprig O' Thyme," HMV6-2238.
3. Grainger, P. (1908) "Collecting with the Phonograph," 153.
4. Anonymous, (undated) *Index to P. A. Grainger's Phonograph Cylinder (also Gramophone Disc) Records*, PG/20, VWML.
5. Grieg, R. (2004) "Joseph Taylor," 392.
6. Peter Kennedy to Rod Stradling, 13 June 2000, PM; "Whiffler" (1934) *Eastern Evening News*, 24 February. For the history of the gramophone's impact on British social life see Lindsay, B (2020) *Shellac and Swing!*.
7. "Whiffler" (1934) *Eastern Evening News*, 24 February.
8. EMG Colonel's YouTube channel is at youtube.com/user/EMGColonel/videos.
9. Anonymous (1959) "Harry Cox," 5.
10. Moeran, E. J. (1936) "Notes on Folk-Songs," 32.
11. *Radio Times* (1929) 10 May, 14.
12. *Radio Times* (1934) 2 November, 382.
13. Barker, J. (undated) Memories. Harry rented a smallholding, too, but it's not clear when he first started to do this.

14. Cited by Marsh, P. (2000) Notes to *BLB*, 14. Portable gramophones became plentiful during the 1920s: see Lindsay, B. (2020) *Shellac and Swing!*, 62ff.
15. *The Scotsman* (1938) 14 February, 9; cited by Marsh, P (2000) Notes to *BLB*, 13.
16. *Radio Times* (1952) 16 May, 13.
17. Kennedy, P. (1958) "Harry Cox," 146.
18. *Radio Times* (1946) 27 September, 32; *Radio Times* (1945) 14 September, 21.
19. (JB).
20. Heppa, C. (2005) "Harry Cox and his Friends," 578.
21. Heppa, C. (2004) "Letter: 'Neglected Pioneer'," 517; Heppa, C. (2019) "Jack Riseborough," 75–80.
22. Heppa, C. (2005) "Harry Cox and his Friends," 584–585.
23. Higgins, D (2009) *The Winterton Story*, 83.
24. Browning, S (2018) *Norfolk at War*, 1939–45, 129.
25. Kennedy, P (1958) "Harry Cox," 145.
26. Moeran, E. J. (1946) "Folk Songs," 4; Moeran (1948) "Some Folk Singing of Today," 152.
27. Collinson, F. M. (1946) "Songs Collected by Francis M. Collinson," 14.
28. Young, R. (2011) *Electric Eden*, 124. Folk song had appeared in other shows, notably an English Folk Dance Society 21st anniversary programme on 6 December 1932, which featured William Kimber and (on disc) Joseph Taylor (See *Radio Times*, 2 December, 692).
29. Arthur, D. (2012) *Singing the Century: the life and times of A. L. Lloyd*, podcastacademy.org/podcasts/singing-the-century.
30. *Radio Times* (1939) 21 July, 16.
31. *Radio Times* (1947) 14 November, 16.
32. Moeran, E. J. (1948) "Some Folk Singing of Today," 153.
33. Sleeve notes to *East Anglia Sings* (2013) Snatch'd From Oblivion SFO 005.
34. Heppa, C. (2019) "Jack Riseborough," 74–77.
35. Christopher Heppa, interview.
36. Brown, M. (1947) "The Broadcasters," *Radio Times*, 14 November, 9.
37. *SLLB* (1959) episode 2.
38. Sam Larner, interview probably by Ewan MacColl and Charles Parker, undated, C/M101.
39. See Holderness, C. (2013) *Sam Larner*.
40. Various Artists: *East Coast Fishermen* (Voices of Suffolk series: No. 6) Helions Bumpstead Gramophone Company NLCD6.
41. Higgins, D. (2009) *The Winterton Story*, 73–74.
42. Sam Larner, interview probably by Ewan MacColl and Charles Parker, undated, C/M101.
43. Lloyd, A. L. (1974) *A Garland for Sam*, 3.
44. David Higgins, interview.
45. Andrew Fakes, interview.
46. Sam Larner, unknown interviewer, possibly Philip Donnellan, undated, C/M100.

8 Building the Repertoire

1. Laing, D. *et al.* (1975) *The Electric Muse*, 87.
2. Stradling, R. (2014) *CRY*, p1; Marsh (2000) Notes to *BLB*, 59–60.
3. Karpeles, M. (1955) "Definition of Folk Music," 6.
4. Roud, S. and Bishop, J (2012) *The New Penguin Book*, xii.
5. Woods, F. (1979) *Folk Revival*, 24.
6. Moore, C. (1980) Notes to Planxty's album, *The Woman I Loved So Well* (Tara 3005); Dave Burland, interview. The resemblance may be wishful thinking on my part.

7. George, R. V. A. (1952) Brief for Collectors, 16 May (BBC), cited in Hall (2017) *Peter Kennedy's Published Recordings*, 35.
8. Seeger, P. (2017) *First Time Ever* (ebook), ch16, 1.
9. Sharp, C. J. (1907) *English Folk-Song*, 3–4.
10. MacColl, E. (1965) *Song Carriers* script #2, C/M.
11. Sam Larner, interview by Ewan MacColl and Charles Parker, ca. 1958–60, C/M102.
12. "Cruising Round Yarmouth," *CRY*, Disc 2, Track 14.
13. Sam Larner, interview by Ewan MacColl and Charles Parker, ca. 1958–60, C/M102.
14. Sam Larner, interview by Ewan MacColl and Charles Parker, ca. 1958–60, C/M102.
15. Sam Larner, unknown interviewer, possibly Philip Donnellan, undated, C/M100.
16. Sam Larner, interview probably by Ewan MacColl and Charles Parker, undated, C/M101.
17. Seeger, P. and MacColl, E. (1960) *The Singing Island*, 110. Other sources identify Larpin Sutton as the man who taught Sam.
18. Sam Larner, *TSTS*; Sam is probably confusing Scandinavia with Scotland.
19. Sam Larner, interview by Ewan MacColl and Charles Parker, ca. 1958–60, C/M102.
20. Harry Cox, interview by Bob Thomson, July 1968, transcript, 1 (PM); Kennedy's diary, 19 July 1956, peterkennedyarchive.org/east-anglia-1956/2/. Most of Harry's songs discussed in this section appear on *BLB*. "I Will Level with Her," "The Cabin with Roses Round the Door," "The Bumblebee Song" and "Mr. Morrison's Pills" only appear on *Every Song a Story* – an early, unreleased, CD-ROM version of *BLB*, the only known copy of which is in PM.
21. Harry Cox, interview by Alan Lomax, (AL)T3347R10
22. Harry Cox, interview by Alan Lomax, (AL)T3341R06.
23. Harry Cox, interview by Alan Lomax, (AL)T3347R10.
24. Harry Cox, interview by Leslie Shepard, October 1965, S434498, VWML.
25. Tudor, J. (1967) "Harry Cox: A Living Legend." *Norwich Evening News*, 23 October; Carole Pegg, email, 14 August 2019.
26. Heath-Coleman, P. (2013) *Harry Cox, ain't that beautiful*, mustrad.org.uk/articles/cox.htm; Reg Hall, interview.
27. Peter Coleman, interview.
28. My thanks to Steve Roud for this information.
29. Harry Cox, interview by Bob Thomson, ca. 1969, C/M103.
30. Jenny Barker, interview.
31. Manuscripts, British Isles 1950–58, image 12, AL.
32. Peggy Seeger, interview.
33. Sam Larner, *TSTS*.
34. Peggy Seeger, interview.
35. Sam Larner, interview by Ewan MacColl and Charles Parker, ca. 1958–60, C/M102.
36. Kennedy, P. (1958) "Harry Cox," 144.
37. Heppa, C. (2005) "Harry Cox and his Friends," 576.
38. Harry Cox, interview by Bob Thomson, ca. 1969, C/M103.
39. Marsh, P. (2000) Notes to *BLB*, 3; Shepard, L (1975) *An Appreciation of Harry Cox*, SR.
40. Harry Cox, interview by Charles Parker, July 1963, transcript, PM.
41. Paul Marsh's annotated list of Harry Cox's recordings, PM.
42. Palmer, R. (2003) "Neglected Pioneer," 158.
43. Moore, A. F. and Vacca, G. (2014) *Legacies of Ewan MacColl*, 114–115.
44. Grosvenor Myer, M. and Thomson, B. (1973) "A Visit to Harry Cox," 8.
45. Shepard, L. (1972) "Harry Cox [Letter]," 241.
46. Godbold, C. (undated) Harry Cox obituary, unknown publication (PM).
47. *The Pierrot Song Book* and others are now in SR.
48. "'Sprite's' Article" (1930) *Eastern Evening News*, 12 March, 19 March.

49. Grosvenor Myer, M and Thomson, B (1973) "A Visit to Harry Cox," 8; Harry means *Country* Magazine.
50. Grosvenor Myer, M. and Thomson, B. (1973) "A Visit to Harry Cox," 8.
51. Myrtle Helsdon, interview by Paul Marsh, 9 September 1994, transcript, 3 (PM).
52. Heppa, C. (2002) "From My Father's Songbook," 16.
53. Copper, B (1975) *A Song for Every Season*, 14–15.
54. "The Bonny Bunch of Roses," *EFS*, Side 1, Track 5.
55. Stradling, R. and Yates, M. (2000) Notes to Walter Pardon's album, *Put a Bit of Powder on it, Father*, Musical Traditions MTCD305–6, 7.
56. Harry Cox, interview by Alan Lomax, (AL)T3346R09.
57. Sabine Baring-Gould Manuscript Collection, SBG/1/3/228, VWML.
58. D'Urfey, T. (1719) *Wit and Mirth*, 96–98.
59. "The Maid of Australia," *BLB*, Disc 1, Track 17.
60. James Madison Carpenter Collection Online, dhi.ac.uk/carpenter/index.html.
61. See Roud Index. Airoland (or Arioland) is the name given to a small loch in Wigtownshire, in southwest Scotland, on maps and documents from the late eighteenth and early nineteenth centuries: see maps.nls.uk/estates/monreith/rec/4047.
62. Kennedy, P. (1958) "Harry Cox," 149; "The Maid of Australia," *BLB*, Disc 1, Track 17.
63. Gemma Khawaja, interview.
64. The transcript is now in JB.
65. *SLLB* (1959) episode 2.
66. Harry Cox, interview by Alan Lomax, (AL)T3341R04.
67. "The Dogger Bank," *CRY*, Disc 2, Track 24.
68. Copper, B. (1975) *A Song for Every Season*, 10.
69. Royal Cornwall Museum, royalcornwallmuseum.org.uk/messages-from-the-royal-cornwall-infirmary; Various Artists (2003) *Here's Luck to a Man*, Track 34, MTCD320.
70. "'Sprite's' Article" (1930) *Evening News*, 12 March.

9 "All We Had for Entertainment"

1. Cited by Holderness, C (2014) *CRY*, 2.
2. Harry Cox, *TSTS*.
3. Heppa, C. (2005) "Harry Cox and his Friends," 575.
4. Sam Larner, *TSTS*; Sam Larner, recorded by Ewan MacColl, Peggy Seeger and Charles Parker ca.1960, British Library, C102/6 S2.
5. Kennedy, P. (1958) "Harry Cox," 145; Holderness, C (2014) *CRY*, 3.
6. Moeran, E. J. (1946) "Folk Songs," 2.
7. Harry Cox, interview by Bob Thomson, ca. 1969, C/M103.
8. Peter Kennedy to Miss M. Slocombe, 10 October 1953, peterkennedyarchive.org/.
9. "Dropsy" refers to the accumulation of fluid in the soft tissues, often causing swelling in the legs and feet. It's a sign of a causative disease such as heart failure. See Medicinenet.com.
10. Lenny Helsdon, interview by Paul Marsh, 9 September 1994, transcript, 9 (PM).
11. Jenny Barker, interview; Barker, J. (undated) *Memories*, 3 and 6.
12. Barker, J. (undated) *Memories*, 7.
13. Barker, J. (undated) *Memories*; Christopher Heppa, email, 18 November 2019.
14. Barker, J. (undated) *Memories*, 3–6.
15. Myrtle Helsdon to the Stricklands, 15 March 1968, VWML; Sheila Park, interview; Harry Cox, interview by Bob Thomson, ca. 1969, C/M103.
16. "Talk About Singing," *EFS*, Side 2, Track 7.
17. Cited by Heppa, C. (2005) "Harry Cox and his Friends," 573. It's not clear which versions of "Amazing Grace" or "Red Sails in the Sunset" Harry most enjoyed.

18. Harry Cox, interview by Bob Thomson, ca. 1969, C/M103.
19. Ken Saul, interview.
20. Higgins, D. (2009) *The Winterton Story*, 88.
21. *Yarmouth Mercury*, 19 March 1954.
22. Barker, J. (undated) *Memories*, 1–2; "Gay" meant pretty. Georgia Shackleton wrote "Harry's Seagull" after learning about the bird when interviewed for this book.
23. Barker, J. (undated) *Memories*, 3; Christopher Heppa, email, 18 November 2019.
24. Wentworth Day, J. (1951) *Broadland Adventure*, 163.
25. Swan, M. (2019) "What happened to the coypu?" *Shooting Times* online, shooting. co.uk; Jenny Barker, interview and *Memories*, 4. Coypu were officially considered to have been eliminated by January 1989.
26. Norfolk County Council Receipt, 19 April 1952, now in JB; Barker, J. (undated) *Memories*, 4.
27. Christopher Heppa, interview. Gunner Blaxell's exercise book is now in JB.
28. Copper, B. (1975) *A Song for Every Season*, 101–102.
29. Evans, G. E. (1975) *Ask the Fellows*, 45; *Here's a Health to the Barley Mow*, produced by Peter Kennedy (1955) eafa.org.uk/catalogue/5.
30. Heppa, C. (2004) "'Neglected pioneer' by Roy Palmer," 425.
31. Heppa, C. (2004a) *Sam Howard*, 425.
32. *Here's a Health to the Barley Mow*, produced by Peter Kennedy (1955) eafa.org.uk/catalogue/5.
33. Jane Roberts, interview.
34. Sam Larner, *TSTS*.
35. Most of them have long-since closed, although the Crown and King's Arms were still open for business in 2020.
36. Shirley Collins, email, 3 December 2019.
37. Heppa, C. (2004) "'Neglected pioneer' by Roy Palmer," 426–7.
38. "Singing in Public Houses," *What Will Become of England*, Track 26; Harry Cox, interview by Charles Parker, July 1963, transcript, 1, PM.
39. Heppa, C. (2005) "Harry Cox and his Friends," 571 and 578.
40. Heppa, C. (2005) "Harry Cox and his Friends," 578.
41. Stradling, R. and Yates, M. (2000) *Put a Bit of Powder on it, Father*, 7.
42. Bellamy, P. (1974) "Interview with Walter Pardon," 11.
43. Stradling, R. and Yates, M. (2000) *Put a Bit of Powder on it, Father*, 1–7.
44. Pegg, B. (1976) *Folk: A Portrait*, 32.
45. Moeran, E. J. (1948) "Some Folk Singing of Today," 153.
46. Heppa, C. (2004) "'Neglected pioneer' by Roy Palmer," 427–429; Christopher Heppa to Paul Marsh, 11 July 2009 (PM).
47. Reg Reeve, interview by Chris Holderness and Des Miller, 17 February 2006, transcript courtesy of Chris Holderness.
48. Harry Cox, interview by Alan Lomax, (AL)T3341R08; Peter Coleman, interview.
49. Harry Cox, interview by Alan Lomax, (AL)T3342R02; Jenny Barker, interview; Pauline Godbold, interview.
50. Sam Larner, *TSTS*.
51. Seeger, P. (2017) 21:4; "Whiffler," (1934) *Eastern Evening News*, 24 February.
52. Kennedy, P. (1958) "Harry Cox," 142–146.
53. Anonymous (1959) "Harry Cox," 5. Plunkett is identified by Paul Marsh in the notes to *BLB*, 18.
54. Pegg, B. (1976) *Folk: A Portrait*, 32–33.
55. Macfarlane, T. J. (1973) "Sing Us an Old Song," 131.
56. Holderness, C. (2013) *Sam Larner*, 1.
57. Damien Barber, interview.

1. Anderson, J. (1964) "Sam Larner," *EDP*, 10 January.
2. Thornber, R. (1999) "Obituary: Philip Donnellan," *Independent online*, 2 March, independent.co.uk/arts-entertainment/obituary-philip-donnellan-1079938.html
3. *EDP*, 20 June 1949.
4. *Radio Times* (1956) 29 June, 10. The programme was broadcast on 1 July.
5. *Radio Times* (1957) 13 September, 26; Contract by courtesy of Chris Holderness.
6. BBC contract, 5 Feb 1959, now in JB.
7. Manuscript of White Squall, courtesy of Chris Holderness; Holderness, C. (2014) 3.
8. Sam Larner, interview probably by Ewan MacColl and Charles Parker, undated, C/M101
9. Anonymous newspaper article, probably *EDP*, Oct 1959, courtesy of Chris Holderness.
10. *SLLB* (1959) episode 2.
11. *SLLB* (1959) episode 4; MacColl's recording is on *CRY*, Disc 1, Track 32.
12. *Radio Times* (1961) 25 May, 18, 26, 36 and 44.
13. Seeger, P. (2017) *First Time Ever* (e-book), 16:1.
14. See bbc.co.uk/radio2/radioballads/original/singingthefishing.shtml.
15. Peggy Seeger, interview.
16. Peggy Seeger, email, 27 April 2019.
17. Seeger, P. (2017) *First Time Ever* (e-book), 24:7.
18. Ken Hunt, interview.
19. Sam Larner, interview by Ewan MacColl and Charles Parker, ca. 1958–60, C/M102.
20. Image of the dedication, courtesy of Chris Holderness.
21. Anonymous (2014) *David Attenborough and the Natural History of Folk*. bbc.co.uk/mediacentre/proginfo/2014/06/r2-david-attenborough-wednesday.html.
22. *Radio Times* (1953) 27 November, 26; Hall, R (2017) *Peter Kennedy's Published Recordings*, 176
23. Cited by Hall, R (2017) *Peter Kennedy's Published Recordings*, 35.
24. Hall, R. (2017) *Peter Kennedy's Published Recordings*, 37.
25. Kennedy, P. (1952) *Report on Midland Region Trip*, October-November, 16–18, peterkennedyarchive.org/midlands-1952/16/.
26. Kennedy, P. (1953) *East Anglian Trip*, 1–2, peterkennedyarchive.org/east-anglia-1953. The list in Kennedy, P (1958) "Harry Cox," 154–5, dates the recordings to 9 October. Hall is emphatic that Kennedy's diary "is wrong. There is no way Peter could have recorded an extensive session with Harry during the day and then recorded … in Blaxhall Ship in Suffolk in the evening." (Hall, R, 2017, *Peter Kennedy's Published Recordings*, 160). Kennedy was known to falsify his records, but his 10 October record is probably correct. Harry and Kennedy could have gone to the Windmill during the morning – the licensee could have allowed him access before opening – and a five- or six-hour session would still give Kennedy time to drive a couple of hours south to Blaxhall.
27. Kennedy, P. (1956) Report on Collecting Trip to East Anglia, July, 2, peterkennedyarchive.org/east-anglia-1956/.
28. *Radio Times* (1953) 25 September, 11.
29. Kennedy, P. (1984) *Folksongs of Britain and Ireland*, 2.
30. Kennedy, P. (1984) *Folksongs of Britain and Ireland*, 1.
31. *Radio Times* (1954) 19 March, 30. The programme was on 24 March.
32. BBC Home Service (1957) *A Ballad Hunter Looks at Britain*: episode four was broadcast on 22 November at 7:00pm – see *Radio Times* 15 November, 43. Lomax's script is in (AL). In the weeks following Parker's session the station broadcast *East Anglian Miscellany* and *In the Country: East Anglian Edition*, either of which might have included content from Harry. See *Radio Times* (1958) 21 November.

33. The contract is now in JB.
34. MacColl, E. (1965) Song Carriers script #2, C/M; "Butter and Cheese" is *NTTFF*, Track 5.
35. The contract is now in JB. The second figure may be thirty-three pounds, but the contract image is blurred.
36. *Radio Times* (1964) 25 June, 59.
37. Myrtle Helsdon, interview by Paul Marsh, 2 April 1995, transcript, 1, PM.
38. Peggy Seeger to Charles Parker (letter) 12 October 1966, PM.
39. Manuscript collection, VWML.
40. Marsh, P. (2000) Notes to *BLB*, 60.
41. MacColl, E. and Seeger, P. (1961) Notes to *NTTFF*, 5.
42. See officialcharts.com.
43. Moeran, E. J. (1948) "Some Folk Singing of Today," 154.
44. Tudor, J. (1967) "Harry Cox: A Living Legend," *Eastern Evening News*, 23 October.
45. Moore, A. F. and Vacca, G. (2014) *Legacies of Ewan MacColl*, 57.
46. Moore, A. F. and Vacca, G. (2014) *Legacies of Ewan MacColl*, 57.
47. Frankie Armstrong, interview.
48. Jenny Barker, interview.
49. Marsh, P. (2000) Notes to *BLB*, 19.
50. "Monitor" (1964) *Coventry Evening Telegraph*, 3 July.
51. Myrtle Helsdon, interview by Paul Marsh, 2 April 1995, transcript, 2, PM.
52. Myrtle Helsdon to the Stricklands, 25 June 1965, VWML.
53. *EDP* (1965) 28 June, 10.
54. Harry's songs are "Just as the Tide was a-Flowing," "The Gipsy Laddie," "Marrowbones," "Edwin in the Lowlands Low" and "The Oxford Girl." Sam's are "Maids, When You're Young, Never Wed an Old Man" (listed as "An Old Man Once Courted Me") and "The Wild Rover."
55. HMV DLP1143.
56. Kennedy, P. (1958a) "Folk Song Recording," 39 and footnote, 19. The magazine interviewed Alan Lomax about his approach to "folk song recording" in its March 1958 issue.
57. Carter, S. (1958) "Folk-songsters find themselves in vogue," *The Tatler*, 1 October, 22–23.
58. Folkways FS 3805.
59. Caedmon Records TC-1162 and TC-1164; Folkways FG 3507; Holderness, C (2014) *CRY*, 3.
60. See *Smithsonian Folkways Recordings*, folkways.si.edu.
61. *Times* (1962) "British Folk Music on American Records," 17 March, 11; Digby, R (undated) mustrad.org.uk/reviews/larner.htm.
62. Anderson, J. (1964) "Sam Larner" *EDP*, 10 January.
63. Folk-Legacy Records FSB-20.
64. DTS LFX4.
65. *Sounds of Sheffield Tramways*, DTS EP EGA8005.
66. DTS LFX1.
67. EFDSS LP1004.
68. Kennedy, P. (1965) Notes to *EFS*.

11 On the Road

1. Bragg, B. (2017) *Roots, Radicals and Rockers*, 92; Barber, C. (2014) *Jazz Me Blues*, 26–27.
2. Bragg, B. (2017) *Roots, Radicals and Rockers*, 246; Martin Carthy, interview.

3. Kennedy, P (1958) "Harry Cox," 145.
4. Burke, D. (2015) *Singing Out*, 7; Laing, D. *et al.* (1975) *The Electric Muse*, 142–143.
5. Frankie Armstrong, interview.
6. Peter Bellamy, interview by Silvia Sass, possibly for a Dutch TV station (ca.1990) youtube.com/watch?v=3bt3tKhVXBc.
7. Bellamy insisted that the Young Tradition was a pop group, due to the power of their performances. See Dallas, K. (1975) Notes to *The Electric Muse, The Story of Folk into Rock*, Island/Transatlantic Records, 1.
8. Bellamy, P (1968) *Mainly Norfolk*, Transatlantic XTRA 1060.
9. Tony Baylis, interview.
10. Damien Barber, interview.
11. Peter Bellamy, interview by Silvia Sass (c1990) youtube.com/watch?v=3bt3tKhVXBc; Young, R (2011) *Electric Eden*, 196; Damien Barber, interview.
12. Frankie Armstrong, interview.
13. Court, C. (1964) "Octogenarian Fame," *EDP*, 2 January.
14. Woods, F. (1979) *Folk Revival*, 32–33.
15. Stradling, R. and Yates, M. (2000) *Put a Bit of Powder on it, Father*, 5.
16. Ken Hunt, interview.
17. Bragg, B. (2017) *Roots, Radicals and Rockers*, 245. Rob Young names Harry Cox as one of the regular singers, but other evidence suggests he made few club appearances in London. See Young (2011) *Electric Eden*, 143.
18. Peggy Seeger, interview.
19. Young, R. (2011) *Electric Eden*, 143.
20. Anonymous (1959) "Harry Cox," 4.
21. Young, R. (2011) *Electric Eden*, 143. Young gives the year as 1957, but the days and dates (Sunday 9, 16 and 23 March) correspond to 1958.
22. Peggy Seeger, interview.
23. MacColl, E. and Seeger, P. (1961) Notes to *NTTFF*, 2.
24. Martin Carthy, interview.
25. See Wilks, J. (2018) *Martin Carthy: the Mega Interview*, jonwilks.online/martin-carthy-interview.
26. Roud Index; Lucy Broadwood correspondence, LEB/5/186, VWML.
27. Peggy Seeger, interview.
28. MacColl, E. (1965) script for *The Song Carriers* (First broadcast 28 January on Midland Home Service), C/M.
29. Christopher Heppa, email, 18 November 2019.
30. Peggy Seeger, interview.
31. "When I sing a Song my Mind is on it," *BLB* Disc 1, Track 6.
32. Shirley Collins, email, 3 December 2019.
33. Collins, S. (2018) *All in the Downs*, 80.
34. Shirley Collins, email, 3 December 2019.
35. Reg Hall, interview; Dallas, K. (1974) "Folk Giants No.1 Harry Cox," *Melody Maker*, 7 December, 9.
36. Plunkett, M. (1976) Notes to *English Country Music*, Topic LP 12T296; Reg Hall, interview.
37. Myrtle Helsdon, interview by Paul Marsh, 9 September 1994, transcript, 7, PM.
38. Myrtle Helsdon to the Stricklands, 15 March 1968, VWML.
39. Jenny Barker, interview; Anonymous (1966) "A Legend Deep in the Heart of Norfolk," *Melody Maker*, 11 June, 8.
40. Dallas, K. (1971) "Harry Cox (Obituary)," *Melody Maker*, 15 May, 4.
41. The song was released in 1966, so Sam never heard it.
42. Court, C. (1964) "Octogenarian Fame," *EDP*, 2 January.
43. *EDP* (1994) "Sam's shanties," 18 March; Holderness, C (2014) *CRY*, 3 and interview.

44. Damien Barber, interview.
45. Hall, R. (2000) Notes to *BLB*, 2.
46. Peter Coleman, interview. Peter would not reveal the identity of the unwelcome guests but confirmed that they were not the Peggs or any of the local visitors mentioned in this book.
47. Barker, J. (undated) *Memories*, 6; Shepard, L (1995) *An Appreciation of Harry Cox*, SR.
48. Myrtle Helsdon to the Stricklands, 17 October 1965 and 25 June 1965, VWML.
49. Peter Coleman, interview; Tony Baylis, interview.
50. Myrtle Helsdon to the Stricklands, 25 June 1965, VWML.
51. Shepard, L. (1995) *An Appreciation of Harry Cox*, SR.
52. Peter Coleman, interview; Sheila Park, interview.
53. Pauline Godbold, interview. Moynihan played fiddle and bouzouki in Planxty and Sweeney's Men; Briggs is a leading revival singer notable for her solo albums and recordings with guitarist Bert Jansch.
54. Peter Coleman, interview.
55. Tony Baylis, interview.
56. Myrtle Helsdon to the Stricklands, 17 October 1965, VWML; The burial is recorded in the Catfield burial register.
57. Myrtle Helsdon to Reg Hall, 7 July 1967, SR.
58. Harry Cox, interview by Bob Thomson, ca.1969, C/M103; Jenny Barker to Paul Marsh, 17 June 2001, PM.
59. Anonymous (1966) "An Evening with Harry Cox," 115.
60. Pegg, B. (1969) "Harry Cox," 9–13; Bob Pegg, email, 8 August 2019.
61. Pegg, B. (1976) *Folk: A Portrait*, 32–33.
62. Pegg, B. (1969) "Harry Cox," 10–11.
63. Pegg, B. (1969) "Harry Cox," 12.
64. Pegg, B. (1976) *Folk: A Portrait*, 33–34.
65. Pegg, B. (1969) "Harry Cox," 12.
66. Bob Pegg, email, 8 August 2019.
67. English Folk Song and Dance Society (undated) efdss.org/about-us/our-history/gold-badge-awards.
68. Jenny Barker, interview; Kennedy (1971) "Obituary: Harry Cox," 162.
69. Peter Coleman, interview; Grosvenor Myer, M. and Thomson, B. (1973) "A Visit to Harry Cox," 8.
70. The writer of the song is unknown; the lyric sheet is in JB.
71. Anglia TV contract for a broadcast on 13 November 1969; BBC contract dated 12 January 1970. Both documents are in JB.
72. Myrtle Helsdon, cited by Marsh, P (2000) Notes to *BLB*, 21.
73. BBC Today contract – the fee was three guineas (JB).
74. For detailed discussion of the sub-genres of contemporary folk, see Leech, J. (2010) *Seasons They Change*.
75. Lenny Helsdon, cited by Marsh (2000) Notes to *BLB*, 22.

12 The Road Goes on Forever?

1. Myrtle Helsdon, interview by Paul Marsh, 9 September 1994, transcript, 5 (PM).
2. Myrtle Helsdon, interview by Paul Marsh, 9 September 1994, transcript, 5 (PM).
3. *EDP* (1994) 18 March.
4. Peter Kennedy to Sam Larner, 6 October 1958 (courtesy of Chris Holderness).
5. *Hansard* (1960) HC Deb 29 November, vol 631 cc42–3W.
6. Jane Roberts, interview.

7. Fakes, A. (2008) Letter on behalf of Great Yarmouth & District Archaeological Society, March.
8. Andrew Fakes, interview.
9. Cited in Smith, B. (1994) *Peter Warlock*, 240.
10. Woods, F. (1979) *Folk Revival*, 32.
11. Cited by Jane Roberts, interview.
12. Keith Skipper, email, 21 September 2019.
13. Anderson, J. (1964) "Sam Larner," *EDP*. An LP cost about £1 10s. at the time (£1.50).
14. Olmsted, T. (2003) *Folkways Records*, 116. Figures for individual albums are not available.
15. Glen Johnson of Topic Records, email, 20 December 2019.
16. All of these documents are now in JB.
17. Serial numbers are, respectively, FTX-032, FTX-033, FTX-034; see folktrax-archive.org/menus/cassprogs/2217norfolk.htm.
18. Myrtle Helsdon, interview by Paul Marsh, 9 September 1994, transcript, 5, PM.
19. Kennedy, P. (1984) *Folksongs of Britain and Ireland*, viii and 4.
20. See Hall, R. (2017) *Peter Kennedy's Published Recordings* for further information; Hall, R. (2017) *Peter Kennedy's Published Recordings*, 1 and 14.
21. Hall, R. (2017) *Peter Kennedy's Published Recordings*, 305.
22. Hall, R. (2017) *Peter Kennedy's Published Recordings*, 305–6. Hall gives the serial number as Folktracks 60–139; details of the cassette release are at folktrax-archive.org/menus/cassprogs/139larner.htm.
23. See folktrax-archive.org/menus/cassprogs/2217norfolk.htm. Kennedy's activities have been the subject of much discussion: Hall's discography gives details of this complex issue.
24. Steve Roud, interview.
25. *EDP* (1994) 18 March.
26. Jane Roberts, interview.
27. Dorcas Larner to the Stricklands, 2 June 1965, VWML. Dorcas dated the letter as "26/65."
28. Myrtle Helsdon to the Stricklands, 25 June 1965, VWML.
29. Death certificate; Palmer, R. (2004) *Cox, Harry Fred*; *EDP* (1965) "Sam Larner leaves £802," 15 November.
30. Buddery, C (2018) Obituary: Kingsley Jones, bmj.com/content/360/bmj.k1265.full.
31. Dorcas died on 5 Sept 1969.
32. Myrtle Helsdon to the Stricklands: 25 June 1965, 15 March 1968, 14 June 1966, VWML.
33. Jenny had married in early March and was no longer living at Sunnyside. Myrtle Helsdon to the Stricklands, 21 May 1971, VWML.
34. Peter Coleman, interview.
35. Myrtle Helsdon to the Stricklands, 21 May 1971, VWML.
36. Information from Mary Haslam, Potter Heigham churchwarden. There is no record of Harry's burial in the church's documents.
37. *EDP*, 8 May 1971 and 14 September 1965.
38. *Times* (1971) "Obituary: Harry Cox," 8 May; Kennedy, P. (1971) "Obituary: Harry Cox," 160; Singleton, T. and Singleton, D. (1971) "Obituary," 114; Dallas, K. (1971) "Harry Cox (Obituary)," *Melody Maker*, 18 May, 4; Dallas, K. (1974) "Folk Giants: Harry Cox."
39. Hall, R. (2001) "Harry Fred Cox," 634; Arthur, D. (2001) "Samuel James Larner," 274.
40. "Whiffler's City" (1971) *Eastern Evening News*, 1 November; the painting was featured in *English Dance and Song* (1970) Spring: 30.
41. *Radio Times* (1967) 28 May, 16.
42. *Radio Times* (1972) 7 September, 55.

43. *Radio Times* (1981) 22 October, 57. See also *BFI online*: bfi.org.uk/fils-tv-people/4ce2b752841f8.
44. *Radio Times* (2005) 20 October, 134; *Desert Island Discs* (2013) 18 January, bbc.co.uk/programmes/b01pt8dj.
45. Information from Katie Howson; Katie Howson, East Anglian Traditional Music Trust letter, 18 July 2000. Katie Howson does not know why this idea failed. It may be that Catfield felt Harry had more connections to Potter Heigham.
46. Wortley, R. (1975) "Review," 81.
47. Bainbridge, J. (2015) "Sam Larner"; Heppa, C. (2016) "Review," 99; Smith, V. (2015) mustrad.org.uk/reviews/larner3.htm (originally published in fROOTS).
48. Peter Kennedy to Rod Stradling of Musical Traditions, 13 June 2000 (PM).
49. Kennedy, P. (1971) "Obituary: Harry Cox," 162.
50. Smith, V. (2001) "Review," 88; Anderson, H. (2002) "Review"; King, T. (2001) "Review," 149; Yates, M. (2000) mustrad.org.uk/reviews/cox2.htm.
51. Burgess (2001) "Review"; Docherty, J. (2001) "Tracking down traditional songs Paul's labour of love," *Hampshire Chronicle*, 23 February; "P. R." (2010) "Review," 85.
52. Yates, mustrad.org.uk/reviews/cox.htm; Fink, M. (2000) acousticmusic.com/frames/fame.htm; Williamson, C. (2000) ramblesnet/cox_england.html.
53. Veteran Records VTDC11CD. The tracks were recorded in Catfield in 1968.
54. Brian Gaudet, interview; SamFest handbill; Gaudet, B. (2016) "HarryFest," 36.
55. Stone Angel formed in 1974; *Lonely Waters* is on Kissing Spell, KSCD 951.
56. Jack, I. (2014) "Inside Llewyn Davis has its pleasures and its flaws, as did the folk movement." *The Guardian online*, 17 January, theguardian.com/commentisfree/2014/jan/17/inside-llewyn-davis-flaws-film. The song is correctly credited to MacColl at the end of the movie.
57. *Readymade*'s other tracks include samples from Lal Waterson, Kate Rusby and Dick Gaughan. "Mr. Stormalong" was released in 2011 on a compilation, *Fresh Handmade Sound, from Source to Sea* (LUSH 003) then in 2015 on the group's album *From Source to Sea* (ECC 100/#004).
58. Philip Underwood, email, 22 October 2019.
59. Smith, C. (2004) "Wide range of lively and varied orchestrations," *EDP* 11 May; John Harle, interview; Cecil Sharp House concert programme, PM.
60. Carole Pegg, email, 14 August 2019; Bob Pegg, email, 8 August 2019.
61. Shirley Collins, email, 3 December 2019.
62. Martin Carthy, Sheila Park, Ken Hunt, interviews.
63. Christine Alden, email, 9 January 2020.
64. Alex Patterson, interview.
65. Georgia Shackleton, interview.
66. Peter Coleman, Damien Barber, Brian Gaudet, interviews.

Selected Discography

HARRY COX

The Bonny Labouring Boy [Topic TSCD512D, 2000]
CD1: "You must get the tune first ..."; The Female Drummer; "People what don't like to hear an old song ..."; The Jolly Butchers; Polka (melodeon); "When I sing a song my mind is on it ..."; Bold Archer; There's Bound to be a Row; Betsy the Servant Maid; Firelock Stile; The Green Mossy Banks of the Lee; The Pretty Ploughboy (song/fiddle); The Watercress Girl; A Week's Matrimony; The Black Velvet Band; A Hornpipe (fiddle); The Maid of Australia; Alone, Alone in London; Miss Doxy; The Bonny Labouring Boy; The Good Luck Ship; The Fowler; In Scarborough Fair Town; I Had an Old Hoss; The Green Bed; A Jig (melodeon); The Bold Drover.
CD2: Georgie; A Schottische (melodeon); Black-Hearted Gypsies O; The Rigs of the Times; The Grand Hotel; The Transports (song/fiddle); Where the Shamrocks Grow; Barton Broad Ditty; Adieu to Old England; Bold Fisherman; A Polka (fiddle); Ekefield Town; A Happy Family; Old Joe, the Boat is Going Over (melodeon); Blackberry Fold; They Told Me in the Gaol; The Fowler (fiddle); Colin and Phoebe; Jack Tar on the Shore; The Turkish Lady; A Slow Stepdance Tune (melodeon); Lost Lady Found; Coming Home from the Wake; The Poacher's Fate; The Poor Smuggler's Boy; A Hornpipe (dancing doll and voice); The Bonny Bunch of Roses O.

What Will Become of England? [Rounder 1839, 2000]
What Will Become of England?; My life (talk); A-Going to Widdliecombe Fair; Working in a gang (talk); The Spotted Cow; Barton Waltz (melodeon); The harvest (talk); The Barley Straw; The Farmer's Servant; The Pretty Ploughboy (fiddle); My father and my grandfather (talk); Jack Tar on Shore; Two Hornpipes: Yarmouth and Meg Merilees (fiddle); On Board of the Kangaroo; Young and Growing; My mother (talk); My upbringing (talk); The Foggy Dew; Hunger and pay (talk); Three Toasts; Nelson's Monument; I used to go along of him (talk); Barton Broad Babbing Ballad; Babbing for eels (talk); Talk and melodeon pieces; Singing in public houses (talk); Charming and Delightful; The old songs (talk); On Yon Lofty Mountain; Learning from my father (talk); She never had time to sit down (talk); The Turkish Lady; Poaching (talk); Henry the Poacher; Windy Old Weather; My father at sea (talk); Sweet William; How my father learned songs (talk); The Yarmouth Fisherman's Song; The Crocodile; The Soldier and Sailor's Prayer; London is as Sharp as the Edge of a Knife; Up to the Rigs of London Town; Up to the present I ain't forgot anything yet (talk); Blackberry Fold; Adieu to Old Eng-e-land, Here's Adieu.

Harry Cox: English Folk Singer [EFDSS LP1004, 1965]
Side 1: Barton Broad Ballad; The 'Prentice Boy; Windy Old Weather; Newlyn Town; The Bonny Bunch of Roses; Adieu to Old England; Blackberry Fold.
Side 2: Widdliecombe Fair: The Ploughboy (fiddle); Talk about himself; What Will Become of England?; Talk about his father; Waltz (melodeon); Talk and melodeon tunes; Talk about singing: Hornpipes (fiddle); The Foggy Dew; Nancy and Johnny; Firelock Stile.

Harry Cox sings English Love Songs [DTS LFX4, 1964]
Traditional English Love Songs [Folk-Legacy Records FSB-20, 1964]
Side 1: Seventeen Come Sunday; The Spotted Cow; Next Monday Morning; The Greasy Cook; Colin and Phoebe; The Birmingham Man; Betsy the Servant Maid.
Side 2: The Bonny Labouring Boy; The Female Drummer; The Squire and the Gypsy; Marrowbones; The Groggy Old Tailor; Up to the Rigs of London; The Old German Musicianer.

78 rpm Single [EFDSS / Decca Record Company Limited: Decca OC87/88, 1934]
Side 1: Down by the Riverside.
Side 2: The Pretty Plough Boy.

SAM LARNER

Cruising Round Yarmouth [Musical Traditions MTCD369-0, 2014]
CD1: The Ghost Ship; When I Went a-Fishing; Maids When You're Young; Before Daylight in the Morning; Rhymes and Sea Lore; The Maids of Australia; A Reckless Young Fellow; The Girls Around Cape Horn; The Wild Rover; The Oyster Girl; As I Lay a-Musing; A Sailor's Alphabet; Duckfoot Sue; Clear Away the Morning Dew; Sing to the Oak; No Sir, No Sir; Old Bob Ridley-O; When I Was Single; The Golden Fenadier; The Wild and Wicked Youth; Now is the Time for Fishing & talk; I Wish, I Wish; The Dockyard Gate; Green Broom; The Dolphin; The Old Miser; The Skipper and his Boy; Blackberry Fold; The Wreck of the Lifeboat; Outlandish Knight; The Tanyard Side; Will Watch; Talk.
CD2: The Bold Princess Royal; The Captain's Whiskers; The Bonny Bunch of Roses; King William & talk; Happy and Delightful; The Chesapeake and Shannon; Coil Away the Trawl Warp; The Jolly Young Coachman; The Loss of the Ramillies; She Said she was a Virgin; Game of All Fours; The Wonderful Crocodile; Donnelly and Cooper; Cruising Round Yarmouth; Barbara Allen; Barney and Kitty; Green Grow the Laurels; The London Steamer; The Bold Young Fisherman; Windy Old Weather & talk; The Haymakers' Courtship; Henry Martin; Just as the Tide was Flowing; The Dogger Bank; Over There in Ireland; The Dark-Eyed Sailor; Butter and Cheese; Napoleon's Dream; Spurn Point; The Barley Straw; Bold General Wolfe; The White Squall; Scarborough Fair Town; Final talk.

A Garland for Sam: Songs and Ballads of Sam Larner of Winterton, Norfolk [Topic TSDL244, 1974]
Alphabet Song; Merry Month of May; Napoleon's Dream; London Steamer; Bonny Bunch of Roses; Barbara Allen; The Smacksman; The Lofty Tall Ship; Raking the Hay; Will Watch; The Outlandish Knight; Haisboro Light Song; Old Bob Ridley-o; The Bold Princess Royal; In Scarboro' Town.

Now is the Time for Fishing [Folkways FG 3507, 1961; Topic Records TSCD511, 2000]
Now is the Time for Fishing; Up Jumped the Herring; The Dogger Bank; Henry Martin; Butter and Cheese; The Reckless Young Fellow; Blow Away the Morning Dew; All Fours; Green Broom; The Dockyard Gate; No Sir, No Sir; Sealore and Rhymes; The Drowned Lover; The Dolphin; The Bold Princess Royal; The Ghost Ship; Happy and Delightful; Maids, When You're Young, Never Wed an Old Man; The Wild Rover.

Selected Various Artist Compilations:

The Voice of the People [Topic Records, 1998]
Volume 1: *Come Let Us Buy the Licence – Songs of Courtship & Marriage* [TSCD651]
Harry Cox: The Bold Fisherman.
Volume 2: *My Ship Shall Sail the Ocean – Songs of Tempest & Sea Battles, Sailor Lads & Fishermen* [TSCD652]
Harry Cox: The Pretty Ploughboy.
Sam Larner: In Scarborough Town.
Volume 5: *Come All My Lads That Follow the Plough – The Life of Rural Working Men & Women* [TSCD655]
Sam Larner: The Pleasant Month of May.
Volume 12: *We've Received Orders to Sail – Jackie Tar at Sea & on Shore* [TSCD662]
Harry Cox: Just as the Tide was A-flowing; Come All You Men Throughout the Nation (The Captain's Apprentice); The Bold Princess Royal.
Sam Larner: The Sailor's Alphabet; The Lofty Tall Ship.
Volume 17: *It Fell on a Day, a Bonny Summer Day – Ballads* [TSCD667]
Harry Cox: In Worcester City; Young Edmund.

The Voice of the People – Second Series
Good People, Take Warning: Ballads by British and Irish Traditional Singers [TSCD673T]
Harry Cox: The Crabfish; The Squire and the Gypsy.
Sam Larner: The London Steamer; Pretty Polly (The Cruel Ship's Carpenter).

The Folk Songs of Britain [Caedmon Records, 1961]
Volume 2: *Songs of Seduction* [TC1143]
Harry Cox: Long Peggin' Awl; The Maid of Australia; Cruising Round Yarmouth.
Volume 5: *The Child Ballads 2* [TC1146]
Harry Cox: The Gypsy Laddie (part); Georgie; Our Goodman (part).
Volume 6: *Sailormen and Serving Maids* [TC1162]
Sam Larner: The Smacksman.
Volume 7: *Fair Game and Foul* [TC1163]
Harry Cox: Polly Vaughan.
Volume 8: *A Soldier's Life for Me* [TC1164]
Sam Larner: Napoleon's Dream.

The Barley Mow: Songs from the Village Inn [EMI 7EG 8288, 1957]
Harry Cox: The Foggy Dew.

Bibliography

Anderson, H. (2002) "Review of 'Harry Cox, The Bonny Labouring Boy'." *Transmissions*, Issue 3. Folklore-network.folkaustralia.com/tranjune.html.

Anonymous (undated) *Ganseys. A Concise Local History of Fishermen's Ganseys*. Cromer Museum Brief History No. 13. Norfolk Museums.

Anonymous (1959) "Harry Cox – The Catfield Wonder." *Ethnic* 1:1: 4–5.

Anonymous (1966) "An Evening with Harry Cox." *English Dance and Song*, Autumn, 115.

Anonymous (2010) *Lydia Eva – The First 80 Years*. Lydia Eva & Mincarlo Charitable Trust.

Arne, T. A. (1741) *Lyric Harmony, Consisting of eighteen entire New Ballads with Colin and Phæbe, in Score. As Perform'd at Vaux Hall Gardens by Mrs. Arne and Mr. Lowe compos'd by Thomas Augustine Arne*. Printed by Wm. Smith, Middle Row, Holborn.

Arthur, D. (2001) "Samuel James Larner," in *New Grove Dictionary of Music and Musicians*, edited by Sadie, S. 2nd Edition, 14: 274.

Bainbridge, J. (2015) "Sam Larner, Cruising Round Yarmouth," *Living Tradition* 107, livingtradition.co.uk/webrevs/mtcd369-0.htm.

Barber, C. (with Alyn Shipton) (2014) *Jazz Me Blues – The Autobiography of Chris Barber*. Equinox Publications.

Barker, J. (undated) *Memories of my Grandad*. Unpublished manuscript.

Bearman, C. J. (2001) *The English Folk Movement 1898–1914*. Unpublished PhD thesis. University of Hull.

Bellamy, P. (1974) "Interview with Walter Pardon." *Folk Review*, August: 10–15.

Bennett, E. and McKay, G. (2019) *From Brass Bands to Buskers: Street Music in the UK*. Arts and Humanities Research Council/University of East Anglia.

Bragg, B. (2017) *Roots, Radicals & Rockers: How Skiffle Changed the World*. Faber & Faber.

Browning, S. (2018) *Norfolk at War 1939–45*. Pen & Sword.

Burgess, P. (2001) "Review of The Bonny Labouring Boy," *Living Tradition* 42, livingtradition.co.uk/webrevs/tscd512d.htm.

Burke, D. (2015) *Singing Out. A Folk Narrative of Maddy Prior, June Tabor and Linda Thompson*. Soundcheck Books.

Collins, S. (2018) *All in the Downs*. Strange Attractor Press.

Collinson, F. M. (1946) "Songs Collected by Francis M. Collinson." *Journal of the English Folk Dance and Song Society*, 5:1: 13–22.

Copper, B. (1975) *A Song for Every Season*. Paladin.

D'Urfey, T. (1719) *Wit and Mirth, or Pills to Purge Melancholy*. Printed by W. Pearson for J. Tonson.

Evans, G. E. (1975) *Ask the Fellows Who Cut the Hay*. Faber Paperbacks. (First published 1956).

Gaudet, B. (2016) "HarryFest: Celebrating Harry Cox." *Mardles*, August–October, 36–42.

Grainger, P. (1908) "Collecting with the Phonograph." *Journal of the English Folk-Song Society*, 3:12: 147–162.

Grieg, R. (2004) "Joseph Taylor from Lincolnshire: a biography of a singer." *Folk Song Tradition, Revival, and Re-Creation*. Occasional Publications (3). The Elphinstone Institute, University of Aberdeen.

Grosvenor Myer, M. and Thomson, B. (1973) "A Visit to Harry Cox." *Folk Review* 2:4: 8–12.

Haines, S. (2019) "East Anglian Stepdancing." *Living Tradition*, 127: 30.

Hall, R. (2001) "Harry Fred Cox," in *New Grove Dictionary of Music and Musicians*, edited by Sadie, S. 2nd Edition. 6: 634. https://doi.org/10.1093/gmo/9781561592630.article.51647

Hall, R. (2017) *Peter Kennedy's Published Recordings of British and Irish Traditional Music and Related Material: an annotated bibliography*. Vaughan Williams Memorial Library.

Harrod & Co's Royal County Directory of Norfolk, with Lowestoft in Suffolk (1877) J. G. Harrod & Company.

Heppa, C. (2002) "From My Father's Songbook." *English Dance and Song*, Summer, 16–18.

Heppa, C. (2004) [Letter] "'Neglected pioneer' by Roy Palmer, in Journal, 8.3 (2003), 345–61." *Folk Music Journal* 8:4: 517–518.

Heppa, C. (2004a) "Sam Howard and the East Norfolk Singing Tradition, 1919–1936." In Russell, I. and Atkinson, D. (Eds.) *Folk Song: Tradition, Revival and Re-Creation*, The Elphinstone Institute, University of Aberdeen.

Heppa, C. (2005) "Harry Cox and his Friends: Song Transmission in an East Norfolk Singing Community c.1896–1960." *Folk Music Journal*, 8:5: 569–593.

Heppa, C. (2016) "Review of Cruising Round Yarmouth," *Folk Music Journal*, 11:1: 99–101.

Heppa, C. (2019) "Jack Riseborough: The Missing Man from the East Norfolk Singing Tradition," in *Old Songs, New Discoveries. Selected Papers from the 2018 Folk Song Conference*, edited by Roud, S. and Atkinson, D. The Ballad Partners.

Heseltine, P. (1924) "Introductions XVIII: E. J. Moeran." *Music Bulletin*, 6: 170–174.

Higgins, D. (2009) *The Winterton Story*. Phoenix Publications.

Holderness, C. (2013) "Sam Larner: the Winterton fisherman and his singing community," *Musical Traditions*: article MT280.

Horn, P. (1981) "Country Children," in *The Victorian Countryside*, Volume 2, edited by Mingay, G. E. Routledge & Keegan Paul.

Howkins, A. (1985) *Poor Labouring Men: Rural Radicalism in Norfolk, 1870–1923*. Routledge & Kegan Paul.

Karpeles, M. (1955) "Definition of Folk Music." *International Folk Music Journal*, 7: 6–7. https://doi.org/10.2307/834518

Karpeles, M. (1974) *Cecil Sharp's Collection of English Folk Songs*. Volume 1. Oxford University Press.

Karpeles, M.; Gilchrist, A. G.; Moeran, E. J.; Freeman, A. M.; Howes, F. (1931) "Humorous and Disreputable Songs, and Ballads of Adventure." *Journal of the Folk-Song Society*, 8:35: 270–279.

Kelly's Directory of Norfolk (1896) Kelly & Company Limited.

Kennedy, P. (1958) "Harry Cox, English Folk Singer: A Personal Narrative Recorded and Introduced by Peter Kennedy. With a Reminiscence by Francis Collinson." *Journal of the English Folk Dance and Song Society*, 8:3: 142–155.

Kennedy, P. (1958a) "Folk Song Recording." *Tape Recording and High Fidelity Reproduction Magazine*, June: 19 and 39.

Kennedy, P. (1971) "Obituary: Harry Cox 1885–1871." *Folk Music Journal*, 2:2: 160–162.

Kennedy, P. (1984) *Folksongs of Britain and Ireland: A Treasure Trove for Anyone Interested in the Traditions of the British Isles*. 2nd Edition (First published 1975). Oak Publications.

King, T. (2001) "Review." *Record Collector*, February, 149.

Laing, D.; Dallas, K.; Denselow, R. and Shelton, R. (1975) *The Electric Muse. The Story of Folk into Rock*. Methuen Paperbacks.

Lee, K. (1899) "Some Experiences of a Folk-Song Collector." *Journal of the Folk-Song Society*, 1:1: 7–12 and 16–25.

Leech, J. (2010) *Seasons They Change: The Story of Acid and Psychedelic Folk*. Jawbone Press.

Lindsay, B. (2020) *Shellac and Swing! The Social History of the Gramophone in Britain*. Fonthill Media.

MacColl, E. (2009) *Journeyman. An Autobiography*. 2nd Edition. Manchester University Press.

Macfarlane, T. J. (1973) "Sing Us an Old Song." *East Anglian Magazine*, 32:3: 130–131.

Malster, R. (2015) *North Sea War 1914–1919*. Poppyland Publishing.

Mansfield, N. (1986) "George Edwards and the Farmworkers Union and Norfolk and the Great War: Oral History in Norfolk Rural Life Museum." *Oral History*, 14:2: 51–58.

Moeran, E. J.; Gilchrist, A. G; Kidson, F; Williams, R. V and Broadwood, L. E (1922) "Songs Collected in Norfolk." *Journal of the Folk-Song Society*, 7:26:1–24.

Moeran, E. J. (1924) *Six Folk Songs from Norfolk*. Augener.

Moeran, E. J. (1936) "Notes on Folk-Songs and Traditional Singing in East Norfolk." *Norfolk Annual* 3; October 1936 31–32.

Moeran, E. J. (1946) "Folk Songs and some Traditional Singers in East Anglia." *Countrygoer*, 7. Moeran.net/pdf/Folksongs.pdf. (Accessed 27 February 2019.)

Moeran, E. J. (1948) "Some Folk Songs of Today." *Journal of the English Folk Dance and Song Society*, 5:3: 152–154.

Moeran, E. J.; Karpeles, M.; Freeman, A. M.; Gilchrist, A. G.; Howes, F. (1931) "Love Songs and Ballads." *Journal of the Folk-Song Society*, 8:35: 257–269.

Moore, A. F. and Vacca, G. (2014) *Legacies of Ewan MacColl: The Last Interview*. Ashgate.

Nicholson, J. (1989) *I Kept A'Troshin*. S. J. Nicholson.

Olmsted, T. (2003) *Folkways Records: Moses Asch and his Encyclopedia of Sound*. Routledge.

Palmer, R. (2003) "Neglected Pioneer: E. J. Moeran (1894–1950)." *Folk Music Journal*, 8:3: 345–361.

Palmer, R. (2004) *Cox, Harry Fred*. Oxford Dictionary of National Biography Online, oxforddnb.com.

Pearsall, R. (1975) *Edwardian Popular Music*. David & Charles.

Pegg, B. (undated, probably 1969) "Harry Cox." *Abe's Folk Music* 5:1: 9–13.

Pegg, B. (1976) *Folk: A Portrait of Traditional Music, Musicians and Customs*. Wildwood House.

"P. R." (2010) "Review," *Hi-Fi World*, April, 85.

Roud, S. (2017) *Folk Song in England*. Faber & Faber.

Roud, S. and Bishop, J. (Eds.) (2012) *The New Penguin Book of English Folk Songs*. Penguin Classics.

Seeger, P. (2017) *First Time Ever: A Memoir* (e-book). Faber & Faber

Seeger, P. and MacColl, E. (1960) *The Singing Island: A Collection of English and Scots Folksongs*. Mills Music Ltd.

Sharp, C. J. (1907) *English Folk-Song, some conclusions*. Simkin & Co. Ltd.

Shepard, L. (1972) "Harry Cox [Letter]." *Folk Music Journal* 2:3: 241.

Shepard, L. (1995) *An Appreciation of Harry Cox, Folksinger*. Unpublished manuscript. (Steve Roud Collection).

Singleton, T. and Singleton, D. (1971) "Obituary," *English Dance and Song*, Autumn, 114.

Smith, B. (1994) *Peter Warlock. The Life of Philip Heseltine*. Oxford University Press.

Smith, V. (2001) "Review: The Bonny Labouring Boy." *fROOTS* 214: 88.

Springall, L. M. (1936) *Labouring Life in Norfolk Villages 1834–1914*. George Allen & Unwin Ltd.

Szreter, S. (2014) "The Prevalence of Syphilis in England and Wales on the Eve of the Great War: Re-visiting the Estimates of the Royal Commission on Venereal Diseases, 1913–1916," *Social History of Medicine* 27:3: 508–529. https://doi.org/10.1093/shm/hkt123

Thompson, F. (2008) *Lark Rise to Candleford*. Penguin Classics. (First published in 1945).

Vaughan Williams, R. and Lloyd A. L. (1959) *The Penguin Book of English Folk Songs*. Penguin.

Wentworth Day, J. (1951) *Broadland Adventure*. Country Life Ltd.

White's History, Gazetteer and Directory of Norfolk (1836) William White.

White's History, Gazetteer and Directory of Norfolk (1845) William White.

Winick, S. D. (1997) "Reissuing the Revival: British and Irish Music on Topic Records." *Journal of American Folklore*, 110:437: 324–341. https://doi.org/10.2307/541167

Woods, F. (1979) *Folk Revival: The Rediscovery of a National Music*. Blandford Press.

Wortley, R. (1975) "Review: A Garland for Sam," *Folk Music Journal*, 3:1: 81.

Young, R. (2011) *Electric Eden: Unearthing Britain's Visionary Music*. Faber & Faber.

Index

www.ingramcontent.com/pod-product-compliance
Lightning Source LLC
Chambersburg PA
CBHW070842100426
42813CB00003B/719